Modern Philosophies of Judaism

A STUDY OF
RECENT JEWISH PHILOSOPHIES
OF RELIGION

Modern Philosophies of
JUDAISM

A STUDY OF RECENT JEWISH
PHILOSOPHIES OF RELIGION

By

JACOB B. AGUS, Ph.D.

BEHRMAN'S JEWISH BOOK HOUSE
NEW YORK   1941

Dedicated to

My Dear Parents

JUDAH LEIB AND BELA DEBORAH

PREFACE

THE PURPOSE OF THIS BOOK IS TO EXPOUND THE BASIC IDEAS of modern Jewish religious thought. We do not attempt to discuss all the problems of Jewish theology which occupy the attention of modern rabbis. Specifically, the problems relating to Jewish law and national aspirations are touched upon only briefly. Our main interest is in the conception of God and in His relation to man.

We feel that a renascence of the Jewish religion is dependent upon a rediscovery of the fundamental truths of Judaism. The battle on the periphery of Jewish life is lost from the start, if, at the center, there dwell uncertainty and skepticism. The effects of inner confusion and vacillation are visible in every aspect of Jewish life—in the shallowness of our leadership, in the progressive deterioration of communal standards, in the substitution of words for deeds by young and old alike, in the empty loudnesses and in the meaningful silences of the American Jewish community. It was through the idea of the One God that our people first emerged upon the stage of history. We shall remain true to our destiny only if we regain once more a profound and significant conviction concerning the Supreme Ruler of the universe.

The plan of this work requires some explanation. The nineteenth century Jewish thinkers are dealt with rather sketchily in the introduction, because our main concern is with the "live" trends in Jewish theology. In all the discussions of this work, we have been guided by one question, "Of what value is this thought to the attempts of our generation to understand the nature of God and His relation to mankind?" We trust that this practical interest has not marred the objectivity and scientific accuracy of our exposition.

The four thinkers whose philosophies are discussed in detail in this book represent extreme viewpoints. They are, therefore, typical exponents of the different movements in Jewish theology. In the last chapter, we attempt to show the core of conviction which is common to all these philosophers.

Our extended treatment of Buber's writings may, at first glance, appear to be unduly overworked. Buber is commonly regarded as primarily a poet, and our serious-minded analysis of his variegated writings may consequently seem to be out of proportion to the real merit of his thought. It is necessary, therefore, to bear in mind that modern philosophy of religion is nearly always based on an alleged religious experience of one kind or another. Religion meets the challenge of modern science through the claim of being itself rooted in human experience. Schleiermacher's "feeling" of religion is, in a broad sense, the foundation of most modern theories of religious faith. Consequently, it is of the utmost importance to study closely the actual reports of any religious experience. The mystics are the modern "witnesses of the faith." Buber's mysticism and lifelong spiritual development is of a most interesting type, and, we venture to add, typically Jewish. Since the life of the spirit cannot be departmentalized, it is necessary to discuss Buber's youthful literary vagaries and his public activities along with his distinctly mystical works.

Kaplan's philosophy of religion is treated at some length, because it is typical of the attitude of a large number of American rabbis.

In the analysis of the systems of thought of Cohen and Rosenzweig, we endeavored to present a systematic account of their basic ideas. Our interpretation of Cohen's system will, no doubt, be disputed by those who are acquainted mainly with his works on logic. An attempt to view all of Cohen's works as one systematic whole will, we believe, bear out the correctness of our interpretation. In the understanding of Rosenzweig's main work, we were guided largely by his published letters.

The term "modern" in the title of this book is used in a double sense—to denote the works which were not only published within the last one hundred years, but those which accept the main theses of the modern historical and scientific views of religion. The orthodox philosophy of Judaism is, in other words, by design excluded from the purview of this work. Our reason for this exclusion is the fact that the philosophical problems of Orthodox Judaism are radically different than those of Conservative or Reform Judaism. For the sake of unified treatment, we have reserved the discussion of Orthodox theology for a separate work.

Our own viewpoint is expressed in the last chapter. We hope to present a more complete exposition of that viewpoint in subsequent publications.

This book is an elaboration and popularization of a doctoral thesis, entitled "The Relation of Man to God in the Philosophies of Hermann Cohen and Martin Buber," which was submitted to Harvard University in the spring of 1939.

My thanks are due to the late sainted president of the Yeshiva College, Rabbi Dr. Bernard Revel; to my teachers in philosophy, Professors Alexander S. Littman, N. Bixler, Harry A. Wolfson, Ralph B. Perry and William Hocking; to Dr. M. Waxman for valuable suggestions; to the officers and members of Temple Ashkenaz in Cambridge, Mass., my former congregation; to the officers, directors and members of the Agudas Achim North Shore Congregation, Chicago, Illinois, whose cooperation and good-will made this publication possible; above all, to my dear wife, Miriam Zelda Agus.

JACOB B. AGUS
July, 1941

CONTENTS

Contents

CHAPTER I

INTRODUCTION

(*a*) ABRAHAM GEIGER
(*b*) L. S. STEINHEIM
(*c*) SAMUEL HIRSCH
(*d*) SOLOMON FORMSTECHER
(*e*) THEROIES OF NATIONALISM

THE PROBLEMS OF JEWISH THEOLOGY IN OUR DAY ARE
vastly different from those with which the Medieval Jewish
philosophers were concerned. The basic principles of Judaism were then fairly definite, inasmuch as the authority of
rabbinic tradition was undisputed. The essential problem of
Jewish theology consisted, therefore, at that time, in proving
the possibility of prophecy. Once this problem was solved,
the authority of Jewish tradition could be maintained on the
strength of the continuous testimony of Israel's literature
and history. The one dogma of the Jewish religion was
"Torah min hashomayim," the belief that both the written
and oral Laws were divinely revealed. And this dogma appeared to the Medieval Jew to be based on such an abun-
dance of convincing evidence as to be no dogma at all, since
no effort of faith was needed for its acceptance. All that
Judaism appeared to demand was the willingness to draw
the proper conclusions from the facts of history.

In our own day, only the Orthodox Jews believe the doctrine that Torah, as a concrete body of learning, was actually
revealed to Moses. The four thinkers whose philosophies
are discussed in this book do not accept this principle. In
accord with the modern spirit of objective historical research,
they reject the Orthodox viewpoint on the ground of its general inconsistency with the modern trend of thought. While
they do not necessarily subscribe to any one theory of Biblical criticism, they accept the general premise of all critics—
to wit, that Jewish "halacha" in general and the Bible in
particular are the products of a long process of development,
in the course of which elements from a variety of sources
were absorbed into the body of Judaism.

3

For these thinkers, then, the problem of Jewish theology is twofold. In the first place, they must prove the validity of the principles of universal religion and, in the second place, they must show that modern Judaism is for Jews the only appropriate form of religion. Both these problems were posed to Jewish thinkers in all their sharpness at the beginning of the nineteenth century. Since then a number of solutions and hypotheses have been proposed, an acquaintance with which is essential to the understanding of contemporary writings on Jewish theology. It is, therefore, necessary for us to preface our discussion of recent Jewish theologies with a brief review of the theories of Judaism of some great nineteenth century thinkers.

The Jewish philosophers of nineteenth century Germany accepted, as a rule, the thesis of Geiger that the worthwhile elements of Judaism were its universal principles of ethics and religion. The great body of laws and customs, which has ever regulated the life of the Orthodox Jew and which has engaged the full attention of the rabbis for well-nigh two thousand years, was regarded by these writers as of merely historical value. The legal expressions of Judaism were but the temporary fence round the garden of Judaism wherein God had planted the eternal and invaluable principles of "ethical monotheism." The philosophical exponents of Reform Judaism were at one in rejecting Mendelssohn's assertion that Judaism was "revealed law" and that the "eternal verities" of religion were accessible to all minds.

Regarding the content of "ethical monotheism," there was no agreement among those writers. Despite their vaunted loyalty to a heritage of beliefs which they conceived it as their "mission" to proclaim to the world, they, humanly enough, were far from unanimous in their views concerning the nature of those beliefs. As was to be expected, they employed the categories of contemporary thought in their systematic formulations of what they conceived to be the essence of Judaism. Some sought their inspiration in Hegel, others in Kant, still others in Schelling or in Schleiermacher. The tremendous upsurge of European thought in the nineteenth century swept all traditional concepts and modes of reasoning in the background, leaving little room indeed for any Jewish "mission" in the field of philosophical reflection.

Yet there were some stout minds that managed to retain their anchors in ancient Jewish thought and thereby to win a secure standpoint from which to judge the whole scope of modern philosophy. While they knew themselves to be students of the great founders of philosophical schools, they knew, too, that they were the recipients of certain principles which were not accessible even to their masters. Thus, though they borrowed much from contemporary European philosophy, they did not do so without a measure of wise discrimination. In recasting and modifying the thought of their age, they often indeed gave more to the body of general European thought than they received from it.

In general, it may be said that the philosophers of Judaism contributed a powerful ethical consciousness to the solution of the theoretical problems of existence. The "twists" which they made in the philosophical systems which they adopted were made in the interest of an active and sane view of ethical life. This observation may be substantiated through a study of the outstanding representatives of Jewish religious thought in the nineteenth century.

(a) ABRAHAM GEIGER

RELIGION, GEIGER TAUGHT, IS NOT A SYSTEM OF BELIEFS, OR a group of practices, or a series of prohibitions; it is an attitude of the spirit. Casting inquiring glances about him, man realizes that, while his reason enables him to penetrate many mysteries, he cannot comprehend the nature of the All or

even his own nature.[1] The realization of the existence of
these limits leads to the feeling of incompleteness and dependence. On the other hand, man possesses a sense of his
own power and worth, for he knows that he is a free moral
agent and that the potentialities of his rational faculties are
enormous. Thus, there is a tension in the soul of man between the desire to be like unto God and "the humiliating
feeling" of finiteness and dependence. Out of this spiritual
tension, the genuine attitude of religion is born. "Now," he
writes, "is not this true religion; the consciousness of man's
eminence and lowness; the aspiration to perfection coupled
with the conviction that we cannot reach the highest plane;
the presentiment of the Highest which must exist as a freely
acting will, of the Wisdom whence also our little fragment
of wisdom proceeds, of an infinitely ruling Freedom whence
also our limited freedom has sprung forth—is not that longing for the higher, that soaring up with all the strength of our
soul, the very essence of religion?" [2]

In this theory of religion, Geiger combined the views of
both Schleiermacher and Hegel. The former taught that
religion is a feeling of dependence, of being no more than a
creature; the latter declared that the essence of religion was
the consciousness of God's perfection. In Geiger's philosophy, the religious consciousness is characterized by the tension between the feeling of dependence and the longing for
perfection. It is particularly significant to note the expression, "the humiliating feeling of his dependence" in Geiger's
description of the nature of true piety. To Schleiermacher,
the feeling of dependence was a mark of nobility, the highest
consummation of man's spiritual development. It is the purpose of religion to direct the hearts and minds of men toward
the goal of attaining this mystical experience of total helplessness and unreserved dependence upon the ever-present

---

[1] This thought is, in modern philosophy, associated with the name of Kant.
[2] "Judaism and Its History," p. 21.

and all-sustaining Power of God. In Geiger's view, this "creaturely feeling" is the beginning, not the end, of religion. The pious man refuses to be content with the attainment of sweet resignation. Rather, he derives from that experience the determination and the energy to drive on toward the goal of human perfection. The battle for the values of ethics which religion inspires is a man's job, requiring the virtues of courage and vision, not the feminine, romantic feeling of being carried along on the mighty current of Being.

Having defined the nature of universal religion, Geiger proceeded to prove that Judaism contained the teachings of universal religion in their original and truest form. While the other nations of antiquity worshipped stocks and stones, the Jews conceived the idea of the One, Who is "Self-existent, eternal, almighty, gracious and merciful, long-suffering and abundant in goodness and in truth." This God is the sole Ruler of the universe. There are no inexorable laws of fate which limit His power, nor are there chains of destiny to tie the hands of man, created in His image. Man is like unto God in the possession of moral freedom. While God is perfect, man aspires toward perfection, to become holy even as God is holy.

Not only does Judaism contain the principles of true religion, but the manner in which it arose points unmistakably to its Divine origin. For the Jewish religion was, from its very inception, permeated with the genuine spirit of religion. Judaism continued to develop through the ages, to be sure, but, in its essential principles, it was an embodiment of true religion even in the earliest phases of its history.[3] Thus,

---

[3] It is interesting to note that Geiger's view of the development of the Jewish religion is shared by Yehezkel Kaufman, who, in his profound work "Toldoth HoEmunah HaYisraelith," defends this thesis with irrefutable arguments. Kaufman's viewpoint is best expressed in the following quotation from his introduction to the first volume. "In this phase (the origin of monotheism in Israel), the difference between the system proposed herein and the system accepted in the science of Biblical studies (and the science

Geiger writes in his letter to Holtzman, "That conception of God has its sole genesis in the secret depth of the Jewish spirit and it is present as soon as that find its expression; it is undisputed in its *entire* literature, that mouthpiece of a nation; it comes out 'finished,' if you so desire, from that

---

of ancient history in general) is largest. It is possible to say, the difference is most fundamental. The dominant tendency is to conceive of the religion of Israel as one of the phenomena of the religious life of Oriental peoples, as connected in its roots to the creeds of the ancient peoples of the Orient. This tendency is dominant though it assumes different forms. Some scholars strive to show that there was a monotheistic stream in ancient Oriental paganism and others, that there was on the contrary an element of paganism in the religion of Israel. But all are agreed in this thought, that there is here an organic connection; that the faith of Israel, even that which is peculiar to it, should be understood and interpreted through the Oriental religions; that the faith of Israel was constantly nourished by the creative genius of the Oriental nations and that even in the period of the literary prophets, it derived from that source essential ideas and symbols. Science labored hard in order to make clear the identical elements in Israel's religion and in the faiths of the ancient nations; to reveal the points of connection, the pagan roots of Israel's creation.

Furthermore, it was an accepted postulate, based on a certain interpretation of the testimony of tradition, that the people of Israel itself was, until the destruction of the first temple, a pagan people. Hebrew monotheism is not a creation of the people. The seed of monotheism was guarded by certain individuals, the ancient property of priests or the creation of later prophets. . . .

In this book, this entire conception is negated in all its forms. The faith of Israel is here conceived as an original creation of the Hebrew nation. This creation is absolutely different from everything which the spirit of man had created in the entire pagan world. Israel's monotheism has no roots in the pagan world. Furthermore, the Israelite form of monotheism was not born as a "theological" doctrine, that individuals or schools have excogitated and developed, and it is not a doctrine that was merely expressed in this or that passage, this or that literary layer. It is a basic idea of a *national culture,* which bears in its entirety and from its beginning all the marks of Israel's creativeness. It is not an idea that was artificially adapted to pagan conceptions, but *a primary style of a national culture.* The religion of Israel is here conceived as an original creation of the people of Israel, as a world in itself, individual and unique, without parallel and comparison. There is in this faith an ancient inheritance from the pagan period, prior to the formation of the faith of YHWH. But, the budding of the faith in God marked the end of paganism in Israel. Israel was not a pagan nation, despite the apparent testimony of tradition."

place of its birth, like the child, even if it does grow up to manhood, it has not put itself together out of component parts blown together from the most various points. You may call that 'dropped in': I know of no genesis. God Himself is its father and Israel its mother, and you cannot find for it parents nor even nurses wheresoever you look for them." [4]

A religion which arose in this spontaneous fashion out of the inner resources of the nation, independently of foreign influences, is obviously the production of the genius of the nation. Its mysterious origin can only be understood as the effect of a special gift of insight, bequeathed by the Almighty to the people of Israel. Just as the ancient Hellenes are commonly supposed to have been, as a people, endowed with an artistic genius, so we may infer that the Jewish people was similarly endowed with a religious genius. While not every Jew was a prophet or a saint, the people as a whole were blessed with the power of producing prophets and saints. "If this be so," he writes, "we may speak of a close touch of the individual spirit with the Supreme Spirit, of the light thrown into individual spirits by the Power that fills everything, so that they could break through their finite barrier; it is—let us not hesitate to speak the word—it is *Revelation,* and that, too, as manifested in the whole nation." [5]

Though Geiger employed the term revelation in speaking of the religion of Israel, it must be understood that the source of authority, to him, was human reason, not any historical event, however Divine. Thus, he did not think of every statement in the Bible or in the Talmud as divinely inspired. The principle of revelation does not accord a blanket certification to the entire body of Jewish belief or practice. The truth of any principle of Judaism is to be examined in the light of the common human understanding. Accordingly, he

---

[4] "Judaism and Its History," p. 402.
[5] "Judaism and Its History," p. 46.

concluded that only the universal principles of Judaism were true.

Are not these universal principles of religion at present the property of all cultured men? If so, then it may be asked whether there is any longer a valid reason for the continued existence of Israel as an organized religious community?

In answer to these questions, Geiger maintained that the mission of Israel was not yet fulfilled. The religions of Christianity and Islam do indeed contain some of the principles of Judaism, but these principles are in those religions intertwined inextricably with pagan ideas. It is therefore the duty of Israel to continue to preach to the world the doctrines of pure ethical monotheism. Furthermore, the Jews today, as the direct physical and spiritual descendants of the people of the Bible, are endowed with the same religious genius as their ancient progenitors and are, therefore, in duty bound to preserve their communal identity in order that the world may not be deprived of their contributions, past, present and future, to the evolution of true religion.

These two reasons for the continued adherence to the Jewish faith—the purity of Jewish doctrine and the Jewish genius for religion, met with widespread approval among the teachers of Reform Judaism. Their insufficiency, however, is quite apparent to the modern student. Concerning the alleged purity of modern Jewish doctrine of religion, it may be pointed out that among many of its Protestant denominations, Christian doctrine is also progressive. In the study of the philosophy of religion, all men employ the same instruments of research—namely, the principles of logic and the available data of human psychology and history. There is therefore no basic reason for the existence of a uniquely Jewish philosophy of religion. In any one generation, it may indeed be true that a definite recognizable cleavage exists between the philosophies of religion of the outstanding Jewish teachers on the one hand and the leading Christian thinkers on the other hand. But then, so long as the liberal interpreters of their respective faiths base their doctrines upon independent scientific observation, such cleavages can only be regarded as temporary and accidental.

As to Geiger's claim of a special genius for religion supposedly possessed by the Jewish people, it is pertinent to recall that he was in favor of eliminating all traces of nationalism from the Jewish religion. To assert that the Jewish people, as a race, are endowed with peculiar characteristics which fit them for their religious mission, and then to deny that the Jewish people are at present a nationality is to hold a very paradoxical position. Geiger seems to think of nationalism as being no more than a voluntary identification with the political fortunes of a group. There is, of course, no conflict between nationalism in this formalistic sense, which makes it synonymous with patriotism, and the attempt to maintain a separate race within the body of the nation. But then, nationalism is more than a formal declaration of allegiance. In the consciousness of European nations, nationalism appeared as a feeling of spiritual kinship or of physical blood-brotherhood. Often enough the political aspirations of a nation were motivated by the claim that that nation possessed a set of special characteristics, a "genius" for something or other. Geiger's endeavors to suppress the element of nationalism in the Jewish religion were therefore bound to lend a ring of pretentious hollowness to his claims concerning the genius of Israel.

(*b*) Solomon Ludwig Steinheim [1]

THE PROBLEM WHICH STEINHEIM POSES TO HIMSELF IS THE one of marking out the bounds between reason and revelation. His solution of this problem is a distinct contribution to the philosophy of religion.

---

[1] Steinheim—"Die Offenbarung nach dem Lehrbegrif der Synagoge," 4 volumes.

He begins with the observation that there is a paradoxical relation between the two instruments of man's knowledge —reason and revelation. On the one hand, he notes, revelation can only be claimed for the kind of knowledge which is not accessible to human reason; otherwise, there would be no need to assume the existence of revelation at all. On the other hand, intellectual honesty and spiritual earnestness impel us to judge all our beliefs and ideas by the standards of cold, impartial reason. Since the truths of revelation are by definition non-rational, are they by the same token anti-rational? Is it possible for reason to admit the possibility of extra-logical knowledge, without stultifying itself?

In seeking the answers to these questions, Steinheim first identifies himself with the position of Kant regarding the limits of human reason. It will be recalled that Kant pointed to four questions which reason, carried along by the momentum of its own development, formulates and seeks to understand, but which lie beyond the limits of its rightful sway. These four questions are the existence of God and His freedom, the beginning of the world and the freedom of man. It lies beyond the power of "theoretical" reason to decide whether God exists or not, whether He is free and creative or not, whether the world is eternal or created, whether man's actions are free or determined. Kant later added that "practical" reason, or the moral law, compels us to postulate the existence of God, the freedom of man and immortality.

Agreeing with Kant's views on the limitations of speculative reason, Steinheim rejects Kant's moral metaphysics, arguing that the rigidity of the Categorical Imperative runs counter to the actual ethical consciousness of human beings and that the "postulates" of "practical" reason are a flimsy substitute for metaphysics. Man can avail himself only of the instruments of reason in his efforts to obtain true knowledge. It is a counsel of despair, Steinheim contends, to resort to the assumption of an ethical or a specifically religious intuition.

In place of an intuitionism, which can only function as a constant threat to the power of reason and as a convenient excuse for all forms of obscurantism, Steinheim offers the age-old hypothesis of Divine revelation. It is revelation, or knowledge breaking in from the extra-phenomenal world, he points out, that is alone capable of providing the answers for the questions, which reason is indeed compelled to ask, but which it is powerless to answer. The relation of revelation to religious knowledge is similar to that of the noumena to our knowledge of the physical world. Just as our knowledge of physical events is derived from two sources—the matter of sense-experience and the form of the categories of reason, so, too, our knowledge of the true principles of religion is derived from the matter of revelation and the form of human reason. There is this difference, however, and an important one it is, between the two relations. While the sense-data impinge upon our consciousness whenever our senses are ready to receive them, the light of revelation is a direct Word of God, Who speaks only at rare occasions and to a limited number of persons. Revelation is not a continuous process, nor is it available to all men; it comes, or more correctly, it came to certain persons at certain times, in accordance with the dictates of a Free Will. God speaks to whomsoever He wills and whensoever He wills. And the burden of His message is the final answer to all the basic questions of reason.

From a study of the history of ideas, we learn that it was through the Hebrew prophets and the Bible that revelation entered into the stream of human thought. As a result, Judaism contains true views concerning man and God—views which are not shared by those who follow the natural trend of reason, when it dares to move beyond its natural limitations.

Thus, Judaism teaches the unity of God, in a manner which is distinctly at variance with the views of all pagan thinkers, including all representatives of natural philosophy. For, to the philosophers who do not rely on the truth of revelation, the unity of God is the unity of an underlying substance, or of some immanent force. The God of Judaism, on the contrary, is a transcendent Being—supernatural, in the correct sense of the word.

In the same way, all pagan thought is in agreement on the principle that nothing ever comes from nothing. The "creation" mythologies of paganism describe creation as a transformation of some primary principle, generally, the dead body of a god. Modern philosophy took over this attitude from pagan thought, maintaining the impossibility of creatio ex nihilo and insisting on the eternity of a primal matter or on the indestructibility of substance. Here, again, Judaism defies a well-nigh universal trend of thought in its bold assertion that the world was created by God out of nothing. Finally, neither pagan thought nor natural philosophy conceives of God as a free, creative Being, or of man as a free and responsible person. The concept of necessity dominates the thought of scientists and philosophers and the idea of freedom is consequently inadmissible to their minds. Those who derive their philosophy of life solely from the study of nature cannot possibly believe in freedom, since the source of this idea is the record of true revelation. Only in the literature of Judaism do we find the categorical assertions that both man and God are free.

The two alternatives in all these four questions are, from the standpoint of logic, equally possible hypotheses. There exists no method in logic by which the validity of one or the other alternative may be proven. This fact was clearly demonstrated by Kant. But, the alternatives selected by pagan thought are those which result from the natural overextension of reason, in that the principles of necessity and non-creativeness are taken over bodily from the phenomenal world to the realm of metaphysics. The truths of Judaism are, on the contrary, from a coldly rational standpoint, apart from the evidence of the documents of revelation, possible, but improbable.

How then does true revelation authenticate itself to the mind of the believer, seeing that its principles run counter to the natural trend of the human mind? If Steinheim had believed that the whole Bible was divinely revealed, he would have been able to point to it as the direct Word of God. But in line with Geiger's analysis, he refused to accord Divine status to the laws of Judaism. He was, therefore, confronted with the task of showing how a supernatural revelation could be recognized as such, even though it became commingled in time with beliefs and principles which are, in his view, neither true nor Divine. It cannot be said that Steinheim found an adequate solution to this problem. He claims that the whole of man, as contrasted with the reason of man, will recognize the testimony of revelation. Faith is the decision of the whole person to accept the hypotheses of true religion, rather than to follow the "natural" course of reason and philosophy. Faith cannot, therefore, be the result of reasoned conviction. It springs from a basic affirmation of the soul, which is transmitted from person to person through the contagion of example. It is the duty of Jews to prove their faith through their actual life, so that more and more people will be led to accept the pure doctrines of ethical monotheism.

In this sketch of Steinheim's thought, we see how he attaches himself to Kant, the greatest moralist of modern philosophy. Not content, however, with Kant's reduction of the ethical life to sheer conformity with a formalistic sense of obligation, Steinheim goes back to Judaism and educes therefrom a view of the ethical life as a devoted service of a free man to his Free God. There can be no question as to which view is more inspiring and more consonant with man's spiritual nature. However, Steinheim realizes that we can only accept the truths of Judaism by an act of faith. This faith, in turn, he preaches, will be generated out of a life of loyalty to the religion of revelation.

(c) Samuel Hirsch [1]

IN HIS VIEWS ON THE NATURE OF RELIGION, HIRSCH FOLLOWS the thought of Hegel. Like his master, Hirsch thinks of religion as an intrinsic element of spirit. Religion is the intuitive apprehension of the Whole, which philosophy seeks to grasp piecemeal, through the slow process of reasoning. What the religious consciousness contains as immediate knowledge, philosophy seeks to comprehend discursively. The religious experience is a self-identification with the Absolute, Who is free, in the sense of being unconstrained by any outside force. The main content of the religious consciousness is therefore the feeling of freedom. The man of piety identifies himself with the self-unfolding Absolute, Who develops through time in accordance with His own laws. Hence, freedom is the content of the religious experience.

Hirsch accepts Hegel's interpretation of religion and its relation to philosophy, asserting that freedom is the content of religion and that the attainment of freedom is the goal of human history. However, he introduces certain fundamental modifications in his own version of Hegelianism. In the first place, he argues that man's consciousness of freedom is coupled with the realization of the fact that nothing in nature is free. Contrasting the inexorable laws of nature with the freedom of God, Hirsch notes that man is closer to God than to the other beings of nature. Conscious of being the one exception to the universal sway of the laws of necessity, man intuitively understands that his freedom is a gift

---

[1] Hirsch—"Die Religionsphilosophie der Juden," 1842.

from God, Who is also free. In being free, man and God are one. To the extent that man achieves real freedom, he unites himself with God. Needless to say that this reasoning is foreign to Hegelianism, which identifies nature and God. To Hegel, the freedom of God is expressed in the hard and unbreakable laws of nature, which constitute the manner of His unfolding through time. God is free because He is true to the laws of His own Being. Man is free to the extent that he accepts the Will of God as his own will. To Hirsch, man and God are free, in the ordinary meaning of this term—they are capable of choosing between two alternatives.

Beginning with this modification of his master's system, Hirsch proceeds to interpret man's freedom in an ethical sense. True freedom must be clearly distinguished from mere capriciousness and ordinary license. Since freedom is a supernatural quality, a gift from God, it can only function in the lives of those who have conquered their natural impulses. To be free, he argues, is to turn one's natural life into an instrument for the spiritual life. In the same manner, Hirsch interprets the freedom of God to mean His supremacy over the laws of nature in the interests of His love for man. Thus, God performed the miracles of which the Bible informs us for the purpose of impressing upon the mind of man the fact that He is the master of nature. The reason miracles are no longer performed today is because the development of human thought, as a result of the influence of the Bible, makes such interference with the laws of nature unnecessary. Miracles are no longer needed in our times for the recognition of human or of Divine freedom; they were only necessary at an early stage of civilization, when they served the purpose of exhibiting and underscoring the truths of religion.

Thus, we see how Hirsch's professed Hegelianism was overlaid with the principles of moral freedom and the creativeness of God, principles which he derived from Jewish

tradition. Hirsch only employed the language of the dominant philosophy of his day to express his thought, which was
really and fundamentally Jewish. His argument is from the
recognition of moral freedom to a God, Who is the source
of the ideals of ethics. It does not lie within the limited
scope of this chapter to point out the many shortcomings of
his theology.

(d) Solomon Formstecher [1]

Solomon formstecher bases his philosophy of judaism
upon the world-view of Schelling. He regards all the phenomena of existence as being manifestations of one underlying force of life. The world as a whole is a living organism
in which every element fulfills a definite function. Nothing
in the universe can be adequately understood without the
concept of organism. By this concept, Schelling understands
the union of many parts into one whole, in so thorough a
manner as to imbue every part with the moving spirit of the
whole. With his master, Formstecher thinks of the movements of the currents of life which underlie and explain the
observed facts of experience, as being from the universal to
the particular and from the objective to the subjective.[2]

Continuing Schelling's line of thought, he attributes the
power of self-consciousness to this underlying force of life,
since man, who is a product of nature, possesses this power.
Taking a leaf from Spinoza's "Ethics," Formstecher proceeds
to argue that the Self, or God, Whose attributes are the
phenomena of nature, possesses also an infinite number of
other attributes. These extra-natural qualities of God's Being are, of course, inaccessible to the limited powers of human comprehension. On the basis of this conception, God

---

[1] Formstecher—"Religion des Geistes," 1841.

[2] See end of chapter, "The Philosophical Background of the Star of Redemption."

is both in the world and outside of it. Insofar as God is in the physical world, He is the motive force of Nature; insofar as He stands outside it, He is spirit.

Formstecher departs from his master, also, in his conception of man. So long as man is conscious of himself merely as a living being, striving for his own preservation and for the continued existence of his race, he is no more than a part of nature. For in all these strivings, man is still the obedient servant of the same natural impulses, which prompt the beasts of the field and the fowls of the air. We may even say that as the most complex manifestation of nature's forces, "natural" man is the "soul of the earth," expressing the dumb drives and yearnings of earthly creatures in the high forms of human consciousness. A radical change in the nature of man took place through the rise of the ethical consciousness. As soon as men became conscious of the demands of ethics, they could no longer be classified as merely natural beings. For, in nature, self-preservation is the one and only rule. The ideal of the Good, which arises in the consciousness of human beings, cannot therefore be regarded as a manifestation of nature. Man's possession of this ideal, Formstecher concludes, can only be due to a "revelation" from God. Ethical man, therefore, partakes of the realm of spirit as well as of the order of nature.

Man's reason is understood as his possession of the categories, the ideal forms, which he possesses in his capacity as the self-conscious part of nature. His esthetic sense may similarly be interpreted as resulting from the application of reason to the sphere of good taste. Man's knowledge of the ideal types provides him with the standards which earthly things seek to approximate, and thereby enables him to be the judge of beauty. But, the ideal of the Good lifts man outside of nature; by virtue of this ideal, man is a denizen of two worlds. This dual source of the human personality explains the incessant conflict in the heart of man between the forces stemming from "nature" and those coming from "spirit." Ever since mankind became conscious of this tug of war, it has sought to find a solution which will do justice to the whole of the human personality. The ideal way of life which man seeks is the one which proves capable of reconciling his "nature" with his "spirit," bringing about an "identity" of common purpose between them. After a lengthy discussion, Formstecher arrives at the conclusion that, if the ideal of the Good is taken as the guiding principle, it is possible to evolve a philosophy of life in which the natural impulses of man and his spiritual ideals are adequately harmonized. Such a philosophy of ethical conduct, he claims, is incorporated in the teachings of the Jewish religion.

Religion may be of two types. It may either be the aspiration toward and the worship of God as manifested in the "universal" life of nature, or it may be the dedication of oneself to the service of God as expressed in the "spirit" of man, the ideal of the good individual life. All forms of paganism, Formstecher contends, are variations of the worship of God as nature. Judaism alone represents the ideal of "individual" life in all its purity.

It is not necessary for us to follow Formstecher through his long historical disquisitions, in which the different forms of paganism are examined; the history of Judaism is divided into three periods to accord with Fichte's conception of history, and the emergence of Reform Judaism is portrayed as the final flower of Judaism; Christianity is described as a fusion of Jewish ethics with Pagan metaphysics, capable of serving as a mission to the Gentiles, but lacking in the complete purity of the ideal of individual life; contemporary German philosophy is shown to be paganism at its height of self-consciousness, since God is thought of as immanent in nature; the longing is expressed for a "second Kant" who will firmly establish ethics as the most fundamental science.[3]

---

[3] "Religion des Geistes," p. 358.

For our purpose here, it is sufficient to note that Formstecher is philosophically a disciple of Schelling, but that he
insists on a correction of Schellingianism in the direction of
an ethical view of life. To Schelling's philosophy of nature,
he adds the ideal of the Good, as the religion of individual-
life. Upon this modification of Schellingianism, he then
founds his philosophy of Judaism, in its relation to other
faiths. With Formstecher, then, as with the other Jewish
theologians, the rule holds good that the Jewish "twist" in
philosophy is inspired by a burning zeal for the ideal of the
Good.

(e) Theories of Nationalism

IN THE FIRST DECADES OF THE NINETEENTH CENTURY, NA-
tionalism, an old-new ideal, appeared upon the scene of Europe with explosive violence. Its growth in popular appeal
since then has been almost uninterrupted. During the Na-
poleonic Wars, the nations of Europe gradually became aware
of the value of their individual identities. The special qualities of the different nations were raised by their respective
members to the rank of ends in themselves. Moreover, the
literary expressions of nationalism were met by a rising wave
of popular acceptance and enthusiasm. Nationalism thus became a mighty political and spiritual force. It was destined
in time to become so all-powerful as to choke the sister-ideal
of democracy, which awoke in men's hearts simultaneously
with the ideal of nationalism.

In its early stages, nationalism appeared to be only an implication of the democratic ideal, finding its foe and contrast
in the principle of "legitimacy." The princes and kings of
Europe claimed the right to rule their peoples as a preroga-
tive inherited by them from previous generations. In mighty
accents, democracy asserted the contrary doctrine. It is
the people who must rule themselves. But, who are the peo-

ple? What limits, if any, should be set to the unit of government? Is every little principality and "free city" to be left to its own devices? Here is where the nationalistic ideal insinuated itself into the politics of Europe. The "natural" units of government, it was pointed out, were the language-groups of Europe. Was not the theory of democracy based upon the doctrine of Rousseau that all men were equal "by nature"? What more logical, then, than that the "natural" divisions of mankind be taken as indicating the "natural" borders of the new democratic state?

Thus, nationalism arose in the modern era as an outgrowth of the democratic revolution. It was not long, however, before its anti-democratic character became clearly evident. The reactionaries of the nineteenth century were the first to discover that nationalism could be employed as an instrument for keeping the masses in check. The final implications of the nationalistic ideal were not revealed until our own day, when they are represented as the "philosophy" of the Nazi-Fascist tyrannies.

In what does the novelty of the new nationalism consist? Obviously, the herd instinct has always been potent among the families of mankind. It is claimed by anthropologists that clan-consciousness long antedated the individual's consciousness of the worth of his own individuality. In the story of humanity, men are seen to fight for the goods of the world in groups. Clans exterminate other clans, tribes subjugate other tribes. That the individual exists for the sake of the group is by no means a novel doctrine. In all its grim brutality, this thought dominated men's minds in the dawn of history. We may well ask, therefore, why nationalism is generally regarded as a new spiritual force, characteristic of our modern era.

The answer is to be sought in the fact that nationalism today is regarded as a supreme, if not as the supreme value in life. In the eighteenth century, the existence of many nationalities was more or less taken for granted by all groups. National lines of division were looked upon as facts of nature, neither to be deplored, nor to be extolled. International life must accommodate itself to the variety of languages in use among men, but, no particular virtue inheres in the existence of this variety. For centuries, European civilization was universalistic. During the Roman era, Hellenistic culture and the Oriental cults put a veil of common allegiance over tribal differences. Later, in the Medieval era, the Christian Church directed the thinking minds of Europe into universalistic channels. In its program, the individual's soul was the only consideration, the wall having fallen, "between Jew and Gentile, Greek and Barbarian." In the nineteenth century, however, as secular values began to dominate the minds of men, the special importance of the different customs of the nations of Europe was asserted with a vengeance. What was formerly just a part of the realm of Being, was now elevated into the nobler realm of the Ought. Nationalism, the preservation of the nation's peculiar characteristics, was now extolled as a supreme virtue. Every nation has a "mission" to perform. The symphony of world civilization would be sadly marred if one or the other national group were prevented from adding its tones and overtones to the common chorus. Thus, it may be said that modern nationalism is ancient tribalism with a Messianic complex. It is the well-known and always important fact of nationality transformed into a conscious all-absorbing purpose, in the spheres of both politics and culture.

The rise of the new nationalism was bound to affect Jewish theology, for the Jewish people occupies in Judaism a role, analogous to that of Jesus in Christianity. Whatever concept of God a Christian theologian excogitates, he is then compelled to weld with the personality of Jesus, who represents to him the revelation of the Deity. In a somewhat similar way, there is an intimate connection in Judaism between a thinker's philosophy of religion and his estimate of the nature and function of the Jewish people. For Israel is the people of revelation. While Judaism is, in point of theory, universalistic, without any qualification at all, in point of fact the Torah is observed only by the people of Israel.[1] The Torah and Israel have become inseparably intertwined through the ages. The symbolism of all the holidays is borrowed from the history of Israel, though their significance is always of a general human content. More important yet, it was the Torah, and only the Torah, that prevented the Jewish people from assimilating in the many lands of its dispersion. It was under the wing of the Torah that the nationalistic feelings of Jews—such as they are, were bred and nurtured. Indeed, it is true, "Israel and the Torah and God are one."

The influence of the new nationalistic ideal is clearly marked in all the expressions of Jewish thought of the last century or so, but it is felt in two opposite directions. Historically, its negative results were first made apparent. When the walls of the ghetto first began to crumble, in the days of Mendelssohn, the Jews thought that all that was demanded of them was loyalty to the fatherland. There was not even a premonition in the mind of Mendelssohn, that liberal Christian rulers may require that Jews forswear allegiance to the Jewish nation before they be permitted to enjoy the rights of citizenship. Nor were the rabbis and laymen of the "Sanhedrin," convoked by Napoleon, conscious of any clash between Jewish and French nationalisms. While they pledged unreserved loyalty to the French nation, Lippman Ber, one of their spokesmen, could say, "we are scattered over the entire face of the earth, but we are one people just the same." [2]

---

[1] See on this point, the discussion of Kaufman in "Goleh V'Naichor," chapter "The Universalistic Character of the Religion of Israel."

[2] "Goleh V'Naichor," II, p. 68.

It was not long, however, before the real implications of the new nationalism became apparent. The Jewish leaders speedily realized that whereas they could conclude covenants and treaties with princes and kings, obtaining the right to settle in their domains on a basis of quod pro quid, they could not conclude treaties of alliance with the masses of the several nations, who now emerged as the rulers of their own destines. The natural feeling of the masses is that everything comprised between "their" earth and "their" sky is "theirs." The Jews had no "national" inheritance of their own. Hence they could obtain equal rights only if they became part of the dominant nation. The new demand, felt more than uttered, was that the Jews become absorbed and digested within the bowels of the nation among which they lived. They might share in the privileges of citizenship, but only on condition that they become indistinguishable, in point of nationality, from the majority population. While liberals of all nations defended the right of Jewry to complete citizenship on the ground that Judaism was only a religion, the demands of the new nationalism were dimly perceived by all. The new god of nationalism was a jealous god, who would brook no partnership.

The Reform movement in Germany was motivated, in part, by the desire to eliminate from Judaism any traces of Hebrew nationalism. It was publicly affirmed that the Jews were now a religious group, no longer a nation. The prayer-book was changed into German and all references to Zion were deleted from Jewish liturgy. No longer would the Jews hope for a Redeemer, "who would gather the exiles from the four corners of the earth." Germany was to be the new fatherland of all German Jews. Thus, a radical transformation of Judaism was undertaken with the view of satisfying the new Moloch of Nationalism.

It goes without saying that the rejection of Jewish nationalism could not have been effected without a thorogoing spiritual revolution. So deeply intertwined have the Jewish nation and the Jewish faith become that the most skillful surgeon could no longer pry them apart and expect to deaden the one while preserving the other. It is of the essence of any faith to believe that it is uniquely true and that its devotees are especially privileged in the possession of Divine Truth, if not Divine Providence. The assertion of this belief on the part of Jews, no matter how reformed, leads to the statement that the preservation of Jewish individuality and Jewish character are of supreme value. For the people of Israel has been the bearer of the message of Israel—this a rabbi must maintain, if he is not to accept the Christian version of the development of the Jewish religion. Hence, the value of the people of Israel cannot but be extolled when the message of Israel is preached. A theologian may, like Geiger, declare that the Jews are endowed with a supreme religious genius, or he may declare that Israel was "chosen" by God to declare His Will to the nations, or he may explain the Jewish past by "natural" causes and point to the values of morality and religion as having evolved out of the peculiar fabric of the Jewish "way of life." Whatever alternative the theologian adopts, he must end up by asserting the value of the Jewish individuality. In Judaism, nationalism and religion imply each other. All that Reform Judaism could achieve, therefore, was to focus the attention of its devotees upon the one ideal of religion, permitting the implied ideal of nationalism to function in the background, unseen and unheeded, but not unfelt.[3]

As it happened, these sacrifices were of no avail. The roots of nationalism are fixed in the vague mass-mind, to which nationalism is not a spiritual movement, but a feeling of blood-brotherhood. The development of nationalism in

---

[3] Achad Ha'Am—"Slavery in Freedom."

Europe was in the direction of racism. No amount of patriotic fervor on the part of Jews was therefore able to erase from the mass-mind the feeling that they were strangers. The very haste and feverish anxiety of some Jews to feel more German than the German, was repellent to those whose nationalism derived more from primitive tribalism than from the new democratic ideals. Despite all the spiritual maneuvers of the Jews of Western Europe, the social fact remained true that the barrier of the Jewish religion demarcated a group, regarded as foreign in blood by the masses of the dominating nationality.

It was not long before the new antisemitism made its appearance, dealing a death-blow to the prospect of immediate Jewish assimilation within the national bodies of Europe. No longer based upon charges of Christ-killing, host desecrating or wells-poisoning, the new antisemitism created an impassable gulf between the European Gentile and the Jew. Chamberlain's "Foundations of the Nineteenth Century," though brimming with inaccuracies and scientific absurdities, became the Bible of a large number of Europeans.[4] In Germany, especially, it helped to put the seal of "science" to the deep-rooted antisemitism and the incorrigible pride of the Prussian people. Curiously enough, the new antisemitism, associated though it was with superheated nationalism, had an international aspect. The English, the Germans, the French and the Russians were blood-brothers, according to the Aryan theory. True, the percentage of Aryan blood in the Russians and in the French may be small, but then, the "elite" of the nations could persuade themselves with little difficulty, and with typical Chamberlainian arguments, that their own blood was indeed entirely "Aryan." Thus, a new international front against the Jews was erected, appealing

---

[4] See the review of this book by Shulman, in the Jewish Quarterly Review, 1914, vol. 5, pp. 163–200.

to the excessively stimulated nationalistic feelings of the peoples of Europe. The net result was to slam the door against wholesale Jewish assimilation.

When the negative influence of European nationalism was thus ended in failure and futility, the positive effects of this movement began to manifest themselves with ever greater clearness and boldness. Jewish nationalism now appeared upon the scene as a secular ideal, exerting a powerful centripetal force. The Jewish religion is a matter of faith, but Jewish nationhood is a fact of history and nature, even as are all the nationalities of Europe. Since the physical circumstances of the Jewish people are unlike those of most nations, it was necessary to "normalize" those circumstances either through the acquisition of a homeland, or through the acceptance by all nations of the principle of minorities' rights. Zionism taught the former doctrine, while Dubnow, the famous historian, and many others pointed to the latter possibility as the only way out.

In this book we are concerned only with the effect of revived Jewish nationalism upon modern Jewish theology. From the foregoing discussion, it has become evident that any profound modification of the theory of Jewish nationalism, was bound to affect the doctrines of the Jewish religion. This result was especially to be expected in view of the weakening of the influence of religion through the spread of secularism and skepticism.*

---

* Even the Orthodox writers were influenced by the new nationalism. Thus, Y. M. Pines, who defended the Orthodox viewpoint, could write of the Jewish laws and ceremonies that "their purpose is clearly apparent—to wit, to unify the nation and to refine the nature of men. And all the seers, prophets and sages are witnesses, whose testimonies are of one accord in confirming and in establishing our national existence as a goal of the Torah and as a purpose in creation." [5] In another connection, he states, "from this we

[5] "Yaldai Ruḥi," p. 2.

For centuries, there was no Jewish life apart from the institutions centering about the symbols and ceremonies of the Jewish faith. The synagogue was the social and cultural hub of the community. There was nothing essentially Jewish that was not associated with the service of God. When the wave of disbelief swept across the ghettoes of Central and Eastern Europe, the "apikorsim," the doubters, who had caught the spirit of modern skepticism, found themselves living in a No Man's Land. They could no longer honestly participate in the activities of the Jewish community. Nor, could they well feel at home in the hostile atmosphere of the non-Jewish secular world. Their natural home was haunted with ghosts of the hoary past, they thought; while the palace of the future, the home of all nations and creeds, that was to be built upon the solid foundations of pure reason, had not yet been erected. Caught thus in the interim between two worlds, the "maskilim" were lonely souls, nobly searching for the truth, yet misled by a thousand illusions, perplexed and sorely troubled.[8]

---

are convinced that the goal of Judaism is to establish a whole nation as a great society, whose mission is twofold, to itself and to others. We are not permitted to hurt this society even with our little finger. For this society, by its sheer existence, fulfills its mission here on earth."[6] We see in these quotations the thought that the national existence of Israel is an end of the Torah and not merely a means to its realization. Israel's nationalism is of supreme value in itself, independently of its being the necessary carrier of the Torah. This thought is a radical departure from the traditional attitude, which could not conceive of Israel's existence apart from the Torah. Thus, Saadiah, in a famous passage, asserts, "our people is a people only through its Torah."[7]

[6] "Yaldai Ruhi," p. 27.
[7] "Emunoth V'Deoth," Chap. II.
[8] The extent of this painful perplexity is seen in the fact that the hero of Feierberg's "L'On" becomes insane through brooding over this conflict of loyalties.

Gradually, the saving implications of Jewish nationalism became apparent. In every nationalism there is a strain of romanticism. National practices and customs are esteemed as uniquely significant, quite apart from their intrinsic rationality or usefulness. As the authentic folk-expressions of the soul of the nation, they acquire a mysterious sanctity. The "folk-ways" of a nation are the repositories of its spiritual life. Stemming from the inner recesses of the nation's character, they embody its hidden strivings, its peculiar insight into things, its genius. The very irrationality of a custom or a legend is proof of its origin in the dim subconscious regions of the national soul, which is the source of genuine creativeness. This aspect of nationalism was thoroughly explored in Germany, and it permeated the mental atmosphere of nineteenth century Europe. In Germany, the politically conservative parties sought their justification in this type of romanticism. Savigny, especially, is noted for his defence of the laws of the *ancien regime,* which were assailed by the liberals of his day as reactionary. The legal structure of a government, he argued, is the crystallization through the centuries of the collective insights of the nation. All apparent incongruities and paradoxes are the necessary forms of the unfolding of the nation's character, for the genius of every nation is unique and unparalleled, expressing itself in patterns of thought or behavior which must needs seem strange to those of another nation or to the sons of the same nation who employ the uniform standards of rationality. It is only through a sympathetic identification with one's nation that the value of folk-ways may be appreciated.[9] Thus, the ideal of nationalism began to draw intellectuals "back to the people," to their ways, their laws, their beliefs, their fears and hopes, their entire burden of tradition.

This phase of nationalistic theory became a powerful in-

---

[9] Savigny—"Vom Beruf unserer Zeit fur Gesetzgebung und Rechtswissenschaft."

tellectual force in Russian Jewry of the eighties. Shocked
by the brutality of the pogroms in the years 1880–1881,
many Jewish intellectuals were overcome with remorse at
their former disdain of their own national culture. Earnestly
they began to search for the road back to Israel, realizing
suddenly that, for better for worse, Judaism constitutes their
national treasure, the product and expression of their national soul. The Jewish religion is the characteristic culture
of Jews, is the gift of Jewry to world civilization. Romantic
reverence for tradition took the place, among these nationalistic "baalei te'shuva," of rationalistic scoffing and super-
cilious attempts at reform.

This bewildered return to a sympathetic view of religion
was greatly aided by the lack of a geographical basis for
Jewish nationalism. All through the ages, it was the religion
of Israel which provided the fence behind which the Jewish
nation was able to live and develop its peculiar genius. Now,
that the intellectual foundations of this wall have been undermined in the eyes of many Jews, what is there to prevent the
total dissolution of the Jewish people through progressive
assimilation and intermarriage, in the course of a few generations? The answer to this question lay near at hand. The
Jewish religion could be utilized as a means of providing a
concrete expression for Jewish national life. Through the
continued observance of many laws of Judaism, no longer as
religious ordinances, but simply as folk-ways, visible form
could once more be given to the national life of Jewry in exile.
Thus, the roles were reversed. Formerly, it was the Jewish
religion which was the end and the Jewish people, the means.
Now, it was proposed that many phases of Judaism be cherished for the sake of preserving the Jewish nation in the lands
of its dispersion.

The first and most ardent exponent of this philosophy of
Judaism is Peretz Smolenskin. In his "Ais Lotaas," he
pointed to the danger of total disappearance which con-

fronted the Jewish people if the rapid flood of defection from
Judaism were not effectively checked. The Jewish people
should continue to live, he pleaded, because they are a nation,
albeit "a spiritual nation." But there is no Jewish life in
exile apart from the ways of the Torah. Hence, it is our
duty, as Jews, to bolster the crumbling faith of Israel by
bringing to its aid a revived sense of Jewish national loyalty.
The practices of Judaism should be interpreted as "national
ties," rather than as "bonds of religion." This change of emphasis, Smolenskin was certain, will halt the tide of assimilation and bring new strength to the tottering structure
of Jewish community life. As the expression of the national
will to live, the Jewish religion would regain the mass-
allegiance of Jews.

This artificial, quack-medicinal, approach to the Jewish
religion could not have exerted any important influence, were
it not for rise of a new mass-movement which infused fresh
energy and hope in all phases of Jewish life. The Zionist
movement, which, in its early stages was known as the "love
of Zion," stirred the hopes of European Jewry for eventual
redemption from the lands of the Diaspora. The cultivation
of Jewish national values was now impelled not alone by
forces which stemmed from the past, but by the attraction
of a brightly beckoning future. The fact that the Jews could
not yet take their nationhood for granted and that they still
had to labor toward the creation of their national possessions
acted as a vivifying force. Nationalism was not just an ideal,
a vague feeling or a theoretical shibboleth; it was a concrete
reality, requiring steady action and patient effort. The collection of funds, the reports of the progress made in Palestine,
the educational problems of the Palestinian settlements, the
struggles between the different views of what an ideal homeland would look like, the revival of Hebrew in Palestine, the
creation of new symbols of the national life—all served to
create a virile national atmosphere. And this atmosphere

was in all its elements a peculiar blend of the past and the future, an inseparable mixture of the old pietism with the new nationalism. Thus, the rise of Zionism served to raise national feelings to new heights and, indirectly, to lend prestige to the opinions of those who sought to provide a new basis for Judaism—to wit, the Jewish national soul.

Of the theoreticians of Jewish nationalism, only two need concern us here, Naḥman Krochmal and Achad Ha'Am. The views of these thinkers exerted a powerful influence on the development of modern Jewish thought. Hence, we shall consider them somewhat more fully, though of course, only from the standpoint of the relevance of their thought to the central problems of Jewish theology.

Naḥman Krochmal, in his posthumous work, "Guide of the Perplexed of our Time," achieved a synthesis of religion and nationalism, that helped to mold the opinions of many subsequent scholars. Yet, he managed to arrive at this result without being conscious of nationalism as a distinct motive force in Jewish life. To him, the "perplexities of our time" were centered round the revived historical sciences of Judaism. How shall we reconcile the historical method, which uncovers the slow development of the Jewish faith, with the accepted views of the Torah? Krochmal was the friend and mentor of a number of scholars, like Rappaport, Erter, Bloch and others. He was, therefore, keenly aware of the manifold details in which the new science of Judaism conflicts with the views current among the Orthodox Jews of his day. Also, beneath the mass of details, he was able to see the deep chasm which separated the underlying viewpoint of modern criticism from that of traditional Judaism.

Krochmal thought he found a way of bridging that chasm. Every nation, he taught, has an "idea" which expresses itself in all the creative work done by its members. There is a certain ideal unto which the entire nation dedicates its en-

ergies and which, in turn, contains the secret of its destiny.
Thus, the search for beauty was the ideal of the classical
Hellenes and the lust for power was the ideal of the ancient
Romans. In the course of history, every "idea" has its day
and the fortunes of the nation rise along with those of its
"idea." The course of human history consists in a gradual
approach to the attainment of absolute truth. The human
mind grasps different phases of Absolute Truth, at the successive epochs of history, assimilating the "ideas" of different cultures in the course of its slow development. In
this manner, the "ideas" of the various nations are gradually
absorbed by the culture of mankind, as the wheel of history
rolls along on its eternal road. Since, however, a people cannot continue to live as a distinct group once its "idea" has
become a part of the general treasure of all mankind, history
reveals to us with monotonous repetition the ceaseless rise,
growth and final decay of nations. The Babylonians, the
Egyptians, the Greeks, the Romans—each had its piece to
say in the cosmic drama. When they had said their say,
when the mind of man had fully digested their particular
"idea," there was no longer any reason for their existence.
Hence, they disappeared as national groups.

Is there any goal to this ceaseless birth and death of
"ideas"? Does the human mind move toward the attainment
of an all-comprehensive idea, or is it that the change of
"ideas" is planless and directionless, blind and capricious?
Krochmal is definitely convinced that there is an Absolute
Spirit (vuḥni muḥlot) which is the goal and end of the human mind. This Absolute Spirit contains in itself the grains
of truth of all the other national "ideas," and represents the
final Truth.

Now, it happens that from the dawn of its history the Jewish people had united its destiny with that of the Absolute
Spirit. From the days of Abraham, it searched for God,
the Creator of all things and the Source of all lesser "ideas."

The Jewish national "idea" is thus the one permanent Idea. Hence, the Jewish people is eternal. Throughout its history, it refused to worship any limited "idea," dedicating its life to the service of God Himself. Therefore, it survives into modern days, while the nations which pinned their respective faiths on temporary "ideas" have long since perished.

Does it mean, then, that the Jewish people have long ago discovered the Absolute Truth, while all mankind is compelled doggedly and by slow degrees to reach that perfection? The answer to this question is not given with any degree of clearness by our author. His thought seems to have been that the "idea" of a nation is an intuitive insight of that nation. The people cannot tell how they came to possess it, nor can they, at least in the beginning, prove its validity. Through its subsequent life, the nation gradually obtains an understanding of its own "idea." So, too, with the Jewish people. Intuitively they have attached themselves to the Absolute Spirit, seeking Him, worshipping Him with all the fibers of their national soul, while, along with the rest of the world, their understanding of Him grows with the cumulative knowledge of the ages. But while others identify themselves completely with the different stages along the path of human spiritual progress, the Jew lives both in the mental atmosphere of his own age and in that of the Future. The progress of reason can only unfold what he already has in intuition. As mankind draws ever nearer to the Truth, the Jew feels he is coming Home. Thus, the Jewish religion is subject to the law of unvelopment rather than of development; like the unwinding of a coiled spring, it reveals new phases of its being, at the different periods in history. It, too, has its cycles of birth, growth and decay, but it rises ever again from the dust, for its "idea" is the final goal of mankind. As different aspects of the Absolute Spirit manifest themselves in the succeeding epochs of human history, the fortunes of Jewry vary in accordance with the revelation, the spread and the absorption of those aspects. Israel's history is unique, then, not in being changeless, but in the fact of possessing the capacity to repeat the cycles, which circumscribe the entire life of other nations.

Many important links in Krochmal's thought were left unfinished in his published book. His conception of the cyclical history of nations and their ideas is manifestly borrowed from the "historical school" of Germany, which derived its inspiration from Herder, Fichte and Hegel. Whether Krochmal's "ruḥni muḥlot" is merely Hegel's Absolute Spirit, which is comprehended through succeeding stages of history, or whether the Absolute Spirit stands for the God of Israel, it is now difficult to decide.[10]

The important point to remember is that Krochmal presented to his contemporaries a view of Judaism which made it compatible with the principle of progress. The essential truth of Judaism, its intuitive view of God, is valid and eternal, while the temporary reasoned concepts of God and, possibly too, the ways of worshipping Him are subject to the universal rule of cyclical progress. Historical criticism could thus continue on its way, revealing the successive layers of Jewish thought. In this work, the scientific historians were, in a real sense, following in the footsteps of Abraham, for, through their labors, the national spirit of Israel was asserting itself. A new cycle in the spiritual development of Israel was begun in the modern era. Those who are earnestly engaged in the search of truth, need not fear that they are deserting the "vineyard of Israel." Through them and their successors in the centuries to come, a new Golden Age of Israel's civilization is bound to arise.[11] For Israel is rooted in Eternal Truth.

---

[10] Ravidowitz—"Introduction" to his edition of Krochmal's "Guide."

[11] This was clearly the meaning of Krochmal when he declared that the last cycle of Jewish history ended in his own day. Manifestly, in his philosophy, the end of one epoch is the beginning of its successor. See end of Chapter XI of Krochmal's "Moreh."

Thus, it is evident how Krochmal shifts the center of gravity from the religion of Israel to the people of Israel. It is the core and center of the religion of Israel that is true unto eternity. But, the guaranty of its truth lies, firstly, in the national genius of the people of Israel and, secondly, in the right reading of general European thought. A Jew's duty is to seek the truth wherever he can find it. So long as his intellectual connection with his people is unbroken, he may rest secure that the national spirit will express itself through his work. God's revelation, mind you, is in the *soul* of Israel, not in its *books*. Herein lies the great importance of Krochmal's philosophy and here, too, the great attraction of his system is to be found. He seemed to unshackle the bold, searching spirit of the Jewish intellectual, for while the letters of the books are clear and unyielding, the concept of a creative soul working in the dark chambers of the mind, offers unlimited freedom in thought and deed.

In a definite manner, too, his thought served to make possible the adherence to Judaism of some of those who doubted the theoretical basis of the Jewish religion. The phrase *ani ma'amin*, I believe, could well mean for them, "I belong to a people that intuitively believes . . ." Personal intuition cannot serve as the basis of religion to those who do not possess that intuition. But, the intuition of a nation is the heritage of all its members, even of those of its sons in whom the national genius is but feebly expressed. Through association with his people, the Jewish intellectual could obtain the needed basis for his faith. The Jewish religion was henceforth to rest on the ground of experience, since unquestioning belief in the infallibility of tradition had been irrevocably lost. But this experience was not a personal experience of the individual believer; it was the experience of the nation, won through centuries of trial, travail and anxious wrestling with God; diffused sparsely and thinly yet no less truly in the hearts of all the nation's sons. What the prophets of Israel felt "as a fire burning in their bones" is thus, through the theory of a national soul, transformed into the possession of the entire house of Israel. As a famous Jewish legend relates: the souls of all Israelites, even of those yet to be born, were present at Sinai, to echo the words of acceptance, "na'aseh v'nishma." In this manner, Krochmal succeeded in grafting the religion of Israel or at least its essential message upon the feeling of national unity.

The philosophy of Krochmal exercised a definite fascination over the minds of many Jewish scholars. Elements of his thought can be detected in the works of many subsequent thinkers. Yet his book failed to carry out the purpose implied in the title. It could not really serve as guide for the perplexed of his day. In the first place, it rested on a conception of national destinies that did not long appeal to the European mind. Whether Krochmal was to be interpreted as a Hegelian or not, the fact remained that his national "ideas" were barely more real than the mythical national idols which were supposed to represent them. Krochmal's philosophy of Judaism was cemented together out of bits of thought that did not enjoy popular credence. Hegel and Herder proved to be poor substitutes for Moses and Akiba.

In the second place, Krochmal assumed that the "perplexed" of his day still believed in the God of Israel, or in what he called "ruḥni muḥlot." He considered it his function to point out that in that belief the guaranty of Israel's eternal life was contained. But what if one entertains doubts even in respect of the reality of this Absolute? Would not, then, the entire argument of Krochmal fall to pieces? Hegel asserted that the philosophical Absolute could not be questioned, because even in the act of doubting, its reality is assumed. This position has been justly assailed. Krochmal's version is even more open to criticism, since his Absolute is not merely a matter of definition, but a Living Being.[12] His

---

[12] This is the contention of Rawidowitz in above-mentioned reference.

proof of the existence of God by the argument of design is neither convincing nor original. There is left the thought that the God of Israel and His Word have been glimpsed in the national, collective insight of the people of Israel. This again is an assertion which thoroughgoing doubters would not accept. So called "national insight" cannot confer the seal of truth upon any proposition. Has not Krochmal himself taught that the national "ideas" of other nations were only relatively true? Why, then, should a Jew assume a priori that the insight of his own national group is infallible? Truth knows no national boundaries whatsoever. Hence, any combination of final truth with nationalism discloses itself upon analysis to be but a temporary makeshift. Krochmal's labors did not result in any exception to this rule.

In the writings of Asher Ginsberg, known under the penname Achad Ha'Am, ideas are presented which have a definite bearing upon the problems of Jewish theology. Achad Ha'Am was not a theologian. He did not believe in the existence of a personal God, and he did not give much thought to the problems of religion as such. But he was vitally concerned with the problem of Jewish survival. Realizing clearly that in the lands of the Diaspora, it was the Jewish religion which kept the Jewish people intact, and that the Jewish religion was by degrees losing its hold upon large sections of the Jewish people, he sought to discover a method whereby the existence of the Jewish people in the future could be assured. Father of the movement of "cultural Zionism," he did not believe that a large part of European Jewry could be transported to Palestine. The major portion of the Jewish people, he predicted, would continue to live as a minority group in the countries of Europe and America. Feeling that world Jewry was confronted with the imminent danger of extinction, he sought to uncover a substitute for religion capable of commanding new motives for Jewish survival. In the course of his search, he proclaimed ideas which have since entered into all branches of Jewish literature and which are bound to influence any Jewish theologian of the future, owing to the intimate relationship in Judaism between nationalism and religion.

In the brilliant essays of Achad Ha'am, two ideas are presented and emphasized by constant repetition—the national will to live and the national spirit. These concepts were axiomatic to Achad Ha'Am, and, armed with them, he sought to recast the Jewish scene. These ideas were the pillars upon which both his philosophy of Judaism and his practical program of action were based.

First, then, he asserted that every nation has a "will to live," even as every person is endowed with the impulse for self-preservation. This "will to live" as a nation is an instinctive force, which, like every instinct, finds the means necessary for its fulfillment, with or without the help of reason. Nay, it turns the power of reason to its own ends, compelling man's rational faculties to invent "good reasons" for its purposes when the "real reasons" are not regarded as honorable ones. Thus, the national will to live may be frustrated by more potent interests; it may be compelled to put on a false face when it rises to the surface of consciousness, but, as a force of nature, it never really ceases to influence human behavior. The national impulse for self-preservation stems from the subconscious regions of the soul and is, therefore, in itself an irrational and primary force. The nation need not justify its existence; it wills to live even as any other organic being.

On the basis of this theory of biological nationalism, Achad Ha'Am offers a complete interpretation of Jewish history. When Israel was young, the national will to live was naively taken for granted. Achad Ha'Am points to the fact that in the older books of the Bible national reward and punishment is regarded as sufficient. The sense of national unity was then so strong that individual happiness was by comparison unimportant. Thus, he wrote in a famous passage, "In all the commandments and laws, the blessings and the curses, which the Torah of Moses put before us, there is one aim held constantly in view: the salvation of the entire nation in its inherited land, and it pays little attention to the happiness of the individual man. Every Israelite is in her eyes but one limb from the people of Israel, and the benefit which will accrue to the group is the reward to the deeds of the individual."

After the destruction of the first temple, when the national spirit was greatly weakened, the individual weal and woe became a painful problem to the teachers of the Jewish religion. The deterioration of the sense of national unity brought the individual's concern with his own fate to the fore. If unchecked, this tendency might have resulted in the complete disintegration of the people of Israel. The prophets and Sages of that day brought the power of the Jewish religion to the aid of the faltering bonds of nationalism. They satisfied the longing for individual happiness with the doctrines of individual immortality and resurrection. During the second Commonwealth, the religious and national motives continued to function together, different parties in Israel laying more stress on the one rather than on the other motive. The progressive destruction of Jewish political power of necessity brought the religious motive more and more to the surface. When the final ruin of the Palestinian center brought the Jewish people to the brink of total national disappearance, the Jewish religion again supplied the needed remedy. By erecting a "fence about the Law," by multiplying commands and prohibitions, it effectively restricted the area of contact between Jew and Gentile. The physical walls of the ghetto were not as important as the spiritual walls of "do's" and "don't's" with which the Jewish religion halted the tide of assimilation and established a Jewish social environment in the midst of a Gentile world. Behind the mighty fortresses of the Jewish religion, the national life of Jewry was assured. The practices of the Jewish religion were the armor needed by the Jewish will to live, in order to maintain itself in the unnatural circumstances of the "galuth." Thus, the national impulse for self-preservation employed the Jewish religion as an unconscious tool with which to effect its purpose of survival. Throughout the years of exile, the Jewish religion was only the conscious "front," while the real force, making for Jewish survival, was the national will to live, a basic motive, which, as we saw, functions in the nether regions of the soul.

When the wave of piety began to recede, in modern times, spiritual confusion resulted. In the hearts of modern Jews, a tug of war goes on between the forces of assimilation and Jewish nationalism. One of the results of this spiritual upheaval is Reform Judaism which represents a new compromise between the national will to live and the ideal values of consciousness. Having rejected Jewish nationalism, the Reformists were still compelled by their national instincts to invent a reason for Jewish survival. The belief of Reform Jews, that to the Jewish people has been given the "mission" of spreading the true ideas of religion, Achad Ha'Am regarded as the outcome of inner perplexity. For the ideas of ethical monotheism are the property of modern culture generally. There is no need and no sense in a particular group arrogating to itself the "mission" of promulgating these ideas. For this reason, he concluded that Reform Judaism is too flimsy and artificial a compromise to serve the national purpose. Furthermore, he declared that through their insistent denial of Jewish nationalism, the Reformists are compelled to continue their activities under false pretences, thus condemning themselves to "spiritual slavery" and intellectual sterility.[13]

---

[13] Essay on "Avduth b'Soch Cheruth."

In his own generation, Achad Ha'Am continued, the national instinct of Israel has attained complete self-consciousness. No longer is it compelled to function behind the scenes. Frankly and without apologies we of the Zionist movement, assert the right of every nation to live its life. However, the national consciousness is still too weak among the Jewish masses to assure in itself the survival of the Jewish people. The forces of assimilation in the modern world are so powerful as to condemn the weaker nationalities to death or total paralysis.

In order to enable the Jewish people to survive, it is necessary to arouse and to strengthen their national will to live. This can be effected through two mutually supplementary methods. The first is the redemption of the Holy Land and the establishment therein of Jewish colonies. By engaging in this national work, the sense of national unity will be brought once again to its pristine strength. The work of Zionism is important, then, from the standpoint of national morale, in that it serves to revive and to strengthen the Jewish national will to live. The national impulse for self-preservation can be aroused and nursed back to normalcy only through the tasks of national upbuilding.

The second method whereby Achad Ha'Am sought to strengthen the Jewish national consciousness is an application of the second central thesis of Achad Ha'Am's philosophy. Every nation, he maintained, has a "national spirit," a certain cultural bent, which finds expression in the national culture and destiny. This thought was popular in the nationalistic circles of all European lands, especially among the reactionaries. Dostoevsky in Russia, Mickiewitz in Poland, Fichte in Germany have already proclaimed national "missions" for their respective peoples. And Hegel had taught that every nation embodies a certain "idea" in the progressive unfolding of the mind of God through the history of mankind. It will be recalled that Reform Judaism had already employed the "mission" theory, in an anti-nationalistic sense. It was the mission of Israel to spread the doctrines of ethical monotheism through the world. In order to accomplish this mission, however, it was necessary that the Israelites become integral members of other nationalities, in order that the truth of their teaching may not be impaired by the nationalistic prejudices of the European nations.[14]

Achad Ha'Am taught that the "national spirit" is a potent social force. While only the great sons of the nation are able to give expression to that spirit, the masses at large are instinctively imbued with it, feeling not merely reverence or sympathy, but a sense of obligation to the national culture. Furthermore, the creative powers of the nation are attuned to its "national spirit," so that it can be truly productive and original only along the lines of its national tradition. There is no such thing as universal, human culture; there are only so many national cultures, each nation feeling the urge and the capacity for its own peculiar style of work and sphere of activity.

The Jewish "national spirit" is expressed not so much in religion, as in morality. At this point, the originality of Achad Ha'Am's viewpoint is most in evidence. Previous writers have sought the expression of the "Jewish spirit" in the Jewish religion, in the belief in the One God. To Achad Ha'Am, on the other hand, the beliefs and practices of the Jewish faith were merely the outer garments of the intuitive and distinctive moral convictions of the Jewish people.

This change in emphasis enabled Achad Ha'Am and his generation to identify themselves, in all earnestness and sincerity, with the Jewish national heritage. For while the Jewish religion includes the acceptance of beliefs that are open to question, Jewish morality is a matter of intuition and will, operating to a large extent outside the sway of reason.

---

[14] M. Gudemann—Nationaljudentum, Wien, 1897.

In direct contrast to Kant, who claimed that all men are conscious of the same Categorical Imperative, Achad Ha'Am asserted that nations differ in the character of their moral insight.

The Jewish view of morality found expression in the fervent outbursts of the Hebrew prophets, who were the instruments of the Jewish national soul. Thus, he wrote in his essay on "Priest and Prophet": "The prophet is one-sided. A certain moral idea fills all the chambers of his heart, absorbing him completely, with all his senses and feelings, so that he is unable to forget about it even for one moment; he cannot see the world except through the spectacles of this thought and all his labors and strivings are toward the end of realizing this ideal in all the phenomena of life. For this ideal, the prophet battles all his days, to the limit of his ability, expending his powers without pity, without calculation and without noting the real conditions of life and the demands of general harmony. He looks only at that which *ought* to be, according to his heart's particular perception, not at that which *can* be, judging by the general conditions outside him. The prophet is then an *original* force. His work influences the structure of the general harmony (of values), while he himself does not accept that harmony, but remains in his particularity, extreme, narrow, the guardian of one aspect, jealous of all other phases of life."

Achad Ha'Am conceded that among other nations, such moral extremists have also arisen and have labored for their cause. "But in far greater measure than is the case among other nations, prophecy rested in Israel in ancient times, not as an accident or as a temporary phenomenon, but continuously over the period of many generations, as if it were an essential quality of its being, bearing the stamp of its national spirit."

What is that central thought of the prophets, which is so

characteristic of the Jewish national spirit? The answer we find stated most clearly in the same essay,[15] "The essential thought of Hebrew prophecy was the reign of absolute justice in all creation; above—through the 'Righteous One of the Universe,' who holds in his hand the category of Justice and judges all his creatures with righteousness; below—through man, who was created in the image of God and who is obligated to imitate his Creator and to help him, as it were, in the conduct of the world in the ways of righteousness. This thought with all its moral and religious implications was the essence of life to the Hebrew prophets; in it, they saw everything and outside of it, nothing was to them of great moment. Righteousness is beauty, is good, is wisdom and truth, and without it—all is vanity."

This doctrine of absolute justice is not worked out completely in our author's writings. To the end of his life, he hoped to carry out the task of writing a systematic work on "The Ethics of Judaism." His illness and his public undertakings prevented him from realizing this dream. Still, there are in his works, brilliant observations concerning the basic intuition of Israel. It envisages, he claimed, the ideal existence of a perfect moral order, abstract and impersonal, functioning in accordance with principles as rigid and as permanent as the laws of nature. This world of Ought is not yet here, nor will it ever be completely realized, but it exists as a beckoning goal in the minds of the prophets and, to a lesser degree, in the minds of the followers of the prophets, stamping itself ever more deeply upon the society of men.

Already the prophets have realized that their moral ideal was doomed to ineffectiveness, unless they could find a group of men, pledged to its realization. In their own people, they recognized this "nation of priests and a holy people." The famous prayer of Moses, "Who will grant it, that all the peo-

---

[15] "Al Porashath D'rochim," I, p. 182.

ple of God were prophets," expressed the longing of the prophets and the subsequent course of Israel's history. For the prophetic message had indeed become the soul and substance of the life of the Jewish people. In all their literature, their religious beliefs, their hopes, their fears and their rituals —the one thought of abstract justice prevails.

"If that gentile who wished to learn all of the Torah while standing on one foot had come to me, I would have told him, 'Thou shalt not make unto thyself any statue or image —this is the entire Torah and the rest is but a commentary.' For indeed, the basic qualities of the doctrine of Judaism, in which respect it differs from other doctrines, is its absolute tendency to lift the religious and ethical perception above any limited sensual form and to present as its *immediate* object an abstract ideal, without an image. . . . And this basic tendency of the Jewish people to rise above any image, in their religious and moral life, is seen not only in respect of the religious and moral *ideal*, but also in regard to the goal of morality and religion. It has already been said and repeated many times, so that it is no longer necessary to explain the matter at length, that the Torah of Judaism sees her goal not in the salvation of the individual man, but in the salvation and perfection of the totality, of the nation, and in the end of time, of all of mankind—that is to say, the goal is a class-concept, having no limited sensual image.

"In yet another respect, perhaps the most important, this same tendency is revealed; in relation to the basis of morality . . ." The ethics of Judaism is based upon justice, rather than love. The former, it will be noted, is an objective concept, capable of being expressed in universal laws. The latter is a subjective feeling, incapable of serving as the basis of any lasting society. Judaism knows the virtue of love. It is supposed to be a distinguishing characteristic of the people of Israel. But, love must supplement justice, and may not take its place. In the beginning is "midas hadin," the category of justice. "And, in truth, 'midas horaḥmim,' the category of mercy, is good only when it is combined with 'midas hadin,' the category of justice, and if the latter is a higher rung in the ladder of ethical development, the former is the moral basis upon which the entire ladder stands." [16]

To this moral theory, the entire Jewish people is dedicated. The rabbis incorporated the prophetic ideal into a body of laws and practices, which rendered it coextensive with life itself. The essence of the rabbis' search was to introduce moral "holiness" in all the activities of men. The motive force of all their labors was the drive to express the national spirit of Israel in the form of practical deeds.

In our own day, Achad Ha'Am continues, this moral ideal of Israel has won the lip service of millions, but its full realization is not yet achieved. In fact, life can always approach but never quite reach the lofty ideal of absolute morality. It is the mission of Israel, to regain hold of this ideal and to become once again "a prophet to the nations."

Reform Judaism, too, preaches the doctrine of the mission of Israel. But, Achad Ha'Am noted significant differences between his own views and those of the Reformists. "A similar call has indeed come forth on occasion, in our times, from scholars and rabbis of the West, authors of the well-known doctrine concerning 'the mission of Israel' among the nations. But, as has been said, the prophetic 'mission' differs from theirs in three respects. (a) Its essence is not the revelation of a new theoretical truth and its spread through the world that all may accept it and thereby fulfill the 'mission.' It is the drawing of the practical life toward absolute justice, without any possibility of attaining at any time a complete victory. (b) This 'drawing,' being practical and not theoretical, demands therefore, as a necessary condition to its possibility, not an absolute dispersion of Israel among the nations, but, on the contrary, a unification and concentra-

---

[16] "Ibid.," I, 141.

tion of its powers, at least partially, in a place where it will
be possible for it to lead the life which is suited to its character. (c) Since there is no hope that this moral attraction
will win a complete victory over the other forces which pull
human society in other directions, therefore it and those who
profess it are timeless, unless men should cease to be men
and lead human lives, being content with the life of 'the
righteous who sit with their crowns upon their heads, enjoying the radiance of the Presence of God.' " [17]

The "national spirit" of Israel is, then, to Achad Ha'Am
as to Krochmal, capable of assuring the eternity of Israel.
Their moral ideals enabled the Jews to endure all manner of
evil in their long wanderings, teaching them to despise the
mailed fists of their oppressors. On the strength of his "national superiority in the realm of ethics," the Jew knew himself, even in exile, to be a priest in the "great temple of the
God of righteousness." [18] The source of the Jew's strength in
the past was not, then, his religion, so much as his standards
of moral value. It follows that even those who no longer are
able to believe in the ancient faith may still maintain their
contacts with the well-springs of the nation's vitality, as long
as they cherish the moral values of Judaism.

If the inner motives of Jewish survival have not been impaired by the impact of modern skepticism, why is the specter
of assimilation and total disintegration so menacing and so
all-pervasive in our age? The answer to this question, Achad
Ha'Am pointed out, is the "petrification of the Jewish heart."
The feelings of national unity were all but atrophied in the
long centuries of exile. In the sphere of religion, this fact is
seen in the lack of adaptability and growth, which is characteristic of present-day Orthodoxy. Among the non-re-
ligious, the decay of the national spirit is manifested in the

---

[17] "Kohen v'Novi," A. P. D., I, p. 184.
[18] "M'dinas HaY'hudim 'vTsoras HaY'hudim"—A. P. D., II, "Shinuy
HoArochin"—A. P. D., II.

wholesale desertion of Jewish community life, in the slavish imitation of foreign patterns, in the unthinking acceptance of modern ideas and standards. What Israel needs is "a revival of the Jewish heart," a new wave of enthusiasm for the ancient values and the creation of new intellectual forms for the old truths.[19]

No one realized as clearly as Achad Ha'Am the inability of the so-called "national spirit" to arouse the sense of obligation of the Jewish masses. With all his emphasis on the moral teachings of Judaism, he was clearly aware of the religious pivot of support, upon which the characteristic Jewish morality rested. Take the belief of the "Righteous Judge" away from Judaism and the entire moral edifice crumbles instantly. The Jewish conception of absolute morality, without the Jewish conception of God, is deprived of the assurance that it is not just an idle dream, an arbitrary human standard without any basis whatsoever in human nature or in the structure of the universe. It may legitimately be argued whether or not morality without religion is possible. Certainly, all relativistic theories of ethics require no religious foundation. But, an absolute standard of morality, the assertion of eternally valid ethical truths—what meaning can any such claim possess if we dispense with the concept of an Absolute Being, Who stands outside the flowing stream of phenomena? Dimly sensing the inadequacy of the moral ideal of Judaism, when deprived of its religious fountainhead, Achad Ha'Am hoped that the return of Jewish culture to Palestine would in the course of time lead to the birth of a new "ideal," thereby giving new meaning to Jewish life, vitalizing the "dry bones" of Israel.

Thus, he wrote in his second introduction to "Al Poroshath D'rochim": "Among the Western Jews there is only one, Israel Zangwill, it appears to me, who understood the importance of the question of an ideal and said explicitly that

---

[19] "Torah she'Blev," A. P. D., 72.

there is no cure to the sickness of our people, which decays progressively, except either a new ideal or the return to Zion. But even he sees only half the problem, in that he separates the two, seeking the remedy in either one or the other, whereas in truth, we need both and the one is impossible without the other. Zionism, as a political movement alone, is not sufficient, powerless as it is to gather the entire dispersion and to end our troubles. On the other hand, no living thought, no great national ideal, can be created in exile, when the powers of the nation which have been uprooted from their national habitat lie bound and hidden, unable to function in the wide open world and to develop in a normal manner. The *spirit of our people* requires liberty, free movement in its historical environment, in order that it may be aroused from its long somnolence and become capable of reviving the national ideal, giving to it a form suitable to our present needs, in order that it become again a shield to our scattered nation, guarding him from moral degeneration and strengthening his power to endure his troubles till the end, with knowledge and clear understanding, knowing the purpose of his suffering and the worthwhileness of that purpose."

In this doctrine of the "new ideal," which the Palestinian Jews were expected to develop, Achad Ha'Am admitted, by implication, the fallacy of the argument that Jewish ethics alone was, throughout the ages, the living core of the Jewish national spirit. For Jewish ethics, in theory at least, is all made, as ready to function now as ever before. What Achad Ha'Am was really looking for could not be supplied by any new ethical theory or even by any tremendous upsurge of moral energy. As has been pointed out by Kaufman and others, a moral doctrine has never in history served as the cause of group divisions. Also, all the groups who departed from the Jewish faith in the past, amalgamated with other nations, unhindered by their alleged "superior morality." Again, Jewish apologists in the Middle Ages appear not to have been conscious of any differences in regard to morality from their Christian and Mohammedan disputants.[20]

The real search of Achad Ha'Am was directed toward a new religion—a new faith, not only in man, but in God. Though he never admitted that the "new ideal" was predicated upon the hope of a return to religion, his ideas attain cogency and coherence only on that basis. A healthy Jewish settlement must be established in Palestine as a pre-condition of the "new ideal," since religions are not created by any fiat of the will or by any intellectual manipulation of theses and antitheses. Understood thusly, the "new ideal" is capable of reviving the Jewish people, for religion is a set of convictions occupying so central a part in the lives of men, that it becomes the focus of group life.

On any other interpretation, Achad Ha'Am's philosophy of Judaism is pitifully inadequate. To render Jewish life in exile tolerable and attractive, Jewish morality with its firm faith in absolute justice and its almost naive contempt for violence and brutality may be sufficient. But, can Jewish morality be maintained against the challenge of skepticism without the conviction of the omnipresence of the God of righteousness? There is surely no reason to assume the validity of absolute morality on the sole ground of its being the product of a "national spirit." Turning from the field of logic to that of social psychology, we may inquire whether the Jewish masses could be expected to adhere to the principles of absolute morality, with the tenacity and the supreme devotion which maintenance of Jewish life requires? Knowing that their morality is but the product of their own minds and hearts, how could they assert its truth? Will it not appear to them rather as a figment of their ancestors' imagination—beautiful, inspiring, noble, but still only an ancestral dream?

The Jewish yearning for the standards of absolute morality, if such a yearning be assumed, does not become a vital

---

[20] J. Kaufman—"Goleh V'Naichor," pp. 202–204.

force until it is converted into a conviction that these standards are indeed fixed eternally in the ultimate scheme of
things. There is a "Power, not ourselves, that maketh for
righteousness," and this Power is strong enough to effect His
Purpose, being the Creator of all things. These convictions
alone possess the dynamic power of turning the abstract
ethical notions of the national spirit into a buoyant faith—a
faith by which Jews could live and the world be saved. But
these convictions Achad Ha'Am and his followers have lost.
Their spiritual life was thus suspended in mid-air. They
hung on to notions with their hands, while with their feet
they pushed away the foundation-stones of those notions. In
their grievous trouble, they sought help in a revived Jewish
life in Palestine. For "what time will do, reason is powerless to achieve." A young nation they hoped, will regain its
naivete, its power of belief, and be saved.

It is idle to attempt a refutation of the different theses
which Achad Ha'Am had combined in his philosophy of
Judaism. Singly, his views have been assailed and refuted
many times over. Yet, what matters is that the general impact of his thought has been felt in all branches of Jewish
literature and life. The four thinkers herein discussed in
detail have felt his influence, and many American rabbis and
religious educators have taken over large sections of his
thought. For while incomplete in itself, the philosophy of
Achad Ha'Am retains a good half of Judaism, with the lines
of insertion for the other half definitely marked out. Judaism derives from the two motives of national life and independent religious conviction. Achad Ha'Am explored the
national basis of Judaism and impressed its value upon his
generation. As to the other half, little light can be derived
from his heroic, if at times confused, efforts to point the way
to "Him who wished to dwell in darkness."

CHAPTER II

HERMANN COHEN

(a) Early Attitudes to Judaism

OUT OF THE GOODLY NUMBER OF GREAT JEWS IN THE LITER-
ary scene of the last generation, there towers head and shoulders above the crowd the giant intellectual figure of Hermann
Cohen. He was a great thinker and Jewish to the core; no
review of general or Jewish thought can possibly ignore his
work. Many will no doubt assert that in his philosophic researches, as in his estimate of Judaism, Hermann Cohen
erred. But, none will deny that, right or not, Cohen's
thought is laid out in the dimensions of rare genius. On any
unprejudiced estimate, Cohen takes his place with the great
Jewish thinkers of all time.

Born in the small German town of Coswig, in the year
1842, Cohen received a good Jewish education. His father,
who was a cantor in the Jewish community, appears to have
been a pious and earnest Jew. The young Cohen continued
to study the Talmud with his father, up to the age of sixteen.
Then he enrolled as a student in the Breslau Rabbinic Seminary, where many renowned scholars were among his teachers.

As a youth, Hermann Cohen lived in an era that was still
seething with Jewish theological speculation and with enthusiasm over the steady process of emancipation. It was
the age of S. R. Hirsch's "Nineteen Letters," of the great
works of Zunz, Geiger, Steinheim, and Formstecher, of the
mighty apologetic writings of Gabriel Riesser. By the six-
ties, the period of intellectual and social struggles had come
to an end and German Jewry settled down to face their newly
expanded world with vigor and earnestness. For more than
a decade, their horizon remained untroubled by the ominous
clouds of antisemitism.

57

Gradually, the interest of Cohen was shifted ever further from the Jewish scene. When the young thinker was introduced to Zunz, seven years after he had first come to the seminary, as "Dr. Cohen, former theologian, now a philosopher," the aged historian is said to have remarked, "a former theologian is always a philosopher." Whether Cohen's philsophic interest was due to his studies in the Jewish religion or not, it is certain that Judaism came to possess for him less and less real value and to be regarded as merely pious sentimentalism. He still occasionally helped his father in the long Yom Kippur services and he continued to attend the *seder* meal at his father's home. But, it appears, he no longer believed that Judaism was even now a significant, spiritual force. When he was thirty-one, Prof. F. A. Lange asked him, "Do not our views concerning Christianity differ?" Cohen is said to have replied, "No, for what you call Christianity, I call prophetic Judaism." Thus, Judaism had become reduced in the mind of Cohen to mere ethical earnestness, which the Bible critics of the period had proclaimed as the essence of the teaching of the prophets.

In his thirties, Cohen was completely absorbed in the study of philosophy. His first work on "Kant's Theorie der Erfahrung" aroused great interest in philosophical circles and served to give direction to the movement "Back to Kant," which had then just begun in German philosophy. How proud must the young thinker have been when a scholar as renowned as Prof. Lange wrote him after the publication of this work, "You begin indeed from the beginning with us all." The brilliance and originality shown in his first book enabled Cohen to overcome the anti-Jewish prejudices of the age sufficiently to become a "privatdozent" in the University of Marburg immediately after its publication and to reach the stage of ordinarius in the short time of three years. Thereafter, for nearly forty years, Cohen continued to labor in the field of philosophy at the university. It was his daring speculation that brought the name of the little town of Marburg to every university in the world. The "Marburg School" in philosophy is nearly synonymous with the works of Cohen and his disciples. As his own system gradually began to take shape, it became apparent that, in those decades, nothing of equal importance in philosophy was produced in Germany. Neo-Kantism, or critical idealism, as Cohen's system is sometimes known, is still a live philosophical tendency today, though it has been cast into oblivion in Germany by the resurgent barbarism of the Hitlerian revolution.

During these forty years of heroic wanderings in the desert of metaphysics, Cohen gave but rare and fleeting attention to the problems of Judaism. At a banquet given in his honor at Berlin, prior to his departure for Russia in 1914, the aged Cohen, then seventy-two years old, was described as a recent *baal te'shuvah* by one of the speakers. "But I am a *baal te'shuvah* already for thirty-four years," the angered philosopher is reported to have interjected. Cohen evidently reckoned his renewed interest in Judaism from the date of the publication of his "Bekenntnis in der Judenfrage."

As in the lives of so many Jews of modern times, the occasion for Cohen's renewed interest in Judaism was an upsurge of antisemitism. In 1879, the historian Treitschke started a campaign of "scientific" antisemitism, reinforcing the lying slogans of rabble rousers with the dignity of his name and the prestige of science. Cohen wrote two open letters to Treitschke, which the latter, however, refused to publish. Thereupon, Cohen published the "Bekenntnis" as his reply to the new assault on Judaism. This pamphlet is distinctly assimilationist in tone. It maintains that the Jews are already Germans and it condones intermarriage by implication. Two thoughts, Cohen maintains, constitute the essence of Christianity in Germany—ethical autonomy, and the uniqueness or transcendence of God. The former concept has gradually evolved in Germany from Luther to Kant, but all Jews now accept it as their own. The latter concept is originally Jewish, but Germans now acknowledge its validity. Hence, Germanism and Judaism are essentially one. This thought was later expressed by him in greater detail in an address entitled "Deutschtum und Judentum."

The reply to Treitschke aroused more criticism in Jewish circles than Cohen's later address, which was more excusable, since it was delivered in 1916, a time of heightened patriotic emotion. In both essays, the peculiar weakness of Cohen's method is illustrated most strikingly. He tends to abstract from actual realities and then to deal with the abstractions as if they were the concrete entities. Two cultures or two religions are not made identical because they contain certain common elements, even if these be regarded by one thinker as the only essential ones.

To this period of assimilationist thinking, belongs Cohen's essay on the Sabbath, which was published soon after the "Bekenntnis." In this essay, he agrees to the change of the Sabbath from Saturday to Sunday. How he was to regret this opinion in his latter years, when, more deeply appreciative of the meaning of Judaism, he wrote his profound chapter on Jewish Law in his "Religion der Vernunft"!

Despite Cohen's own statement, we should perhaps reckon the beginning of his return to his religion from 1912, the date of his coming to Berlin with the avowed aim of devoting himself to the instruction of his own people. While yet at Marburg, he did indeed occasionally write essays on Jewish themes. But, at the age of seventy, the gray-haired, yet intellectually alert philosopher, determined to consecrate the rest of his life entirely to the study and the teaching of the Jewish religion. He hoped to reach the wide Jewish public through his lectures in Berlin's "Lehranstalt für die Wissenschaft des Judentums." As the years rolled by, the aged philosopher became progressively more conscious of the worth and significance of Judaism and he longed to awaken his fellow Jews to a realization of the value of their faith. But he was sorely disappointed. His circle of influence in Berlin remained small. The "Western" Jews were engrossed in other interests. His listeners were mostly recruited from among the Russian-Jewish students in Berlin. It was from these students that Cohen came to learn at first hand the plight of the Jewish student body in Russia. Accordingly, he conceived the idea of establishing a Jewish University in Russia, and he actually undertook a journey to the land of the Czars for this purpose. The World War destroyed this laudable plan and Cohen was compelled to confine his educational efforts to the Jews of Germany.

Throughout the years of the war, Cohen continued to lecture to a small group of students about the philosophy of Judaism. Undaunted by the evil forces which the great war had let loose, the aged thinker kept his attention riveted firmly to the great ideals of mankind. There is not the faintest trace of bitterness or despair in his writings of the war-years. The book which resulted from those years of labor, "Religion der Vernunft aus den Quellen des Judentums," is a massive contribution to the philosophy of religion. Franz Rosenzweig, his beloved disciple, hailed it as another "Guide of the Perplexed." The aged author knew that it represented his last supreme effort in his long search for truth. He died before the book was published, confident of having left a legacy to the world, that was worthy of ranking him among the great religious teachers of Israel.

(b) General Philosophical Position

IN THE HISTORY OF GERMAN SPECULATIVE THOUGHT, HERmann Cohen occupies a pivotal position. He was one of the founders of the neo-Kantian movement which began in the seventies of the last century, and he continued to be the moving spirit among that group of philosophers down to the end

of the World War. The neo-Kantian movement was a revolt against the speculative vagaries of absolute idealism
which seemed to spin forever about the same point, the all-
absorbing Self or Absolute, remaining oblivious alike of the
growth of science and of the needs of practical life. At the
same time, neo-Kantism was a protest against the materialistic philosophies of the latter part of the nineteenth century,
which gave due—perhaps more than due, weight to the conceptions of the physical sciences, but which failed to do justice to the nature and destiny of man. Together with Friedrich Lange and later Paul Natorp, Hermann Cohen undertook to mold philosophy into a strict science and thereby to
place speculative thought on the road to sure and progressive
development, insisting however that the spiritual elements
of life be given equal emphasis with the purely cognitive
interests.

Thus, neo-Kantism can be described as being at once a
form of positivism, idealism and humanism. With the posi-
tivists, Cohen shares the view that the mathematical sciences
are the typical sciences, properly so called. The biologic
sciences he regards as being only on the way to becoming
sciences, as tending in the natural course of their progressive
development to abandon their merely descriptive methods, to
become more analytic and more exact, and eventually to dissolve into the mathematical sciences. Allied with this view
of the nature of the sciences is the philosophy of the naturalists, which regards the qualitative world of our senses as only
subjective. But, whereas naturalists regard such entities as
atoms, energy, waves, etc., as ultimate metaphysical elements, the neo-Kantians look upon these elements of physics
as so many "given" entities, with which thought may not begin. Thus, Cohen's system can be described as idealistic, in
that true Being is viewed as identical with the operations of
thought, will and feeling, not with anything given in experience. The humanist strain in the neo-Kantian movement is

seen in the fact that the ethical and esthetic values of man are not explained away through reference to physical causes or to a metaphysical Absolute, but are regarded as ultimately real and valid.

It must be observed at this point that the term neo-Kantian is now employed in reference to a great variety of German thinkers, who have little in common except similarities of method.[1] In this book, the term neo-Kantian will henceforth be used as referring specifically to the philosophy of Hermann Cohen.

Following Kant, Cohen begins his system with an examination of the processes of thought. He accepts Kant's Copernican revolution—the assertion that whatever reality may be in itself, it cannot for us be other than what our forms of thinking will permit it to be. Philosophy must be a critique of reason, for the categories of our thought are the inescapable molds of reality. This argument did not drive Kant into subjective idealism, because he regarded the Categories as objective forms of the human understanding. Yet, in a sense, Kant remained a subjective idealist, since, in his view, the "Ding an Sich" remained forever hidden from the eyes of men. Mankind as a whole was condemned to deal with the phenomenal world, the Categorical Imperative being the only ray of noumenal reality to penetrate into the life of humanity. Kant's system remained a dualism of matter and form— the matter of experience and the form of intuition and reason. It was therefore exposed to the attack that it failed to account for the fact that the noumenal matter somehow submitted passively to the forms of the intuition and of the understanding. Thus, it is possible to maintain that Kant's analysis did not go far enough, since he was constrained to resort to the assumption of a mysterious noumenal world in order to account for the actual experiences of men. Hegel's philosophy, it will be recalled, was an attempt to prove that

---

[1] See Hastings' "Encyclopedia of Religion and Ethics," Vol. IX, p. 306.

the development of the concept of the Absolute accounted completely for the experiences of the phenomenal world.

Cohen's development of Kantism resembles in many ways that of Hegel. Like Hegel, his principal question is, how does thought actually proceed in the development of a concept? (Begriff). Every concept is the unity of a manifold, the synthesis of a many into a one. How is this process of unification effected? Hegel's answer that thought proceeds by way of thesis, antithesis and synthesis is well known. Hegel's methodology was probably based on the observation that thought is the medium wherein subject and object meet and are synthesized. From this simple generalization, he concluded that all thought is a synthesis of opposites. Posing the same question to himself as Hegel, Cohen resorted to mathematics to find the solution.

The progress of any science can be measured by the extent to which its principles have been reduced to the form of mathematical formulae. The goal of the application of reason to nature is consequently the understanding of all phenomena as merely special cases in one all-embracing formula. Historically, the progress of the sciences has been from biology, to physiology, to chemistry, to physical chemistry, to mathematical physics. The transition from mathematics to physics, however, has been regarded as involving the yawning gulf between the realm of essence and the realm of existence. Mathematics must begin with something definite and existing, it was said, before it can be turned into mathematical physics. Thus, in the first stages of modern science, the ultimate elements of physics were assumed to be molecules. The subsequent progress of science, however, has made necessary the assumption of more tenuous units. The atoms were then seen to be composite products, consisting of so many protons and electrons; the electrons in turn were in the course of time, shown to be foci of waves in an ether. In our own day, scientists no longer assume the existence of an ether and the waves of the electrons are, therefore, left undulating in a nothingness of any number of dimensions. This development indicates, to Cohen, that the course of thought is simply and solely mathematics. No analysis will be ultimate for thought which requires the assumption of any irreducible data of experience. Between mathematics and physics, there is no ultimate boundary line, at which thought must needs pause to take up a new and elementary datum. When the development of thought shall have been completed, all physical events will be understood in terms of mathematical constructs only.

The idea that logical thought is neither more nor less than mathematics is basic to Cohen. No part of his system can be understood apart from this hypothesis, that thought is not a matter of passing data before the mental eyes; that it is not the visualization of general classes and of the particulars that belong therein, as syllogistic logic claims; that it is not the mental tracing of "lines of influence" and, "lines of meaning" between data of experience, as James argued.[2] Thought, in the exact scientific sense, is mathematics. Logic is only the abstract schematization of mathematics. At this point, Cohen appears to meet Russell and Whitehead, the English philosophers who endeavored to reduce all mathematics to logic. But, this parallel is quite misleading. Whereas Russell and Whitehead regarded thought as a way of seeing, Cohen viewed thought as a continuous self-regulating process.

In the study of the philosophy of mathematics, a most fundamental problem is the relation between finite numbers and infinities. In actual life, of course, only finite numbers are encountered. But, if mathematical thought is indeed a

---

[2] Logic, pp. 21, 49, 297.

continuous process, then the basic unit should be the symbol
of an endless process rather than of a discrete object.[3]
Cohen, accordingly, takes the derivative $\dfrac{dy}{dx}$ as the beginning

of all mathematics.[4] The derivative represents a relation between two rates of change. It is an indefinite and shifting
entity, reaching a more and more definite value as the
changes are made to approximate zero. The derivative is in
no sense a given or perceived datum; yet, all the changes and
motions of the universe can only be described accurately by
formulae which involve its use. For this reason, Cohen
takes the derivative of calculus as the beginning of thought.[5]
It does not represent a discrete entity, to be sure; but, in
that very fact lies its unique significance. Since thought is
a process, its beginning cannot be a definite object, or the
abstraction of an object or a class of objects, but the segment of a process. The beginning of thought is itself shifting into non-Being, reaching definiteness only asymptotically.
The method of the derivative represents the emergence of
things from the naught, definite values from the realm of the
infinitesimal. The ultimate essences of all physical sciences, Cohen argued, are really no more than derivatives.[6]
At the base of all exact thought lies the notion of process, of
endless becoming.

In Cohen's terminology, the beginning of thought, the
mathematical derivative, is termed Idea. The "idea" takes
the place of Kant's noumenon, for, out of it, the whole
scheme of Being is evolved. The Idea is not a metaphysical
reality, a "Ding an sich"; the whole problem of things in
themselves is left out of the province of philosophy. The

[3] It is interesting to note that already Plato, in the Timaeus, had represented the finite numbers as secondary, maintaining that they emerged out
of the Indeterminate Dyad.

[4] Logic, pp. 105, 106.

[5] Logic, p. 113.

[6] Logic, pp. 114, 141.

"idea" is, to Cohen, the ultimate element of objective, as distinguished from absolute, reality.

What does thought do with the derivative? From mathematics we know the procedure. When integrated, the derivative provides us with a series of terms, $y=f(x)$, a series which is not a mere haphazard collection, since every term is related by a definite law to the other terms in the series. The integrated function represents a continuous series, in which every term is deducible from the qualities of the preceding term. At the same time, when integrated between definite limits, the function yields finite numbers, each of which is the product of a summation of an infinite number of terms.

Examining now these mathematical processes, we note that thought begins with an Idea, the derivative, applies the judgment of totality, the process of integration, and obtains as a result a plurality of terms, obeying one law. The causal nexus of the observed universe, in which every event is determined in all respects by preceding events, is thus seen to be a mathematical or a logical necessity. This schematization of the process of thought, Cohen calls logic. The requirement to begin with an Idea is called by our author the Category of Source (Ursprung). The categories of totality, plurality and causality are all derived from the process of integration, as indicated herein.

Time and space, we may recall, were regarded by Kant as a priori intuitions. Noumenal reality was presumably outside the dimensions of both space and time. The world which our senses reveal to us is the result of the application of our intuitions and categories of thought to the noumenal matter that comes to us from the outside. Thus, he assumed a duality in the making of objective reality—receptive and spontaneous elements. Cohen, on the other hand, reckons both time and space as mathematically produced categories, products of the judgment of totality.[7] He thus eliminates

---

[7] *Logic*, p. 170.

the need of assuming a priori forms and a posteriori matter. Nothing need be assumed except the process of thought itself. Whereas with Kant, the production of thought alone did not yet give knowledge, as he insisted that "conception without perception is empty," Cohen accords thought complete independence. It begins with its own Idea, and, following its own laws of continuity, produces its own object. This does not mean that thought possesses the power to fathom the mysteries of metaphysics. As a critical idealist, Cohen professes to eschew metaphysics as sheer fantasy. Nor does the independence of thought mean that experience is of no importance in the framing of ideas and concepts. On the contrary, Cohen insists that the deeper meaning of purity is the essential and indispensable relation of terms to experience.[8] The ideal end of thought is to dispense completely with the data of experience, but this goal can only be reached through the constant checking and rechecking of the basic concepts of thought with the hard facts of experience. Knowledge begins with, but does not end in, scientific observation. Mathematical thought, Cohen asserts, is the one avenue to certain and "pure" knowledge.

A fundamental axiom of Cohen's is that Thought and Being are one. This is really a tautological statement, for Cohen does not deal with metaphysical, but with objective reality—that is, the reality apprehended by all thinking minds. The identification of Being with Thought becomes significant in its negative implications. Whatever is not pure thought, however obdurate a fact it may be, belongs to the realm of becoming and is not yet Being. While the realm of Being can be understood in itself, the realm of Becoming can be understood only by reference to Being. The boundary between the realm of Being and the realm of Becoming shifts with the progress of thought.

---

[8] Ethics, p. 370.

The data which our minds receive by way of perception Cohen calls the facts of actuality (wirklichkeit). The realm of actuality, as it is revealed to our senses, is a confused mixture of quantity and quality. But thought, mathematical thought, that is, cannot take any note of quality. Hence, the progress of Thought or of Being is really a progressive encroachment of quantity and mathematics upon quality and perception. Cohen appears to think of the end of the process of thought as being a complete understanding of the qualitative world in terms of sheer quantity. This final end or goal of thought, Cohen describes as the attainment of a complete concept (Begriff). From this viewpoint, actuality is to be understood as not-yet Being and, hence, as constituting the task for knowledge. Perception is not itself a rightful avenue of "pure" cognition, but it sets the goal which thought must reach.[9]

Cohen speaks of three "pure" directions of "culture-consciousness": pure thought, pure will, pure feeling.

These tendencies are pure in the sense that they do not begin with anything externally given and arrive, or tend to arrive at their respective objects. The elements and contents of all these directions of mind, Cohen calls Being (Sein). Thus, there are three realms of Being, alike in methods of development but differing in essence.

It is important to note the difference in the significance of the term "pure" as used by Cohen, from the meaning of this term in Kant's writings. To Kant, "purity" meant the absence of any elements of experience or of any data of intuition, the possession of form without matter. To Cohen, matter itself is only a relative opposite of form, since matter passes into form by continuous and imperceptible stages. "Purity" in the neo-Kantian sense is a term of order, not of content. It means the rejection by thought of data, not de-

---

[9] See Joseph Soloveitchik in "Die Begründung des Seins und Seinsprinzip bei Hermann Cohen," pp. 41, 91.

duced by means of rational laws from their respective and proper sources.

What makes the processes of thought or will or feeling go? What determines their course of development? Cohen seems to think of the endeavor to produce the final concept as the drive of each of the processes of Being.[10] The search for truth is part of the process of thought itself.

It is necessary to remember, in reading Cohen's writings, that the process of thought is, to him, not identical with consciousness, and that it is in no way subjective. Thought is a general objective process, in which human individuals happen to participate. Thought was there in all its completeness and subtlety, when men were still in the pre-thinking stage. The growth of culture takes place through the ever greater participation of human beings in the three processes of Being. The flow of consciousness is not thought itself, but a production of thought, standing for the ability of thought to objectify itself. How this process of objectification takes place and how the unity of thought is preserved in that process, are questions that cannot be dealt with in this study.

We noted before that Cohen shunned emphatically the attempt to construct a metaphysics. In his writings, the speculations of mere metaphysicians are dismissed with undisguised contempt. It is sheer folly, in his view, for man to presume to discover what is existent in itself. Yet, Cohen's own system of philosophy can hardly be regarded as anything other than a metaphysics. Being, to him, is that which must be assumed to make experience possible. But, since experience is here and now, does it not mean that the conditions of experience have been fulfilled? True, it may be that ultimate reality possesses additional qualities; it is possible that processes more profound and basic than our three processes of mind take place in the ultimate recesses of metaphysical reality. But those processes, if there be such, can-

---

[10] See ibid., p. 52.

not, on Cohen's hypothesis, intrude within our ken. They are, therefore, irrelevant to us, and on a par with Spinoza's infinite number of God's attributes. Moreover, the fact that the actual world is regarded as a term in the process of thought is incomprehensible apart from the view that there does exist a real thinking entity, in the consciousness of which our actual world is the passing object. Thus, Cohen's "System of Philosophy," which is written throughout from the standpoint of a theory of knowledge, could be construed, with minor modifications and with the necessary concessions to philosophic pedantry, as a theory of reality, though the author himself seems to disavow any such interpretation.

The principle of the self-sufficiency and objectivity of thought cannot be regarded as other than a metaphysical reality. Since Will and Feeling are accorded the same status as Thought, we really seem to have a thinking, willing and feeling Reality, that is transcendent to the actual world.[11] This Reality could well be called God and thereby form the basis of a philosophy of religion. From the viewpoint of religion, Cohen's arguments would have been immensely strengthened if he had employed the language of being, instead of the language of epistemology. On any such interpretation, Cohen's view of God as "truth," which will be explained in the following chapters, if translated into metaphysical terminology, would mean the drive and the direction of the thinking and willing processes of Being.

From all the above, the divisions of Cohen's system of philosophy will have become evident. The foundation of the system is given in the "Logic der Reinen Erkenntnis." Both "ethics of pure will" and "esthetics of pure feeling" are treated in works bearing these respective titles. Cohen con-

---

[11] This too is the conclusion of A. Kewkowitz in the "Zeitschrift für Philosophie und Philosophische Kritik," Bd. 144. This interpretation is based on the assumption that to Cohen there is no element in Actuality which cannot become Being. See reference in footnote 12.

ceived of a fourth branch of the system, "Psychologie," dealing with the manner in which unity of consciousness is produced. However, he never managed to write that work.
Hence, there remain some ambiguities in his thought. In
particular, the relation between Being and Actuality or
Thought and Perception remains uncertain.[12]

By way of a summary of Cohen's view of the nature of
thought, we may say: insofar as human consciousness is
"cultured," it moves along with the three basic processes of
Being—processes which begin with one infinity, the Source,
and end at another infinitely distant goal, the Object. The
determinate world, which our senses seem to give us, is, from
the viewpoint of thought, an endless process and an endless
task. For, science knows only the eternal becoming.

(c) The Concept of Man

Thought, as was noted before, is not the only direction of "culture consciousness." Will and feeling, too, are
construed as creative processes, producing their respective
forms of reality. These two processes, however, are ultimately dependent on logic, for they, too, are manifestations
of reason, (Vernunft).

Like Kant, who thought of the qualities of universality
and necessity as constituting the part of reason which is common to both mathematical logic and "practical reason,"
Cohen maintains that there is a core of reason which is
shared by all directions of culture consciousness. Ethical
guidance derives neither from the actual struggles of life, nor
from a peculiar light of intuition, but from a rational faculty.
Art and esthetics, too, are based on "sittliches Vernunft" and
are, therefore, to be clearly distinguished from arbitrary

---

[12] See on this point, the conclusions of J. Soloveitchik in the above quoted
"B. d. S. u. S. bei H. Cohen," pp. 91–110.

felling. The common core of reason in all the three directions of spirit is the list of the categories from the one of
Source down—the scheme whereby the concept of Being is
produced. The justification of this claim is found in the
quality of lawfulness attaching to both ethical and esthetic
judgments, a quality which can be defined only by logic.

The term "Vernunft" is employed by Cohen in a special
sense, as meaning rational thought and, also, in a broader
sense, to signify the three processes of Being.[1]

Like mathematical thought, accordingly, both ethics and
esthetics must start with characteristic Ideas and apply the
categories of thought to their respective forms of Being. At
this point, Cohen encounters a fundamental choice. Since
the infinitesimal was found to be the idea of thought, is the
same idea to be made the source of ethics? If so, then the
independence of ethics is lost, and the study of human conduct is given over to the sciences of biology and psychology.
If not, then the question arises, how far may ethics differ
from logic in its starting point without sinning against the
demand of purity? Cohen resorts to the concept of analogy
to overcome this obstacle. The idea of ethics is to be
"analogous" to the idea of thought.[2] What Cohen conceives
to be the formal requirements of "analogy" is not entirely
clear. Thus, an element of arbitrariness is introduced into
the very foundation of ethics.

Before applying this method to the problems of ethics, we
have to determine whether there is such a direction of spirit
—that is, we may well ask whether the activities and emotions that we denote as ethical cannot be wholly accounted
for by certain psychological principles. These principles
may in turn be explained in terms of physiology, which again
will in time become amenable to mathematical treatment.

---

[1] See use of term "sittliche, Vernunft" in R. d. V., pp. 481, 482, etc. True
religion is "Religion der Vernunft," in the larger meaning of that term.

[2] See "Ethik," p. 402.

Is it necessary to assume, we inquire, another movement of spirit apart from that of mathematical thought?

The answer of Cohen is, in effect, that it is our moral duty to assume an independent ethical realm of being, as it is our intellectual duty to search for the mathematical realm of being. As critical idealists, we feel that intellectual honesty compels us to reject empirical data and to place exclusive reliance on pure thought. Similarly, moral honesty compels us to discard all empirical explanations as unworthy and to regard our ethical will as capable of producing its own determinations in accordance with the laws of reason inherent in it. Just as we err intellectually if we do not seek for the starting point of reason in reason itself, so we sin against ethics if we do not seek its foundation in the ethical consciousness itself. Thus, he states in one of his earlier works,[3] "Wer dieses Soll nicht anerkennt, nicht zum Problem macht, der will keine Ethik." ("Whoever does not recognize this Ought, does not make it as the problem, does not want to have an ethics.")

In strictness, then, we note two grounds for the independence of ethics in Cohen's system. One is the argument by analogy. Since, in the case of thought, we assert that knowledge begins with the idea, we ought to apply the same method to will and feeling. This argument is strengthened by the fact that mathematical thought cannot prove the impossibility of other kinds of being, corresponding respectively to pure will and pure feeling. The other argument is really an appeal to our own insight. We are asked to probe our inner soul that we might discover whether it would permit the dissolution of ethics. Thus he states that cultured men feel this certainty: "that man simply cannot be viewed as a beast of prey." [4] This certainty, however, he admits is

---

[3] "Kant's Kritik der Erfahrung," p. 187.
[4] Ethics, p. 37.

"a certainty of a different kind than the one of logic."[5] But if this certainty, that ethical laws of right and wrong do indeed exist, is not based on the principles of logic, are we not compelled to assume that it derives either from our emotional background or from some basic intuitions? In either case, according to Cohen, it would be impossible to regard ethics as a "pure" science. Cohen is thus faced with a fundamental paradox. Ethics is a "pure" direction of spirit, though, clearly, it is founded on a feeling of certainty that is not rational in origin.

To save ethics, it is necessary to find a view of certainty which will offer common ground for both ethics and logic. Such a view, Cohen finds in the "basic law of truth" (Grundgesetz der Wahrheit). This law of truth states that although ethics and logic are in fact independent directions of spirit, they must agree in their methodology. This law of truth is not an after-thought or a deus ex machina, invented to save the system; on the contrary, it is the basic insight upon which the entire system is built. Obviously, one cannot start constructing a philosophy of life without assuming some one principle or experience as fundamentally certain. However rationalistic our philosophy may be, we cannot escape the conclusion that certainty is an experience. This apprehension of truth, then, is the ultimate foundation of Cohen's system. Truth, he feels, has both ethical and logical implications and stands outside these directions of consciousness.

Logic is a formal series of rules that must be employed in passing upon questions of correctness; it cannot, however, be used to judge the "basic law of truth," since the feeling of truth is the final source of all human certainty, being more primary even than the principles of logic. Truth, or rather truthfulness, is a basic human insight, directing us to seek

---

[5] Logic, p. 516.

"purity" in all the directions of spirit. In the field of ethics, this truthfulness compels us to assume that will is not determined haphazardly or by intuition, but that it contains an element of reason—i.e. lawfulness.

Despite this assumption of a law of truth, Cohen states in numerous places that the certainty of ethics remains different in kind from that of mathematical thought. He finds Kant's lasting contribution to philosophy to be the recognition of that philosopher that ethics and logic do not contain the same kind of certainty. The reason for this distinction is the fact that an Idea is regarded by Cohen as a hypothesis which must continually approve itself by its application to the actual world. In the case of ethics, there is no concrete actuality by reference to which the Idea may be proved. To be sure, "ethics is the logic of the spiritual sciences." [6] But the spiritual sciences are still only in the first stages of their evolution and are, by their very nature, incapable of attaining uniform standardization.

With ethics recognized as an independent science, we now have to determine what its subject is. It cannot be simply human conduct, as we have learned from logic that the object of a direction of spirit must be a concept of a completed order, or rather, the concept of a system. The object of "pure will" is, therefore, the concept of mankind. The "pure will" of men directs all their activities toward the goal of the ideal human society. It is the task of the science of ethics to describe this goal and to outline the different stages in the evolution of the ethical will.

Our next task is to discover the "Idea" from which the process of pure will is to begin its development. In the case of logical thought, the necessary idea was found in the mathematical concept of the derivative. We should, therefore, inquire whether there is a science standing in the same

---

[6] B. d. R., p. 11.

relation to ethics as mathematics does to logic. In his commentary on Kant, Cohen stated that ethics lacked such a science. However, in his "System," he declares that the pure will of ethics finds its concrete expression in the science of jurisprudence.[7]

Now, the science of jurisprudence is concerned with units of human action. From the standpoint of the law, it does not matter how many psychological and physical elements are comprised in one legal action. This fact is clearly illustrated in the legal fiction, according to which the transactions of a corporation are treated as if they were those of a single person. This view of the acts of a corporation is not due either to convenience or to accident, Cohen declares. It is the expression of the fundamental nature of jurisprudence as an independent science, evolving and defining its own basic terms. This welding of a many into a one, in the concept of action, is the characteristic mark of an independent direction of spirit. Translated in terms of will, a unit of action means a "willenstendenz," a tendency of the will. We conclude, therefore, that the "idea" of ethics is an incipient tendency of pure will.

What is the nature of "pure will"? Cohen is at pains to distinguish it from "pure affect"—that is, from feeling. "Pure affect" is the background against which both thought and will move. It drags along after those two processes of spirit, but the law of truth, decreeing the purity of reason and will, forbids that it direct them. Pure will, Cohen concludes, is a basic movement, or process. It differs from thought, which is also a fundamental movement, in that for thought an object is the content, whereas for will, an object is a means to the production of its own essential process. Again, the progress of thought is mainly analytic in character, depending upon the recognition of distinctions among the diverse

---

[7] *Ethics*, pp. 63, 587.

data of experience (Sonderung), while the tendency of will is consistently in the direction of synthesis.[8]

The corporation as a juridical person is, to Cohen, the model of ethical self-consciousness, showing as it does a functioning unit of responsibility, which arises out of a multiplicity of tendencies and interests. The human personality is similarly endowed with ethical responsibility, despite the fact that it consists of many and diverse impulses and aspirations. Thus, the assertion that men are responsible for their actions is the original "idea" of pure will and is not at all based upon the false notion that there is an indivisible essence, corresponding to the word "I." It is possible to accept the conclusions of modern psychology concerning the non-existence of a soul or a self and still assert the ethical responsibility of human beings. The "I" of ethics, subject of the judgments right and wrong, good and bad, is a primary postulate of pure will, having no relation whatsoever to the physical realm of existence.

Applying the judgment of totality to the "willenstendenz" of each person, we obtain, as in the case of integration, the concept of a whole group of persons acting as a unity. An actual example of such a group is the political unit of the state. But the actual state is not that concept, inasmuch as it includes only a segment of mankind. This concept of man, the goal toward which men ought to strive, contains, in accordance with Cohen's principles of logic, inner purposiveness—that is, the ideal society of mankind is to be regarded as the supreme end of ethics. The goal of human society is to attain perfect organic unity, the time when all men will so completely subordinate their own individualities to the interests of the whole of mankind as to function like cells in the all-embracing body of the universal state. The ethical concept of man is the view of humanity as an evolving and

---

[8] See Johannes Weise—"Die Begründung der Ethik bei H. Cohen."

self-perfecting personality.[9]   Thus, we see that Cohen began by asking what man should be like and he ended by telling us what the state ought to be like.   Plato in the "Republic," it may be recalled, followed a similar line of reasoning.

This "concept of man," which acts as the driving force of ethical life, is not a mere idle dream.   It is very real, Cohen insists, constituting a part of Being even as the truths of logic.   It is important to note the complete parallelism in Cohen's philosophy between the processes of logic and ethics. Just as thought ends in the concept of the universe as one organism, so does will end in the concept of human society as one organism.   Both goals will never be actually reached, but, in the course of human progress, they will be approached ever more closely, in the same manner as the ends of the hyperbola tend to approach the axes.   The concept of man sets the task for the ethical will, even as the actual world performs this service for logical thought.

This tendency to perform the task set by a concept of the realm of Being is the root of the sense of obligation which is associated with the commands of morality.   The attraction of the goal of ethics functions even when that goal is not clearly envisaged.   Guided by what we know we ought to do, we help to realize the universal society of mankind.

It may seem that in setting a goal for ethical action, Cohen contradicts his own assertion that for the process of pure will every object can only be a means, not an end.   However, there is here no real contradiction, for the ideal state is itself conceived as being in a state of perpetual evolution.   It is therefore a process, rather than an object.

Does ethics possess the concept of man as an individual,

---

[9] The influence of the socialistic movement is here quite obvious. Cohen was early captivated by the messianic-socialistic ideal. See F. Rosenzweig —"J. Sch.," p. XXIII. Cohen's concept of society as a person must be sharply distinguished from the sociological school of Emile Durkheim. The latter thinkers regard society as being already a person, whereas, to Cohen, society is only ideally so.

not merely as a member of the totality of mankind? In his "Begriff der Religion," [10] Cohen condemns as a misunderstanding the criticism that his system sactions the total obliteration of individuality. On the contrary, he insists, the individual attains his highest dignity in his union with mankind.[11]

Thus, Cohen claims that, from an ethical standpoint, the individual is important only insofar as he contributes to the evolution of the ideal society. This totalitarian view of life is counterbalanced, however, by the viewpoint of religion. Our author concedes, as we shall see later, that there is a residue of legitimate need for individuality which is not satisfied by ethics and cannot in fact be satisfied by its methods. This need arises particularly in the consciousness of sin. The person who knows himself to be sinful cannot feel that he, too, is part of that endless army of men, which marches toward the eternal ideal. He feels himself isolated, rejected; at this point, Cohen claims, ethics ends and religion begins.

To be sure, in his "Ethics," he attempted to show the development of the self-consciousness of the individual from the resources of ethics alone. The basic concept of law, he pointed out, is action, but, in legal action, two subjects are necessarily implied. Thus, the emergence of ethical consciousness contains not only an "I" but a "Thou" as well. Accordingly, Cohen calls the "fellow-man" the source of the "I." [12] He formulates the tendency toward ethical individuality as the endeavor "to learn to think and will my 'I' only in the correlation of 'I' and 'Thou.' " [13] Again, in the enumeration of two sets of virtues, Cohen distinguishes the

---

[10] Pp. 52, 53.

[11] "So darf es daher gar nicht zu verstehn sein, dass der Mensch durch die Menschheit zunichte werden konnte; vielmehr soll er durch sie erst das wahrhafte Leben des ewigen sittlichen strebens, das Leben der Ewigheit erlangen und immerdar behaupten." "B. d. R.," p. 53.

[12] Ethics, p. 212.

[13] Ethics, p. 256.

motive of "Ehre" from that of "Liebe." [14] It is the function
of the latter set of virtues to direct the person to an improvement of individual groupings and the individualities of those
related to him.[15] Still, it is only a tenuous and vague sort of
individuality, an individuality that is related to at least one
other person, that we are ethically permitted to have. It was
left to religion to evolve the final view of individuality.

Freedom of will, in the sense of the ability of empirical
man to rise above the sway of mechanical causes, is denied
by Cohen. He accepts the Kantian argument that "Ought"
implies "Can," transferring it, however, from the sphere of
individual action to that of the destiny of mankind. Accordingly, he asserts that the task of attaining the ideal of
mankind must be capable of realization. This logical necessity leads, as we shall see in the next chapter, to the idea of
God. Clearly, "Can" is not deducible from "Ought" without
the assumption of a beneficent Deity. A malevolent creator
or a fortuitous arrangement of particles may well lead to
the rise of wishes and ideals that are totally hopeless and
futile. Individual freedom of action exists only to the extent
that the individual identifies himself with the cause of humanity. In its perfection, therefore, freedom exists only in
the ideal society of the future. The last meaning of ethical
freedom, Cohen concludes, is not that it is given as a fact,
"but that it is a task and must remain a task." [16]

The question, "how does the empirical will change into
the will of the practical reason?" remained unanswered in
Kant's system. In Cohen's system, where the concept of
man is the concept of ideal humanity, this question takes the
form, "how is it that the actions of men, which are largely

---

[14] Ethics, Chap. 10.

[15] Ethics, p. 462.

[16] See "Jüdische Schriften," vol. 1, p. 28. To act in freedom means, as in
the case of Kant, to act in accordance with the laws of "practical reason"
or "pure will."

determined by mechanical causes, tend to the realization of the ethical ideal?" As in the case of Kant, the "how" remains a mystery, but the fact of this process is grounded by Cohen in the idea of God.

(d) Concept of God

THE CONCEPT OF GOD OCCUPIES THE CENTRAL POSITION IN Cohen's system of philosophy, containing the seed and substance of his entire thought. However, Cohen's intellectual development was such that this concept did not receive its full and adequate treatment until the very last period of his life. "Der Begriff der Religion" and the "Religion der Vernunft" contain a substantial enlargement of the idea of God which is expounded in the earlier works of Cohen.

In this section, we shall deal with the idea of God as presented in the "Ethics," and reserve for the following section the consideration of the additional meaning which this idea received in the last works of our author.

Ethics, as was noted before, deals with a form of being, as distinguished from the sciences which deal with the realm of becoming. Just as logical thought and the being of the physical universe are one, so is pure will and spiritual being one. But, the form of being which is will, is not the same kind of being which is identified with logical thought. The main point of difference is the absence of an unmistakable and obdurate realm of ethical existence, corresponding to the ethical realm of being. The actual world which we apprehend with our senses is, as we have seen before, the task for our thought. Employing its own constructions, thought strives to understand the sensible world by means of them. To be sure, it is an endless task that human thought is confronted with—to reach the stage when all the irrational elements of experience will have been dissolved into the continuous, "pure" and rational flux of thought, when all quality

will have been comprehended as sheer quantity. But, mean-
while, the actuality to which thought refers is right here,
confronting our gaze in all its stubbornness.[1] This actuality
is perceived only because the Category of Space, which is the
result of the judgment of totality, presents us with the idea
of infinite externality as given all at once.

In the case of ethics, we do not have any (Wirklichkeit)
actuality corresponding to the ethical will. It is true, there
is the science of jurisprudence which Cohen regards as being
related to ethics in the same manner as mathematics is to
logic. Mathematics, it must be remembered, Cohen views
as being actual.[2] But then law is only "analogous" to mathematics,[3] not really as exact and as uniform as the latter
science. Moreover, even mathematics, actual as it may be,
is still a part of the realm of being. We are forced to conclude, therefore, that, in the world of space, ethical being is
denied "adequate actuality." [4]

To find the nature of ethical being, we have to resort to
the concept of time, which, even as space, is a constitutive
concept of cognition. While space, however, produces the
external world, time forms the inner world, the subjective
picture of nature.[5] Time, Cohen states, is not the inert board

---

[1] We touch here again a fundamental ambiguity in Cohen's philosophy.
Is thought a metaphysical or only an epistemological entity? We may recall that Kant's "Bewusstsein Uberhaupt," which in our author's system is
replaced by "Kulturbewusstein," is beset with the same vagueness. In
this paper, the metaphysical interpretation is accepted. For impersonal
thought then, the infinite to come is here and now. But this thought, in
thinking itself employs time, thereby forming the actual world, which is, in
truth, Being held up to the mirror of time. (See Walter Kinkel—"Hermann
Cohen," chapter on Logic.)

[2] Note the criticism of this view in A. Lewkowitz's "Die Religionsphilosophie des Neukantianismus." He points out correctly, we think, that
the being of mathematics is only the possibility of being.

[3] Ethics, Chap. 8.

[4] Ethics, p. 401.

[5] It will be recalled that Kant makes this distinction. See Max Muller's
translation of Kant's "Critique of Pure Reason," p. 18.

on which the series of phenomena are marked as they appear. It is rather "the shaft out of which that series is dug." In other words, the future is implicit in every perception of time. The element of anticipation, of seeking the future, is the "pure" perception of time. Anticipation, clearly, is a modification of will, not of pure thought. Thus, we see that pure will and the apprehension of time are intrinsically connected. Time, not merely as a mathematical relation, but as an actually felt pull toward the future, is to be understood through ethical terms.

The mathematical judgment of totality may be applied to the apprehension of time and thereby yield us the concept of infinite time, which is a very useful concept in the study of the physical sciences. However, this application really does violence to the "pure" perception of time, since time is properly to be regarded not as a summation, but as a summing. Time is not merely another dimension of our space-time world; it is a unique process, in which the past and the future are contained in every present moment. Genuine time eludes the net of all logical and mathematical research.

While the concept of infinite time may be employed in the scientific investigation of nature, the true analogue to infinite space is not infinite time but the ethical concept of eternity. This concept is not to be regarded as signifying a point in time, or as representing a summation of all points of time. It is an ethical concept and it relates only to will. It means, "eternity of the progress of ethical work." [6] The ethical will at work is conscious of the infinitely distant point in time where still the ethical striving goes on, though the extent of ethical achievement is then greater. "Dieser unendlich fernen Punkt bildet die Ewigkeit für jeden endlichen Punkt." [7] (This infinitely far point forms eternity for every finite point).

---

[6] Ethics, p. 388.
[7] Ethics, p. 389.

Eternity is thus an ever shifting point in time, which point is apprehended as marking the furthest advance of humanity on the road to ethical achievement, the highest contemporary vision of the ideal society of mankind. This evaluation of the present in the light of the utopia of the future is the characteristic mark of the ethical life and is the only knowledge we have of an ethical realm of actuality. The actuality of the ethical will does not signify a time when human beings will be so morally perfect that ethical insight will have the force and certainty of an instinct. That eventuality is distinctly undesirable in Cohen's view, since it implies the cessation of ethical striving, and the substitution of automatic responses for conscious, free decisions. The overcoming of resistance and the supremacy of reason in directing human conduct are essential elements of the ethical will. Hence, eternity must imply eternal striving toward the ideal—a striving which begins from a new level at every moment of time, which continually wrestles with and overcomes the resistance of human nature, advancing ever closer toward, though never actually reaching, the organic society-state in which all mankind feel and act as if they were one person.

Thus, eternity is not a concept of logical thought, since as we have seen, mathematical logic produces through the judgment of totality only the concept of infinite time, which is an abstraction, a form of spatialised time having little in common with the experienced feeling of anticipation. Eternity is the anticipation in the present moment of the goal of ethics in the infinitely distant future. In every act of pure will, there is a straining toward the infinite and an affirmation of an endless progress, a feeling of infinite endeavor, of consistent moral advance, of ultimate accord with truth. All these elements are comprised in the one word eternity. As the promise of the future, eternity sets an eternal task for the life of ethics. Accordingly, eternity is the actuality of ethics, performing the same task-setting service for it as the

sensible world does for logical thought. Thus, he writes,
". . . will and eternity become the analogies to thought and
nature." [8]

What kind of being can we ascribe to ethical actuality?
Obviously, Cohen asserts, it is the being of an ideal. The
concept of ideal arises in art, where it signifies the picture of
perfection. In every work of art, an ideal, envisaged by an
artist, is realized to a degree, but it is never completely actualized. We thus recognize three phases in the nature of an
artist's ideal: 1. Perfection, 2. The process of perfecting, 3.
The recognition of the imperfection of the perfected work.
These characteristics of an ideal, it now appears, are true of
the ethical goal of eternity, which shines in the distance as a
beckoning light, but which is never quite reached. "Accordingly," he concludes, "we determine the art of ethical being
as the Ideal." [9]

Having discovered this quality of eternity as the goal and
content of pure will, we now possess for ethics a kind of
reality, which is, in one sense less, in another sense, more,
than physical reality. For while the eternal goal of ethics is
not now actually present, it extends as an ideal and as a
promise of fulfillment through all of time. Physical reality
contains no such assurance. The fact of its existence in the
present moment does not assure its continued existence in the
dim future. What if the law of entropy were eventually to
reduce all life and all movement to a state of lifeless equilibrium! Think of it! What assurance is there that the
laws of nature will continue to operate from moment to moment? All laws of science are proved on the basis of what
has been, not of what will be. May not living nature somehow end at some mysterious point in time? But in that
event, ethical eternity would also cease to exist, since there
can be no ethics apart from men and nature. Hence if the

---

[8] Ethics, p. 402.
[9] Ethics, p. 400.

apprehension of eternity is not to be viewed as a senseless delusion, it must be assumed that nature will always exist, providing the necessary background for human, or human-like beings to live ethically.

This proposition, stating as it does a consequence concerning the sensible world, must be deducible from the resources of mathematical thought. Certainly, ethics cannot be a source of mathematical knowledge. But mathematical logic cannot of itself prove the infinite duration of the physical world. Hence we are in need at this point of a border concept—one which will have implications for both logic and ethics.

Such a concept Cohen finds in the idea of God. From the dawn of history, the belief in God or gods always implied certain conclusions regarding the physical world and the realm of human conduct. In all its mutations in the course of the evolution of human culture, the idea of God contained the connotation of a basic harmony between the structure of the universe and the aspirations of mankind. It is, therefore, permissible to employ this term to stand for the proposition that the physical world is somehow kept up for the sake of the eternity of the ethical task. The idea of God establishes a relation between the actuality corresponding to mathematical logic and the actuality of ethics—i.e.: eternity. It is important to note that God does not merely relate the two beings, but the two actualities.[11] In this respect, the idea of God stands outside both pure thought and pure will, since the methods of these directions of spirit relate only to being and cannot be employed in their "pure" states on data of the realm of actual existence (Dasein).[12]

Since the idea of God is not deducible from thought or

---

[10] See F. Rosenzweig in his "Einleitung," "Jud. Schriften," vol. 1, on the significance of this idea in idealistic thought.

[11] See Siegfried Ucko's "Der Gotterbegriff der Philosophie H. Cohen's," p. 48.

will, are we to conclude that it is to be accepted on faith, that it is a mystery transcending the limits of knowledge, to be received only by a fiat of the will?   Such a conclusion would be utterly at variance with the whole trend of Cohen's thought.   Are we to regard then the idea of God as a stop-gap employed to fill a lacuna in the system, a veritable deus ex machina?

Cohen points out in reply, to these questions, that the "basic law of truth," which, methodologically is the starting point of the system, contains implicitly the idea of God. The law of truth states that both ethics and logic must agree in their rational methodology.   Logic and ethics must not be dissolved into one another, nor are they to be regarded as having no relation to each other.   In the previous chapter, we saw how ethics was founded upon logic, depending upon the latter science for the method of determining the nature of a concept.   This dependence of ethics upon logic was made necessary by the law of truth.   But the same law now demands that the actuality corresponding to logic be accommodated to the actuality of pure will—that is, that physical nature endure endlessly in order that the experienced eternity of the ethical task be not stultified and that the goal of ethics be anchored in reality.   Thus the idea of God which effects this connection between the two actualities is seen to be a deduction from the law of truth.[12]

Accordingly, the ideas of the future, God, and truth, are intimately connected—a fact for which the simultaneous emergence of these three concepts in prophetic religion is cited by the author as historical confirmation.[13]

It is evident that in deducing the idea of God from the law of truth, Cohen makes a mental leap from the realm of being to that of actual existence, the justification of which, on the basis of his own thought, is doubtful.   His reasoning

---

[12] See supplementary notes.
[13] Ethics, Chap. 9.

is as follows: the deepest significance of the method of purity, demanded by the law of truth, is to be found in its eventual applicability to the actual world. The deductions of pure will must be applicable to the actual world. But the eternity demanded by the pure will would be denied by the actual world, unless the latter were construed as endless in time. Hence the actual world is infinite in time.

There is an error in this argument which derives from the ambiguity of the term eternal. It may be taken in a relative or in an absolute sense. The artist envisions a perfect ideal. He knows that his own productions, though made in the effort to embody that ideal, are yet infinitely below it in perfection. His endeavor as an artist to represent that ideal contains the quality of eternity, in Cohen's sense, since the ideal is apprehended as unattainable except by an infinite number of exertions. The artist mastered by his ideal goes on fashioning inadequate images of it, knowing full well that the ideal may never be represented in the actual world, in its complete perfection. This realization does not contradict his perception that the relation between his efforts and the ideal is that of a finite number to infinity. Now the actuality of the ethical endeavor, it was shown above, is that of the ideal. The eternal task of ethics is really the relation between our finite acts and the ideal of the one humanity. There is no necessary implication therefore in the feeling of eternity which is said to accompany all ethical striving for the assumption that the actual world must endure endlessly.

Cohen assures us that eternity is not produced by the application of the judgment of totality to the moments of time. "It (eternity) means so little in itself, an eternal time, as an eternal place, but only the eternal work." [14] Eternity is a construct, not of thought, but of will. He further states that the quality of eternity distinguishes the manifestations of

---

[14] Ethics, p. 388.

pure will from those of sheer desire.[15]   But what can this
quality of eternity mean if not the apprehension of the infinity of the goal in comparison to the paltriness of one's
efforts?   Eternity is a qualitative concept, not a quantitative
one.   Is it not clearly inconsistent, therefore, that Cohen
should feel justified in reasoning from eternity to infinity,
after he had taken so much pains to establish an absolute
distinction between these two concepts?

Cohen's deduction of the necessary existence of the actual
world from the eternity of the ethical will could only be justified if the concept of eternity were originally construed as
being infinite time plus a qualitative advance along the path
of ethical perfection.   But how, we may ask, can an act of
will contain reference to infinite time?   Thought deals with
infinite series by picking out a character in them which is not
in itself infinite and which serves to define the series.   Every
infinite is defined by a specific relation, which implies that
the series may not be ended.   But no mathematical infinite
is ever produced by the addition of term to term, no matter
how long the process is continued.

In this case, the action of the will is itself one of the terms
of the infinite progress which it is supposed to postulate.
This is psychologically impossible for all that the person can
feel is the relative infinity of the distant goal toward which
he strives.   From a logical viewpoint, it is impossible to
argue from the qualities of any one term to the infinity of
the series.   But if the relatively infinite goal is the sole content of the feeling of eternity, then all that the reality of
ethics demands is that the goal shall always be elusive, not
that in all infinite time these must of necessity be a constant
advance toward the ideal.

Cohen's reasoning is perhaps better understood if eternity
is construed as a demand that ethical progress ought not to
cease.   The idea of God now appears and effects the change

---

[15] Ethics, p. 392.

from "ought not to cease" to "does not cease." This interpretation, however, does not seem to accord with Cohen's
definitions of eternity, as quoted in this chapter. Furthermore, on the basis of this argument, there would be no reason
for refusing to grant so many other ethical desiderata.
Cohen seems to think of eternity as being a quality of the
ethical will, not as a demand of it. Pure will at every present
moment demands the kind of actions which will tend to
realize the infinitely distant goal. The "ought" of ethics
applies to the here and the now.

If our analysis of the meaning of eternity is correct, Cohen
is not justified in deducing the idea of God from the law of
truth. We are to regard therefore his introduction of the
idea of God into his system of philosophy as an attempt to
satisfy the longing of men to believe that the ethical ideal is
real in a more solid sense than that of an esthetic ideal.
Since this longing is itself ethical, Cohen insists that the idea
of God is part of the objective structure of ethics, not merely
a means to keep up the courage of men. "Nicht der Mensch
also fordert für seine subjective Stützung Gott: sondern zur
objectiven Begründung der Sittlichkeit wird Gott gefordert."
(E. 2nd ed. p. 55) (It is not then, that man demands God for
His subjective support, but He is demanded by the need for
the objective grounding of ethics.) The idea of God is then,
despite Cohen's own protestations, to be regarded as an addition to, not deduction from the law of truth.

What is the nature of the being of God? To this question
Cohen replies: "God is idea." He is neither alive, nor a
person, but an idea. As an Idea, God is founded in the
structure of spirit. Again as an idea, God cannot be described, but we can tell that which, barring Him, would
not be.

As an idea of pure thought and pure will, God does not
have to be "believed" in, for He can be discovered by the
processes of reason itself. This does not mean that the same

certainty attends the thought of God as that which accompanies mathematical reasoning. "Die Ehrlichkeit des neuen Weltalters beruht auf der schlichten Einsicht, die sich nicht bemanteln lasst, dass ein Anderes die mathematische, ein Anderes die moralische Gewissheit ist." [16] (The honesty of the new world era rests on the simple insight, which cannot be covered up, that the certainties of mathematics and ethics are different). The certainty of ethics and of the spiritual sciences based upon it is nonetheless superior to that of mere faith.

God is transcendent, which is to say: that as the idea of truth, God stands outside both ethics and logic, and that He constitutes their ultimate justification; that neither nature will be transcendent to ethics nor the reverse; that He has no (Dasein) existence of His own, apart from nature. What is the content of the Idea of God? The content of any Idea is the sum total of events which require it as their presupposition. Thus far, the only content of the idea of God that we have noted is the aspect of eternity attending all ethical action. In the later works of Cohen, this idea was considerably enlarged in meaning, as we shall see in the subsequent chapter. The growth of the idea of God in the "B. D. R." and the "R. D. V." is due to its being set in correlation with the idea of man. For the present, we know God as, on the one hand the idea of truth and hence as the foundation of the entire system of philosophy, and, on the other hand, as the maintainer of the physical world for the ethical task. Thus God is at once a purely logical concept of harmony between two domains of Knowledge and a Power, transcending the existence of both man and nature.[17] This apparent contradiction is partly removed by the fact that in Cohen's view, concepts are constitutive of reality and hence control the

---

[16] Ethics, p. 420.

[17] See the conclusions on this point of A. Lewkowitz in Zeitschrift fur Phil. and phil. Kritik. Bd. 144.

course of nature. This, however, is never explicitly stated by Cohen. The idea of God really reveals the essential ambiguity inherent in Cohen's system concerning the relation of the actual world to the realm of Being or Thought.[18]

To summarize the discussion in this chapter, Cohen's idea of God is derived from his studies in the field of ethics. God is at once at the beginning and at the end of ethics. At its beginning, ethics requires the idea of truth to point to the fact that there is indeed a realm of Ought, a science of what is intrinsically, "lawful" to do. Our feeling of truthfulness forbids us to assume that selfish desires and interests may explain all human actions. In this way the independence of the science of right and wrong is assured. The goal of ethics, the attainment of the ideal society is somehow felt in every ethical act. This goal is the actuality of the ethical will, standing in the same relation to it as the actual world is to mathematical thought. The idea of God ties together the two actualities, assuring the maintenance of the physical world for the ethical goal.

(e) The Relation of Man to God

We saw above that Cohen recognizes three directions of culture-consciousness: Thought, Will and Feeling. Religion, obviously deals with all three of these phases of culture. It centers about the concepts of God and man; it involves the voluntary acceptance of what is conceived to be the will of God and the effectiveness of its rites and symbols is largely in the field of emotion. What therefore is its place in the system of philosophy? Cohen rejects the attempt to arrive at a solution of the problem of religion by the assumption of a fourth direction in consciousness, or by postulating a special religious intuition of the Infinite, after

---

[18] See the series of articles by Prof. D. Neumark in the "Hatoren" Hebrew magazine, the issues from April 1924 to July 1925, where Cohen's idea of God is criticised.

the manner of Schleiermacher, or more recently, Rudolf Otto. The easy way of finding a place for religion in the modern scheme of things is to assume a "religious feeling," which obeys its own laws and carries its own justification. In this way an honored and secure place is provided for theology and all intellectual difficulties are avoided. The apprehension of the "sacred" or the "feeling" of "creatureliness" is an experience and is, as such, entitled to the respect which all facts command. But Cohen would not take the easy road. Accordingly he is compelled to find a place for religion within one or all of the three directions of spirit.

In his long essay, "Religion und Sittlichkeit," Cohen declares that the origin of religion is found in mythology. (Mythos.) Primitive, pre-scientific man was puzzled by many things in the ceaseless round of life and death. Not being conscious of the demands of reason, he resorted to that conglomerate of fantastic explanations that we call mythology. In his attempts to placate the mysterious forces of nature, man gradually invented the rites of magic and religion.

While the results of primitive imagination are endlessly varied and complex, there are certain ways of thinking that are peculiar to it. "Soul" and "fate" are the two central ideas of mythological thought. Primitive man explains all events in terms of the activity of souls, while above all nature, he sees the iron chain of fate. Out of this tendency to attribute souls to things, the gods arose. To the pre-cultural man, the nature of the gods and their relation to the world and to man are of prime concern. At that stage of mental evolution, neither the ethical concept of man, nor the scientific view of nature are even dimly perceived. The gods, or the one god—the number does not matter, are the forces of nature which must be coerced or propitiated for the sake of terrestrial happiness or post-mortem salvation. It is the business of the gods to help men conquer other men or to fight the inimical powers of the universe, not to aid man to subdue the evil in himself, in society, or in nature. The mind which constructs and finds satisfaction in mythology knows only the polarity of success or failure, not the tension of good and evil. All historical religions, clearly, still bear the marks of their mythological origins. According to this broad view of the mythological attitude, the religions of most so-called pious people, of the pillars of all established churches, would be classed as mythology. For so long as people inquire, "What shall I gain by it?" instead of asking, "Will it improve my character?" they are still following the mythological line of thought.

Religion, properly so called, arises with the emergence of the ethical consciousness. Thus, the Hebrew prophets with their thunderous insistence on "justice" and "righteousness" are the true originators of religion. Against the mythological view of a plurality of gods, they asserted the oneness of God. The difference, Cohen argues, is not merely one of numbers, but of kind. The gods were, to the heathen, forces of nature; they could bring rain and sunshine, famine and pestilence. Apollo was the god of the sun, Aphrodite the goddess of love, Demetrius the god of fertility, the Baals, the gods of rain. The purpose of worshiping any god was to obtain the favors that he could give. Hence there was no inconsistency in the worship of many gods, since the needs and interests of men are many and various. But the one God stands outside and above nature. His essence must forever remain unknown. He is not identified with any natural force or with the totality of all forces. Every attempt to represent God as a being of nature, even if only symbolically, may detract from the purity of the conception of God. For this reason, the prophets of Israel were violently opposed to the making of any images or representations of the Lord of the universe.

The essence of the prophetic message, Cohen finds in the statement of Micah—"He hath told thee, O man, what is good." [1] God tells men what they should regard as good and what they should condemn as evil. The "function" of God is not to provide prosperity, or even happiness, but to aid the efforts of man to discriminate between right and wrong. God had thus become the originator of ethics. In this transformation, Cohen finds the end of mythology and the true origin of religion. In his view, the sole purpose of religion is to help men live an ethical life. It was the historical function of religion to develop the ethical conscience of man. The slow growth of "culture consciousness" gradually enabled ethics to dispense with the aid of religion and to emerge as an independent science. If this course of development should continue, it is clearly evident, religion would progressively disappear, giving way to ethics.[2] Cohen does not in this work evade this conclusion. Thus he states [3] "Wenn sonach der wahrhafte Ursprung der Religion in der Sittlichkeit liegt, so ist es nicht ihr Ende, sodern ihre Vollendung, wenn sie aus der Verflechtung mit dem Mythos befreit, und in die reine Lehre der Sittlichkeit verwandelt wird." (If therefore the true origin of religion lies in ethics, then it is not its end, but its completion if it is freed from its entanglement with mythology and is transformed into the teaching of ethics.)

Since the raison d'etre of religion is to be found in its supposed usefulness for ethics, we should inquire whether religion in the modern world does in fact help to induce men to accept the ethical ideal?

Answering this question in the affirmative, Cohen points out these services of religion to the cause of ethics.

1. Religion keeps up the idea of God for ethics. The God-idea is perennially reinterpreted by thinkers, but without the aid of religion, ethical philosophers might not have produced it. The idea of God is indeed part of ethics, being

---

[1] Micah VI, 18.
[2] See supplementary note 1 at end of volume.
[3] R. u. S., p. 68.

the promise of its eventual fulfillment; still the fact remains that so many philosophers failed to recognize this logical relationship. A godless ethics necessarily lacks the idea of the reality of mankind, the assurance that the existing lines of division between classes and nations will be overcome in a blazing sense of the unity of all humanity. It is therefore in danger of being dismissed as a mere illusion. Religion has not fulfilled its historical mission so long as the idea of God and all that it implies have not yet become integral elements of man's ethical convictions.

2. Religion trains the individual for the ethical task, thru the regimen of conduct and observance that it imposes upon him. More specifically, the ethical virtue of loyalty is maintained and nourished by the allegiance offered to the inherited religion. Character is built and ennobled thru the discipline of Church and Synagogue. One's institutional religion, is, after all, a matter of accident.[4] Possessing it, however, it is our duty, on the one hand, to interpret it in the light of our ethical conscience and, on the other hand, to adhere to it faithfully, for the continuity of religious tradition is alone capable of developing that integrity and strength of character, which may be described as the "piety of loyalty." Also, when a man lives in the realization that he shares in a continuous tradition, he is constantly made aware of the reality and significance of spiritual values; he is thereby rendered immune to the lure of materialism and is consequently prepared to recognize the merits of "scientific idealism." [5]

In the "Begriff der Religion" and later in the "Religion der Vernunft," Cohen modified somewhat his earlier views. He argues in these works that while religion cannot indeed be regarded as an independent direction of consciousness, it ought to be recognized as possessing characteristic value of

---

[4] R. u. S., p. 74.
[5] Ibid., p. 74.

its own, "Eigenart." This value is due to the specific content of religion, which is now regarded as extending beyond the limits of ethics and hence as not destined to disappear into the latter science with the progress of culture. In addition to the value of its own content, religion gains further .in significance in that it synthesizes the three directions of consciousness. Sharing in thought, will and feeling, religion helps to evolve out of these diverse movements, the unified "culture consciousness" of every age.[6] Since it rises above the special disciplines of ethics, esthetics and mathematics, religion brings into focus their respective contributions and evolves therefrom a unified and all-embracing world-view. In this sense, religion is the final philosophy of life of each epoch, registering and interpreting the progress of every direction of spirit in terms of the needs and problems of life. Thus, while religion does not produce new knowledge, it concentrates attention on new relationships, thereby evoking fresh meaning in the concepts of logic and esthetics.

This thought is illustrated in the manner in which monotheistic religion employs the concepts of unity and being, concepts which are clearly derived from the sphere of logic. In religion, the concepts of unity and being are fused into the idea of God, who is the One Being.

For the religious consciousness God is the Unique Being (Einzig.). "He alone is Being." [7] In comparison with His Being, the being of everything else sinks into the "world of shades." True religion is necessarily monotheistic; it sets up God over against nature and declares that true being belongs only to the former.

How can the religious attitude be permitted by the august majesty of "pure reason" thus to distort the concepts of logic? The concept of being, it will be recalled, is approached

---

[6] See sup. note (2) at end of volume.
[7] B. d. R., p. 27.

thru the mathematical study of nature while the idea of God stands only for the eventual agreement of physics and ethics. Does not religion here conflict with, or more correctly, usurp the place of logic?

Cohen's reply to this question is two-fold. He points first to the physical implications of the God-idea, the fact that God "preserves" nature for ethics. In this sense, God is more primary than the being of nature, which is the object of logical study. Secondly,—and here the true significance of Cohen's view is revealed, he declares,[8] "monotheism is only one standpoint of the spirit to the world, which is in need of being supplemented by other standpoints." The statement "God is the one Being"[9] is therefore to be regarded as a value judgment, an assertion of emphasis.[10] He is the only Being that matters to the religious consciousness. If the ethical ideal is ever to be approached, the obstructions of nature must needs be flouted. Mighty streams of water and impassable walls of fire are regarded as of no real significance by the man of piety, who fixes his gaze steadfastly upon the ethical goal, which is in turn assured by the being of God. It is the mark of the religious person that his attention is entirely concentrated on the guaranty of God for the realization of the ideal of humanity and that, in consequence, he refuses to be swayed from his path of duty by the obduracy and intractability of the forces of nature in his own person, or in the environment about him.

On this interpretation, Cohen's insistence on the Uniqueness of God's Being does not represent a modification of his earlier views on the nature of God.[11] Religion is a subjective viewpoint, an attitude of the spirit, which is avowedly one-sided. "Pantheism is not religion."[12] Religion is

---

[8] B. d. R., p. 25.

[9] B. d. R., p. 27.

[10] See sup. note (3) at end of volume.

[11] See sup. note (4) at end of vol.

[12] R. d. V., p. 47.

brought about only through selective emphasis. It should be remembered that the concept of being in Cohen's philosophy is regarded as the goal to which each of the directions of spirit tends. For religious thought, then, God as the ethical ideal, is the One Being.

Another concept which religion borrows from logic is that of correlation. Religion deals with a three-fold correlation: the correlation of man to man, of man to God, and of God to nature. The concept of correlation belongs, in Cohen's logic, under the general classification of purpose. "It is a purpose-relation (Zweckbeziehung), that we apply between God and man, as between God and nature." The formation of a concept, it will be recalled, entails the presence of a purposive relation in our author's logic. "When I accordingly desire to form the concept of God, I must establish a purposiveness between man and God. . . ." [13] In non-technical language, the correlation is a method of relating two mental data in terms of what they mean for each other. In strict logic, we have the right to set up a correlation between any two terms at all. The system as a whole cannot gain thereby any additional knowledge concerning the nature of the world, but it may well attain greater coherence and increased significance by such a procedure. The establishment of a correlation between two entities amounts really, from the strictly logical viewpoint, to the development of a special terminology, which is useful for the expression of new spheres of meaning. Hence the question of whether or not a certain correlation is to be set up must be decided on the basis of practical considerations. [14]

For the present, however, it is clear that religion, which is the complex of motives and data, clustering about the correlation of man and God, cannot be regarded as containing its own standards of value. Consequently, it must approve

[13] B. d. R., p. 47.
[14] See sup. note (5) at end of vol.

itself by its ethical or esthetic fruits. But the values of esthetics are, in Cohen's view, dependent upon those of ethics, since "Ethics is a second logic for all the sciences of the spirit." [15] Nothing is beautiful which is not also good, Cohen contends. Amoral beauty, let alone anti-moral beauty, is sheer sensuality. Hence, the ultimate justification of religion is to be sought in ethics, though the content of religion may well be such as ethics alone is incapable of evolving by its own methods.

In ethics, as we saw, God is related to both man and nature. He assures the continued existence of nature for the ethical work of man. But the term "man" in this connection really stands for humanity, not for an individual person. From the standpoint of ethics, the true self of every individual is humanity. This is a very noble viewpoint, to be sure, but, Cohen asks, is the individual to regard his own empirical being as of no ethical consequence at all? This problem arises with particular sharpness, in the case of a person who has sinned. The sinner has disassociated himself from the march of humanity toward the ideal society. It is not the sin in itself, but the fact that its perpetrator may thru it lose the vision of a united humanity that is of crucial importance. Since the sinner, even if repentant, does not feel himself part of eternal humanity, and does not identify his individual self with the ethical concept of man, he may be lost for the ethical task. Here is where the correlation of the individual man with God may prove helpful.

Before pursuing this line of thought any further, we must emphasize again, for the sake of clearness, that while the ethical correlation of humanity with God is, to Cohen, a fact of Being, the correlation of individual man with God is a human, subjective device, of no ontological significance, to be used only for what it is ethically worth. There are no objective and permanent laws, regulating the "lines of in-

---

[15] B. d. R., p. 11.

fluence" between empirical man and God, other than those which the religious man fashions out of his own resources.

When the individual becomes conscious of a bond of relation between himself and the God of ethics, religion is born. The guaranty of God concerning the progressive attainment of the ethical ideal by humanity is then applied by the religious person to his own destiny. "Mein eigener Gott ist der Gott der Religion." [16] The individual sinner feels that if he should mend his ways and make the ethical ideal the guide of his life, God will again accept him in the ranks of eternal mankind. The God who, as a "methodological concept" unites ethics and physics, is now seen in the role of a "personal" god, One Who is concerned with the weal and woe of every individual, Who pities and "redeems" every poor sinner.

Is there any self-deception in this belief, this transformation of an impersonal idea into the God of redemption? No, Cohen maintains, pointing out that God is here used only as the name, signifying the attainment of a victory over sin; "Man does the work of redemption, but God is thought of as the sign (Wahrzeichen) that the liberation from sin was achieved." [17] In other words, God as the Redeemer is a subjective conception, of value from the psychological standpoint, since it helps the despairing and repentant sinner to find his way back to the straight and narrow path of ethics.

Thus, religion arises when man deliberately attributes qualities to God, which are to serve as an inspiration for his own conduct.[18] The God of ethics is not the God of the individual, any more than He is the God of any particular physical object. He is not even the God of humanity, as His function will be performed even if all mankind should perish, provided other spiritual beings arise to take their place. But

---

[16] B. d. R., p. 116.

[17] B. d. R., p. 64.

[18] See sup. note (6) end of book.

each man can, by an act of will, make this general, abstract and aloof God, his own God. Religion is wholly the result of the fiat of man. It is a heroic stratagem of the spirit, a psychological instrument employed by man for the sake of improving his character.[19]

As an instrument, religion must be judged by its efficiency. Our next task, therefore, is to inquire whether it does indeed perform the ethical work for the sake of which it is practiced? Can modern religion be an effective force for the good? Can we strip God of the power to change the natural course of events and ban from the sphere of religion all manner of selfish concern and still possess a faith that is vital and significant?

This question can only be answered after an analysis of the whole structure of religion which Cohen rears on his conception of the correlation of man and God. Accordingly, we set forth here in brief outline Cohen's view of the ideal religion.

1. Religion begins with the establishment of the correlation between the individual man and God. "Not God alone and in Himself, but always only in correlation with man." [20] So long as men think in objective terms, seeking to discover the facts of being, they will attain a knowledge of logic, of ethics and of esthetics, but they will never arrive at religion. When men, however, turn to ask whether their own individual characters are in accord with the ethical processes of being, then genuine religion is born. For, then, the individual man is concerned with what God means to him, not with the objective meaning of the God-idea. God is in that event not just the "Lord of the Universe," but, "my God, the Savior of my soul from the power of evil." The God of the individual is the God of religion. Thus, the Psalms always refer to God as "my God" or "our God."

---

[19] See supplementary note (7) end of book.
[20] B. d. R., p. 32.

2. God is conceived as unique, in the double sense, of transcendence to both logic and ethics and exclusive interest for the religious person. In the first sense, the uniqueness of God is the fact that the idea of God stands at the very beginning and at the very end of the philosophical system. As we have seen before, the law of truth directs the development of both logic and ethics, leading them to the ideal of "purity." At the same time, the physical world which is the object of logic and the ideal society of mankind, which is the object of ethics, are welded together in the idea of God, for God assures the continuance of the actual world for the ethical goal. The uniqueness of God in the second sense is an expression of the emphasis of monotheism, as discussed above. It need hardly be pointed out that the uniqueness of God's Being is an authentic Jewish doctrine. God is "echad um'yuchad," One and Unique in His Oneness.

3. The attributes of God can only be negative, since every quality of (Dasein) actuality—including those of power, life, will, and wisdom, which Maimonides does ascribe to God, cannot be justly applied to His Nature. The positive attributes of God are to be wholly restricted to the realm of ethics. When Moses asked to see the glory of God, he was told that he could only see the back of God, His actions. These, Moses described in the famous "sh'losh esrah midoth," which enumerate the ethical attributes of the Deity.[21] "Thus the attributes of action are not so much the qualities of God, but rather in accordance with their concept, the ideal for the action of man." [22]

In Cohen's system, the proposition that God is merciful and just cannot be taken literally, since as an idea, God is but one aspect of the system; in Himself, He is neither good nor bad. In religion, however, when the attention of man is riveted to God as the Redeemer, then God is envisaged as

---

[21] Ex. 34, 6.
[22] R. d. V., p. 110.

the ideal ethical personality. Objectively, from the standpoint of knowledge, God is an idea, a conception transcendent to the three directions of consciousness; subjectively,
from the standpoint of the repentant soul seeking to rise
higher in the realm of the spirit, God is the beckoning light,
the perfect moral Being, Whose one message is "be ye like
unto me." The qualities of God are meant to be standards
for human life. In attempting to understand the attributes
of God in a "Religion of Reason," we have only to know what
the virtues of "pure will" are. Cohen classifies all ethical
virtues under the motives of respect and love. Like Kant,
Cohen thinks of the motive of respect as being respect for an
objective law. Thus, the virtue of justice is derived from
the motive of respect.

Both love and justice are forms of pure will—the former
containing a larger admixture of feeling to reason than the
latter. In any conflict between the dictates stemming from
the two separate sources, priority is always to be accorded to
the one motivated by Respect or Justice. For reason must
ever remain supreme. Love which is not directed by principles of abstract justice is apt to be clannish, narrow and
blind. It follows that God cannot be conceived simply as
Justice or as Love, if His qualities are to be the norms of
human conduct. He is both just and loving. The relative
strength of Love and Justice in His Being cannot be calculated by man. "The connection between God's Justice and
Love is the secret of His Being." This conception permits
us to view the presence of pain in life either as the punishment of the just God, or as the purgative acts of the loving
God, or as the expression of both aspects of God's will.
There are "yissurim shel ahavah," pains of love, as well as
"yissurim shel tochachah," pains of punishment. The latter
are seen by the pious soul as punishment for sins, for, in
Cohen's view, justice demands proper punishment for crimes.
The former comprises the evils that come to men, in order to

refine their nature.[23]   Thus the Will of God in any special situation is veiled in mystery.

The statement that the Will of God is inscrutable is an important principle in theology, since ignorance of the full
intentions of the Deity is an essential component of the feeling of piety.   Only the humble can pray to God.   In this
case, the inscrutability of God's will is due to the possibility
of viewing His actions from either of two ethical standpoints.

4. God is creator of the world.   This does not mean that
He brought the world into being at a certain moment of time.
Reason knows only its own laws which are permanent and
valid for all time.   Since to Cohen, mathematics and the
physical sciences are direct developments of "pure reason,"
the existence of the world is a logical necessity.   Therefore,
the belief in the creation of the world can only be regarded as
the result of pre-logical, non-scientific thinking.   That belief
must consequently be reinterpreted.   By attributing the
creation of the world to God, Cohen suggests, we mean that
He maintains the world for the ethical task of man.   How
God effects this preservation of the world must forever remain a mystery.   It does not lie within the purview of reason
to discover how God unites the processes of ethics and logic.
Reason can only follow separately the three directions of
spirit.   Their union and eventual harmonization is somehow
contained in the Being of God.   This again is part of the
mystery of God's uniqueness.[24]

The relation of God to the world is that of Being to Becoming, where in Cohen's sense, Being is the ground for Becoming.   The actual physical world is the realm of Becoming,
since it is ceaselessly in motion.   The sciences of ethics,
esthetics and physics are the realm of Being, containing as
they do the constant laws, regulating the changes in the realm
of Becoming.   The idea of God is the primary idea in the

---

[23] B'rachot, 24.
[24] See sup. note (7) at end of book.

realm of Being, transcendent even to logic and ethics, as we have seen before.

5. The transcendence of God permits us to say that revelation comes from God, in the sense that both logical and ethical reason are conditioned by the idea of God. Revelation also means the testimony of reason that it does not derive from "beastly sensibility."[25] To say, with the empiricists, that all human thought comes from experience, is to defy the voice of revelation. In this connection the idea of God is employed as synonymous with the idea of truth, which demands that both ethics and logic begin with a Source-Idea, not with any empirical data. On the basis of this view, the refusal to recognize the autonomy of reason becomes an act of impiety. In this way, the theological principle of revelation is reinterpreted to stand for the gradual evolution of human thought, down to its final culmination in the philosophy of "critical idealism." The first principle of this school of thought, to wit, that theoretical and practical reason must produce its own starting point, is the final revelation of the God-idea.

6. The term, "Spirit of Holiness," Ruaḥ Hakodesh, in the Jewish religion, is to be reinterpreted to mean the highpoint of the correlation between man and God.[26] Thus the holy spirit is not an attribute of either man or God, but of their relation. Holiness is but another name for the ethical life— that is, for life with God as the ideal of conduct. The command "and be ye holy, for I am holy" is interpreted by our Sages in an ethical sense, as follows: "As He is merciful, so be ye merciful, as He does deeds of loving kindness, so do ye likewise, etc."[27] The "Spirit of Holiness" may be said to be present during moments of great ethical insight, such as conversion or repentance. The conception of the "Holy

---

[25] R. d. V., p. 97.
[26] R. d. V., p. 122.
[27] Sabbath, 133 b.

Spirit" serves to limit the domain of possible union of man
and God to the ethical field, thus avoiding the errors of
mysticism and pantheism.   The Holy Spirit is between God
and man, not in either.   Any form of religious technique
which assumes that man can be completely holy must be rejected, for holiness is the eternal task.[28]   The goal of ethics
is never actually reached, though it is approached ever more
closely.

7. The content of the correlation of man and God grows
with the ethical development of the concept of man.   In
ethics the problem was posed, how the "next-man" (Neben-
mensch) changes into the "fellow-man" (Mitmensch), how,
that is, man comes to include the welfare of others within his
own sphere of interest.   Religion helps to bring about this
most important change, thus serving a vital function in the
development of ethical feeling.   At this point, ethics and religion are mutually supplementary, for "the relations between man and man form the lower, or rather, the inner correlation within the one of man and God.[29]

The perception of social suffering is felt as spiritual pain
by the religious person.   When we realize the extent of
poverty and distress that even now harass the greater portion of mankind, and then reflect on the undeniable fact that
these evils are really the results of the imperfections of our
society, then we are deeply saddened.   It grieves us to see
how far we still are from the ethical ideal of life.   This grief
at the suffering of others brings home to us the essential unity
of all mankind.   Thus by means of the sympathy aroused at
the sight of social injustice, the religious man is enabled to
perceive his fellow-man in every human being.   "Mitleid" is
the source of the feeling of human solidarity.

8. Suffering now receives its religious meaning.   Misery
and pain are needed in order to awaken the conscience of

[28] R. d. V., p. 129.
[29] R. d. V., p. 154.

men and thereby to advance the cause of ethical progress. There can be no ethical progress without the stimulus of poverty and distress. There can be no sympathy unless there is pain and there can be no ethical progress unless there are multitudinous occasions for sympathy. Our insight into the conditions needed for progress, therefore, should lead us to say that the unfortunate section of society is not punished for its own sins, but for those of the whole society. "The poor are the pious;" God heaped upon their weary shoulders the burdens which must needs be borne, if mankind is to continue to advance toward the goal of ethics. For, "him whom God loveth, He punisheth." Social pain is needed to arouse man's love of man. Poverty is "the optic device" by which we discover that the stranger is our brother.[30] Hence those who suffer are the true servants of God.

It is in this sense of "the suffering servant" that the election of Israel as "the people of God" is to be understood. The martyrdom of Israel's long history is proof of God's choice of Israel to be the perpetual goad of humanity's conscience.[31]

Cohen does not deal with the question of the origin of evil, in a physical or in a metaphysical sense. Physics, he declares, knows no evil and metaphysics is superstition. He is concerned solely with the religious meaning of social misery. Social suffering must not be ignored or sanctimoniously glossed over with hollow explanations—such as, "evil is unreal, being only a negative entity, like darkness," or "evil is the necessary background of good," or, "evil only appears to be evil to our limited understanding," or "evil is a 'chair' for the good." Such explanations are really attempts to explain evil away and to blind the minds of men to the only social facts which are capable of rousing them from the lethargy induced by smug self-satisfaction.

---

[30] B. d. R., p. 79.
[31] See sup. note 8 at end of book.

Mythology is indeed conscious of social evil, but its explanation is always in terms of "guilt." To the mythological mind, suffering is punishment for guilt incurred in the infraction of some Divine law. This guilt is non-ethical in nature. It is like a defiling substance, which can only be removed through pain and death. The "Mythos" declares, "the poor are the guilty ones." Thus, it adds insult to injury, flattering the mighty and reviling the weak. Monotheism, on the other hand, demands a live realization of the injustices of society, plus an accompanying sympathy, love and even reverence for the unfortunate. They bear the brunt of human progress. They are collectively the tragic hero of the Divine Drama, which is perpetually unfolding on the roll of world history.

This view of Cohen's implies certain assumptions in regard to human psychology, which are, to say the least, open to question. The monotheistic consciousness, which takes such a lofty view of social oppression—would it not take an equally altruistic attitude in regard to human joy? Why cannot the infectiousness of joy, the delight of men at the sight of human happiness, serve to awaken in us the sense of the unity of mankind? If so, then suffering is no longer needed for human love. Is there no truth to the common proverb, "Laugh and the world laughs with you; weep, and you weep alone?" As a matter of fact, Cohen recognizes the virtue of "Mitfreude," which causes a person to rejoice in the joy of others, as the crown of monotheistic virtues. It is his claim that "Mitleid" comes much easier to men than "Mitfreude." For, to lack the latter is to miss a noble virtue indeed, but to lack the former is to be devoid of all ethical insight.

9. The correlation of man and God is not so much an affair of cognition as of love. God loves man and man loves God. While the love of man to God is real, that of God to man is merely a way of speaking that is congenial to the

mood of piety. The man standing in this correlation is further understood as loving other men. Love in any of these three relations is neither sexual nor esthetic. The artist loves the beautiful, the successful, the impressive; the religious consciousness loves the ugly, the unfortunate, the wretched. The artist finds it necessary to gloss pain over with things beautiful; the religious man translates the perception of pain directly into sympathy and the latter again into love. Also the artist sees not the individual, but the type; whereas religious love is directed to the individual as such.[32]

What is the order in which these three love-relations arise? First, Cohen states, comes the perception of the misery of the unfortunate. This perception is immediately followed by sympathy. Attention is then turned to the activity of God. Why does God permit such evil? Can it be that the poor are the guilty ones? No, one's conscience is bound to reply. The suffering of the poor is a kind of sacrifice for the sins of all mankind—a sacrifice which each succeeding epoch of human history demands as the price of progress. It is the saints that suffer. God loves the miserable. This high estimate of the lowly classes transforms arrogant sympathy into unpretentious, humble love.

The next step is the love of man to man, which is derived directly from the love of the unfortunate. This step is easily taken since, in a real sense, every man is a sufferer in more ways than one. The bond of sympathy is all-embracing. And the final step, by way of gratitude, is the love of men to God. God is loved by man as the idea which makes possible the love of men to each other. The meaning of God's love to man is seen in the sympathy to the poor that He, or rather the idea we have of Him, arouses in us.

The love of men to God is love of the ethical ideal. This love is not idle longing for or basking in God's grace; on the

[32] B. d. R., ch. 3.

contrary, it produces energetic social amelioration and is fed in turn by the needs of the social situation. Look at the wretchedness of the poor, Cohen counsels us, then think of God as their supporter and their avenger in world history and see if love for God is not kindled within your breast! "This avenger of the poor I love," exclaims Cohen.[33] From another viewpoint, love of God is the love of the "nearness of God," of the ever closer approach of society to the demands of the ethical ideal.[34]

The psalmist's exclamation, "But it is good for me to draw near to God," [35] is, to Cohen, the most profound expression of monotheism. It is not union with God that is held out as the ideal by the psalmist, but "drawing near" to God. And this "drawing near" to God becomes the highest ideal in monotheism, in clear contrast to the goal of union with or absorption into the Deity that mysticism and all pantheistic religions seek. "God Himself is not desired. Mythological love is directed to God. Monotheistic love, on the other hand, desires only the nearness of God; the nearness of God to man." [36] Monotheistic piety is a perpetual seeking of God, a quest that never ends. But this seeking "is always love, always longing, always an emotion, never only an intellectual attitude." [37]

10. Religion is alone capable of producing the ideal of individuality. In ethics, every person is only a sample of the total group, just as, in physics, every object is but a juxtaposed aggregation of so many relations. Selfhood, in the ethical sense includes all humanity. The individual attains selfhood only to the extent that he identifies himself with the ethical society of the ideal future. Ethics can only recognize defection from the right path in the preoccupations

[33] B. d. R., p. 81.
[34] R. d. V., p. 190.
[35] Psalms 73, 28.
[36] R. d. V., p. 190.
[37] R. d. V., p. 442.

of an individual with the state of his own soul. The ethical self is oriented outward; "the other" lies in its very inception. Hence the only form in which individuality could be an ethical ideal is expressed in the question, "How can I make my empirical person more serviceable in the cause of the ethical ideal?" [38] Phrased thus, the question is a practical one and it affords room in ethics for the ideal of a good individuality, though as a means only, not as an end.

Not being content with such a limited conception of the ideal of individuality, Cohen points out the line of spiritual development which is unfolded when the same question is expressed in theological terms: The man has sinned. He wants to be redeemed. How can this redemption occur? This formulation of the question does not restrict the range of its application to a special group, since in the face of the endless ethical task, all men are sinners. For, "there is not a just man upon earth that doeth good and sinneth not."

The conception of sin may properly be applied to an individual only, not to a social group. It has been Cohen's contention in the "Ethics," that the verdict of the judge concerning a plaintiff does not involve the idea of guilt. All the judge has to determine is whether a violation of the law has taken place. He then steps out of the picture, allowing the processes of society as expressed in the penal code to run their course. Codes of law do not contain judgments of value; their principles and ordinances are merely descriptive of society, in exactly the same manner as the architect's blueprints are of the skyscraper.[39] This does not mean that the individual criminal should adopt the same amoral attitude. On the contrary, the criminal should be deeply conscious of his sin, for the remorseful, heart-breaking recognition of his own sin, with its accompanying emotional background is essential to ethical progress and to spiritual life generally.

---

[38] See sup. note 9 end of book.
[39] See sup. note 10 end of book.

But, sin is always against something—against certain ideals, against certain rights, against the Divine Being. There can be no sin per se. In charting the path of repentance, we have therefore to indicate the object of sin. Superficially, it may appear that all sin is sin against society. However, Cohen points out, this is not an ethically fruitful conception, since it does not show the sinner how he can be rehabilitated. Society is a large bookkeeping organization concerned only with criminality, not sin, and what is once inscribed as criminality can never again be erased.

Sin should be interpreted as sin against God, "Sünde vor Gott." It is the ethical ideal of a united humanity, assured of eventual fulfillment through the concept of God, that the criminal had sinned against. Sin is now expressed in terms of the correlation of man and God, as a weakening of the intensity of the relation—a weakening, but not a breaking of the relation. The sinner has fallen away from God, but God is still his God. Expressed in these theological terms, it is easily seen that the cure of sin is not punishment but redemption, Erlösung. Thus the criminal, by recognizing his act as a sin against God, finds himself capable of redemption by God.

The redeemed individual marks a high ethical achievement. He now recognizes his former sin as a grievous error and he has the satisfaction of knowing that he had overcome the contradictions which had prevented him previously from reaching the unity of "I." [40] This new united "I" embodies a higher ethical value than is represented by the innocent person who, not having sinned, did not go through the purifying processes of repentance and redemption. The repentant sinner is the "new man," possessing the "new heart" and the "new spirit" of which Ezekiel prophesied. He is an individual in the sense that he is oriented toward himself, toward the raising of himself from sin, and he knows further

[40] R. d. V., p. 221.

that he had once overcome sin and that he can do so again. The state of his soul is now independent from his relations with other men. "He is an independent spiritual being because of his ethical unity.[41] This new individual is never an accomplished fact; it is to be regarded as a perpetual task. Just as the ethical totality-individual is an ideal that may ever be approached, though never quite reached, so is the religious "I-individual" an ideal which demands an endless progress for its eventual fulfillment.

The significance of the "I-individual" is missed if it is understood as referring to a succession of acts of sin and states of redemption. Before God, we must all know ourselves to be sinners, all the time. Examining his own conscience, the religious person recognizes his many shortcomings in the light of his ideals. He then proceeds to redeem himself, or rather, to be redeemed by God, thus attaining, to a degree, the new "I-individuality." Whenever he performs this spiritual exercise, through prayer or meditation, he climbs a new rung on the ladder of the perfection of "I-individuality." It will be remembered that God's redemption of man does not in Cohen's system involve a mysterious flow of grace from Heaven. All that he postulates in his scheme of redemption is a set of terms. It is part of the terminology of religion, Cohen asserts, to declare that God is the Redeemer.

This device of religion for the attainment of self-sanctification possesses the assurance for its success in the goodness of God.[42] No new arrangement in the being of God is needed in order that He may be construed as Redeemer. Figuratively speaking, man sinking in the morass of sin throws a rope about the solid tree of God and then pulls himself out to spiritual safety. What saves this procedure from being a mere verbal jugglery, a hollow attempt at virtuous self-

---

[41] R. d. V., p. 228.
[42] R. d. V., p. 251.

inflation, is the fact that God is conceived not as a human, but as a cosmic ideal, rooted in Being, or rather as the root of Being. The three movements of spirit converge in the idea of God. Hence when the soul turns its face to God, it finds real grooves, prepared in all eternity, leading it on toward redemption. It should be remembered that the term "Redeemer" as applied by Cohen to God does not mean that He must redeem, but that He may redeem. The attribution of the power of redemption to God amounts therefore, in the last analysis, to the statement that men are capable of improving their character through their periodic reflections on their own personal relations to God.

11. How is reconciliation between man and God to take place? Can it be that a mere rededication to the ideal of ethics is sufficient to bring about this reconciliation? Cohen insists that much more is involved. The person, who recognizes his own sin must take upon himself the punishment which is appropriate for that sin. It is true that other men must not apply the correlation of guilt and punishment to him. But, to the ethical consciousness, sin requires expiation. Quite apart from the fact that society must impose a penal code in self defense, Cohen declares, every man who sincerely wrestles with his soul knows that there can be no true repentance without penance. The voluntary acceptance of pain is an essential part of true remorse. Since all men, in moments of honest self-examination, know themselves to be sinners, there is no one who cannot regard the evils that befall him as so much penance. Job's friends, who argued that his suffering was the punishment for his sins, were wrong only because it was not for them to entertain such thoughts about a friend, but Job too was wrong, for, as a pious man, who is never entirely satisfied with the state of his soul, he should have accepted his suffering as a necessary preparation for redemption.[43]

---

[43] R. d. V., p. 268.

The truly repentant sinner desires pain, as a means of atonement, for, the process of redemption involves a whole-hearted acceptance of punishment. Individual suffering acquires new meaning on this view, quite apart from the value of social suffering discussed above. It is a preparatory step for the process of redemption, for the acquisition of a moment of the I-individual. "Mein Leiden ist nicht eine Wirkung, sondern ein Zweck für mein Selbst" (My suffering is not an effect, but a purpose for my self.)

On this view, the painful trials of Israel's history are seen in a new light. Israel is dedicated to the task of achieving the I-individual. Consequently, its way is necessarily steeped in martyrdom, for without pain there is no redemption. The manifold trials of Israel are "Yissurim Shel a'havah," troubles and sorrows sent by God to His people, out of His deep love, in order to chasten and purify their character. This pain is useless, of course, unless it is accepted in a humble, repentant spirit, as a penance, and is followed by moments of redemption. If suffering is accepted in this spirit, however, it becomes an effective instrument for the attainment of moral grandeur. To reach the heights of spiritual life, one must wade through the morass of distress and despair. Happy, easy-going good fellowship is but a low ethical level. The crown of thorns is indeed the only crown of dignity.[44]

12. The possibility of immortality for man is to be understood in two different senses. As we saw before, the ethical person finds his self in the totality of human beings. Since the continuity of the human race is assured by the idea of God, the self, in this sense, is unaffected by the death of any individual. The I-individual of religion is also conceived as an endless task involving an infinite number of the cycles, sin, atonement and redemption. Hence, the I-individual, too is immortal in the sense in which every unrealizable ideal is

---

[44] See sup. note 11 at end of book.

timeless. This does not mean, of course, that our soul survives the body, continuing to exist as a ghostly substance, as
it were. The I-individual exists only in moments of intense
correlation between man and God—moments which have
been previously described as exemplifying the "Holy Spirit."
The Holy Spirit is alone immortal.[45] Empirical men only
partake of the Holy Spirit during their lifetime insofar as
they attain the momentary stages of reconciliation with God.
To the extent, then, that we possess the Holy Spirit, we cannot die. For the correlation of man and God is assured of
continued progress in intensity, as a corollary of the irresistible march of ethical progress.

Cohen might with equal justice have added that insofar as
men possess Pure Thought and Pure Feeling they are immortal. For he conceives of thought at least as impersonal
and timeless and there is no reason why these qualities should
be denied to feeling. That he does not allude to these aspects
of human immortality can only be explained by the fact that
he recognized their irrelevance to the religious life.

13. Immortality in both the ethical and religious senses
finds its concrete expression in Judaism, in the ideal of the
Messiah.[46] The hope for "the days of the Messiah" is
really an expression of the belief that human society will
advance perpetually along the endless road to perfection.
This belief necessarily involves the assumption that the
correlation of man and God will attain greater strength, since
ethical progress, in the last analysis, depends, for Cohen,
upon religious progress.

But religious progress by way of sin and redemption includes as an essential element the acceptance of pain. Hence
the ideal of the Messiah must be conceived as associated
with the enduring of physical and spiritual agony. Only
"the suffering servant" can be the Messiah. He offers him-

[45] R. d. V., p. 359.
[46] See sup. note 12 at end of book.

self as a substitute for all men—a substitute for their share of suffering, though not for their guilt.

The substitution of another person to bear the retribution for one's own guilt is the result of mythological thinking. The scapegoat rites are based upon the notion of guilt as a kind of defiling substance, which, magnet-like, draws punishment upon its bearer. Thus, guilt could be literally transferred from person to person by the appropriate rites. In the Christian view of Jesus at the cross, taking the sins of all mankind upon himself, there is unmistakably embodied a characteristic seed of mythological thought. In Judaism, the fifty-third chapter of Isaiah which describes the suffering servant is applied to the people of Israel. As the Messiah-people, Israel is destined to the career of martyrdom. That one person or group of persons must, as a matter of fact, bear the burden of progress for the rest of society, is a common-place social insight. It is the discontent of the humble and the oppressed that generates the social energy which drives mankind ever forward on its path of progress. The malefactors of fame and fortune do not, as a rule, endure the hardships, which their evil practices impose upon the less favored sections of society. Clearly, then, the effects of human sin are not evenly distributed. Some men must suffer that all may live. Thus, Cohen concludes, the Messiah, as the agent of ethical progress, suffers for all mankind, suffers that true humanity may evolve; the Messiah is, in fact, the symbol of the tragic heroes of humanity, perpetually battling in the front lines of progress.

Cohen considers the Messianic ideal as the characteristic product of monotheism. Since belief in it is so important for the ethical progress of mankind, he regards monotheism as an essential constituent of modern culture.[47]

Who is this suffering Messiah? To this question, several answers are given in Cohen's writings. Israel as a religious

---

[47] See supplementary note 13 at end of book.

unit was proclaimed by our prophets and sages to be the
Messiah, since it was to be dedicated to the task of preserving the ideals of monotheism for modern culture. Furthermore, the suffering of Israel is in direct proportion to the
defection of other groups from the ethical ideal. The slow
birth of humanity, out of the historical mess of races, creeds
and classes, is accompanied by divers woes and hard travail,
by waves of tribalistic reaction which strike Israel first by
reason of its physical helplessness. To the extent that it accepts these evil visitations as its contribution to the evolution
of the perfect society, Israel is the Messiah. Yet in another
sense, the poor and oppressed classes in every age are the
Messiah, for upon their weary backs the iron tracks of the
new age are laid.

14. Prayer is the method whereby the correlation of man
and God is brought into being and whereby it is periodically
strengthened. Longing to and love of God find expression
in prayer and the intense forms of these emotions are poured
forth in lyric poetry. In prayer, man is reconciled and
brought nearer to God.

But prayer is more than an expression of love to God. A
mere glance at the prayer-book suffices to show that we pray
largely for other things than the improvement of our character, that we pray in fact for our own well being, for life
and happiness. Is this kind of prayer proper for a man of
culture, that ideal man who recognizes as worthy only the
three "pure" directions of Spirit? Strangely enough, Cohen
answers this question in the affirmative. Even as the physical
world is kept up by God for the task of ethics so are our
physical bodies maintained by Him, in their vitality, for the
sake of the Holy Spirit. Thus we may well pray for the
elimination of worry and trouble from our lives, in order that
we may be enabled to attain greater ethical and religious
heights.

Does not such prayer however involve the belief that God

will grant our petition? Is not such a belief, in Cohen's view, wholly unwarranted? To be sure, it is unwarranted, on Cohen's view of the nature of God, since the physical world is conceived as operating in accordance with inflexible laws, without any interference from God. Nevertheless, he declares, it is our duty to believe that God will grant our rightful requests. "Wenn aber der Glaube an den Erfolg notwendig ist für die Zaubermacht meiner Andacht, so ficht mich kein Gift der Skepsis an." (But if the belief in success is necessary for the magic power of my intention, then the poison of skepticism will not stand in my way.) [48] After all, Cohen argues, neither pessimism nor optimism is capable of actually proving its contentions. Hence it is our duty to assume an optimistic attitude. At this point Cohen comes unexpectedly into agreement with James' "Will to Believe," who, in his famous essay under this name, advocated the acceptance of those ideas as true, which reason cannot disprove and which are necessary for healthy living.

15. The ultimate value of religion is to be sought in the habits, standards and ideals, which constitute its concrete expression in actual life. "It is by their fruits that you shall know them." Obviously, the fruits of religion are the virtues of ethics. But, religion adds a basic ideal to ethics. Through concentrating attention on the idea of God, it teaches the ideal of the imitation of God. Man must ever strive to be like unto God, straining at the unattainable, even though it hurts. One aspect of the Deity is the law of truth, as we have seen. Hence, truthfulness is the first virtue of religion, as it is also the basic virtue of ethics.

The cultivation of our intellectual faculties is, therefore, a religious duty, a principle which in Judaism finds expression in the fact that the study of the Torah is virtually the highest sacrament. Justice and love are in religion, as in ethics, the two parent motives of the other virtues. The

---

[48] R. d. V., p. 447.

highest religious virtue is that of inner peace, which is the perfect harmonization of man's ethical habits. At that stage, no hate is possible and contentment reigns supreme, as man learns to rejoice in the happiness of others. Having overcome both hate and fear which are grounded in ignorance, the man of peace lives unperturbed in eternity.

From the above outline of "the religion of reason," we note how the concept of correlation enabled Cohen to loosen the tongue of religion, so to speak, to express in sacred phraseology and ritual the truths of his philosophy of life. We have now to determine whether Cohen's religion is anything more than a rephrasing of philosophy from the viewpoint of the individual seeking a reconciliation with the God of ethics. Surely if religion does not bring to the aid of ethics the force of another human impulse, its value to the latter science is indeed very questionable. It will be remembered that religion arises, according to our author, in the attempt of the remorseful individual to reinstate himself as an ethical person by achieving a reconciliation with the ethical ideal. If this attempt is impelled by the ethical motive alone, religion is well-nigh superfluous, since when it appears upon the scene of consciousness, there is no longer any need for it. The whole scheme of religious terminology would, on this supposition, appear to be a psychological adaptation of the proverbial attempt to lift oneself by one's bootstraps. Clearly if religion is to be of any significance, its roots must be shown to extend beyond the field of ethics.

In the last essays of Cohen, we do indeed meet with an assertion, which was disavowed in his earlier writings, to the effect that religion derives its effectiveness from esthetics as well as ethics. There is a natural longing for God, a pure lyrical yearning for the "nearness to God." This longing constitutes the emotional driving force of religion being the real source of the high exaltation of the psalmist, prophet and martyr. We seek the "nearness of God," not only because as ethical persons we feel the rightness of doing so, but because we are drawn by the attraction of the beauty of holiness. The three directions of spirit, which aim at attaining their respective goals in the True, the Good and the Beautiful, are uniquely joined together in religion to produce the feeling of trust in God. (Vertrauen) This trust in God, as the basic feeling of religion, is at the same time the parent of all the virtues, generating emotional energy which causes the acceleration of the process of development in all pursuits of the spirit. Historically, this phase of religion is illustrated in the fact that nearly all the arts and sciences were born and cultivated under the aegis of religion. Thus religion is constituted by a fusion of ethical and esthetic motives. The psychic power of the correlation is trust in God (Gottvertrauen).[49]

In the final analysis then, religion is rooted in feeling. There is an irrational residuum in religion which no analysis can ever dissolve and which must be assumed as a fact of human experience. The "religion of reason" is despite its jealous "purity" and complex dialectics, religion as well as reason. "Der Monotheismus ist ein psychologisches Mysterium. Wer das nicht anerkennt, der versteht ihn nicht in seiner Tiefe." [50] (Monotheism is a psychological mystery. Whoever does not recognize this, does not understand it in all its depth.) Again he writes, "wie das Wesen Gottes ein Geheimnis ist, so nicht minder auch das Wesen des Menschen

---

[49] That the driving force of religion is basically emotional is emphasized by Cohen particularly in his "Jüdische Shriften." See especially, the following citations "Es muss eine asthetische Grundform sein, der diese schöpferische Kraft beiwohnt. Wir erkennen sie in der Grundkraft der Lyric: das ist die Sehnsucht." Also, "diese Zartheit, Innighkeit, schmerzliche wie freudige Intimitet vermittelt das Vertrauen des Individuums aut Gott." See Jud. Schriften, p. 241. Jud. Schriften, p. 240. See also p. 253—"Die Sehnsucht bildet die Vermittlung von der Gotteserkenntnis zum Gottvertrauen, und ohne dieses kann die Erkenntnis nicht Liebe werden."

[50] Jüd. Schriften, p. 239.

in seinem Verhältnis zu Gott." [51]   ("Just as the essence of
God is a mystery, so too is the essence of man in his attitude
to God.")

The longing which is thus seen to be the source of the effectiveness of religion is not to be identified with esthetic
longing as such. Though this identification is made in the
essays from which the above quotations are taken, the earlier
writings of Cohen on religion endeavor to draw a distinction
between esthetic longing, which is a product of love, and the
religious forms of the same emotions. Thus, Cohen points
out that esthetic love is directed toward the typical man of
nature, whereas religious love is directed toward the unfortunate. Esthetics knows no pity; it covers pain up with a
haze of glamour and the idea of God with which it operates,
in Cohen's system of esthetics, is not the one of religion. [52]

Accordingly, we have to think of the feeling of trust in God
in religion as being a peculiar blend of the three directions
of spirit. There is no original and irreducible religious mode
of feeling, as Schleiermacher claimed. Thought, will and
feeling are fused together into the mysterious unity of simple piety, the unquestioning trust in God.

It is this phase of Cohen's view of religion which comes
closest to Buber's description of the basic religious attitude.
With both thinkers, religious faith is not alone a logical,
ethical or esthetic process, but a fusion of all three processes.
While both agree that the fusion is psychologically ultimate
—the mystery of monotheism, as Cohen puts it, the "primary
word" as Buber describes it—they differ fundamentally regarding the metaphysical implications of the religious attitude. Moreover, it must be noted that while for both Buber
and Cohen, religious feeling is an act of the total self, the
former thinker means by the phrase, "the total self," the
actual empirical person, whereas the neo-Kantian philosopher

---

[51] J. S., p. 253.
[52] B. d. R., p. 86.

can mean by the same phrase only the three pure directions of the spirit.

This introduction of the element of feeling in religion is certainly a great gain, but it brings up a question of fact. Is it true that Cohen's view of God arouses that feeling in men? To be sure, Cohen adduces the Hebrew psalms as containing perfect expressions of the longing for God, while being at the same time, typical examples of pure lyrical compositions. His argument seems to be that the "pure feeling" which finds expression in the lyrical style of the psalms must have been due to their authors' dim perception of the idea of God, as this idea is grounded and described in his own system. Surely, this is carrying philosophy a bit too far. If we are to use the psalms as data of the psychology of religion, we have to place them in their historical context. The God of the psalmists was a personal God, with all the clearness and ambiguity of that term. Clearly, not all ideas of God excite within us the same emotional response. Hence we conclude that Cohen's claim to have discovered as a fact of psychology, a longing toward God, as he conceives the term, is necessarily without historical confirmation.

We are compelled, therefore to conclude that, the assurance of the experience of a longing to God when God is conceived in the Neo-Kantian manner rests on Cohen's own religious experience. No one can read the writings of Cohen without noting the exalted emotion and noble fervor that his language betrays whenever he deals with the literature and ceremonies of Judaism. The oral testimony of those who have known this philosopher during his lifetime fully confirms this evidence.

Nevertheless, there is reason to doubt whether Cohen's view of God could arouse that mysterious feeling of pious trust, of which he writes in his essay on the "Psalms," and thereby serve as the focus of the religious consciousness. To be sure, there is nothing intrinsically impossible in his con-

ception of religion. As we have outlined Cohen's version of
the progress of religious experience, the reader may have obtained the impression that it was largely sheer verbalism and
artificiality. This impression is very natural for one who is
not acquainted with Cohen's method of thinking. Believing
that the task of philosophy is to replace the jumble of confused data that we receive from the world, by a system of
mutually connected ideas, he sees the goal of reason in the
establishment of just such chains of ideas, characterized by
the quality of lawfulness. Cohen's logic is as "artificial" as
his religion. To appreciate his method, we have to accept
his viewpoint that the basic question of philosophy is, how
does culture-consciousness actually operate? The answer
to this question can only be in the form of a succession of
ideas and states of feeling. Still the indubitable fact remains
that, from a purely psychological standpoint, the structure
of the religion of reason is extremely shaky.

It is based upon an idea of God which, apart from its intellectual difficulties, seems hardly to fit into the pattern of
religious emotion. In one sense, the idea of God is a methodological concept. Hence it can be reached with any degree of clearness only by the method of rigorous, ice-cold,
logical analysis. Such a procedure is not easily compatible
with the attitude of prayer. True, hair splitting arguments
for the existence of God were, in the past, offered and believed in by the most pious persons. The point here is that
as a methodological concept, the idea of God has no meaning
at all apart from the attitude of rational inquiry, an attitude
which is not congenial to the emergence of the religious experience of trust in God.

If we think of God in the second sense as the maintainer
of the physical world for the ethical task and as the avenger
of oppression in world history, the needs of the religious attitude are better satisfied. Yet two major difficulties remain. In the first place, this God of history is indifferent to

the concerns of the individual. Before this God can become the God of religion, He must be set into relation with the individual—a process which introduces ambiguities in both the concepts of God and of the individual. God is taken either as the God of ethics or He is interpreted as if He were the God of the individual. Also the individual is taken in certain contexts as the empirical individual or as the Holy Spirit. When ample allowance is made for these ambiguities, the nature of God remains exactly what it was in the "Ethics" —namely, one who is unconcerned with the problems of the individual.

In the second place, there is the difficulty noted by our author, "How can one love an Idea?" [53] His reply to this query fails to take into account the special nature of the idea of God. Of course, one can love an ideal; Cohen is right in insisting that only an ideal is really loved, but an idea in a rational system is a trifle silly to love, though it is not psychologically impossible to do so. An idea has neither meaning nor effectiveness apart from the other ideas in the system. In a rational system, all ideas are internally related. This observation applies to the idea of God, transcendent though it may be, with equal force. As a matter of fact, in the actual development of his view of religion, God is described as loved as an ideal, rather than as an idea.

It must be noted that Cohen's rigorous exclusion of all "mythological" interests from religion makes it extremely difficult for him to do justice to the spiritual needs of the individual.

In conclusion, the value of the Religion of Reason for Cohen's ethical system should be considered. The "Ethics of Pure Will" requires to borrow from religion not only the concept of God, but also the concept of individuality. In the "Ethics," the ideal of totality was presented as the determining category of ethical values. Man was to act so

---

[53] R. d. V., p. 187.

as to hasten the advent of the time when all humanity will be organized as one large personality. While in individual conduct, acts conceived in this spirit would no doubt be, in the highest sense, good and noble, there remained the danger that the acceptance of such a philosophy by a large number of persons would lead, in the political sphere, to the aggrandizement of the ideal of the totalitarian state. There could be no objection in principle, on the basis of the arguments in the "Ethics," to the claim of the state to become all-powerful and to invade whatever domains of private life it deemed advisable.

The development of the ideal of individuality through the correlation of man and God corrects, in a measure, this defect in Cohen's ethical system. Through this personal relation, man acquires a unique value. He is now significant not alone because he is needed by the whole, but because of his own intrinsic value. True, this ideal of individuality is achieved at moments only and some men never attain it. Still, it remains within the reach of all men, and it counterbalances the attraction of the ideal of totality, which would otherwise have retained unchallenged dominion.

Cohen himself nowhere explicitly recognizes the great political significance of the religious ideal of individuality. He died in 1918, long before the rise of the great totalitarian states. We, today, made wiser and sadder by the events of the last few years, are keenly conscious of the truth that the progress toward totalitarian organization of the state, made inevitable by the complexity of our economic structure, needs to be accompanied by the cultivation of the ideal of individuality, which, in the last analysis, can only be grounded in relation to God. If man's possession of reason is the source of his power, his relation to God, in whatever form this relation is conceived, must remain the source of his ultimate value.

CHAPTER III

FRANZ ROSENZWEIG

CHAPTER III

FRANZ ROSENZWEIG

(a) THE LIFE AND INFLUENCE OF
    FRANZ ROSENZWEIG
(b) PHILOSOPHICAL BACKGROUND OR "THE
    STAR OF REDEMPTION
(c) CONTENTS OF "THE STAR OF
    REDEMPTION"
(d) PHILOSOPHY OF RELIGION
(e) PHILOSOPHY OF JUDAISM

(a) The Life and Influence of Franz Rosenzweig

"Ins leben" are the words with which the main book of Franz Rosenzweig closes. This practical note is heard in all his writings. Philosophy is no idle speculation. Rooted in the deepest experiences of mankind, it ascends into the ethereal heights of abstraction only in order to bring back therefrom a message of cheer and comfort. It is the fear of death which leads men on to philosophize, and it is in the actual stress of day by day life that philosophies acquire their final meaning, are tested and proven true. Rosenzweig's own philosophy came to him as a sudden brilliant revelation, and it brought about an actual conversion in his religious life. Thus, the philosophy of Rosenzweig cannot be studied apart from his life; the two are as inseparable as body and soul. It were unfair and quite unrewarding to study the works of our author as if they were merely the reasoned analysis and systematization of objectively known facts. We should then be viewing the message of this original philosopher from a standpoint which the entire tendency of his thought aims to repudiate. His works are to be read, as the expression of a real religious experience, as the actual records of the progress of a great and pious soul, in the course of its grappling with the ultimate mysteries of the Universe. The story of his life and the chart of his intellectual development are the two complementary expressions of the same series of intuitions.

Franz Rosenzweig was born at Kassel, Germany, in 1886. His parents had already travelled far on the road to assimilation which German Jewry embarked upon in the early decades of the nineteenth century. They were wealthy and highly cultured people, intensely loyal to their German fatherland.

131

Georg Rosenzweig, the father of Franz, was a successful man of affairs, a millionaire, possessing the title Commerzienrat, with an excellent local reputation as a kind and wise philanthropist. His wife, Adela, was a deeply sensitive woman of high culture, who sought anxiously to understand and to follow her son's intellectual Odyssey. Despite their assimilationist background, the Rosenzweigs retained a measure of loyalty to Judaism in the abstract. When a cousin of the family, Hans Ehrenberg, was converted to Christianity, Georg and Adela were deeply grieved, though their own attachment to Judaism was too vague to enable them to formulate a logical objection to this step. Rather pathetically, they suggested that Hans should have visited a Jewish "theologian" at least three times, before deserting his ancient faith.[1] Their attitude was typical of the great number of "liberal" Jews, whose adherence to the "Mosaic persuasion" is verbally correct, but actually very confused, since it derives more from habit and convention than from a sincere, deep conviction.

Early in the life of Franz, it became apparent that he would not rest content with this colorless religion. His deep earnestness, even as a youth, showed that to him, bare religious formulae would not long serve to take the place of a living religion. However, his first interest was art and esthetics. It appears that in his adolescence Rosenzweig was not much interested in religious problems. At the age of nineteen, God was to him no more than a "weathermaker."[2] He was then enrolled in the faculty of medicine at the University of Freiburg. In his letters of this period, we note a sensitive soul, thrilling to the beauty of musical and literary masterpieces. Deeply revealing is his comment on Italian art, with which he became acquainted during a

[1] "Briefe," p. 45.
[2] "Briefe," p. 14.

visit to Venice. "It is absolute music," he writes to his parents, ". . . it is something so incomprehensible that one could found a religion on it."[3] In truth, esthetics was then his sole religion and, later, as his own thought matured, the esthetic motive in it was still strong, though of course it was then overshadowed by other, more compelling considerations.

The young Franz gave up the study of medicine after a while and turned instead to history. For a long time, he wavered between history and philosophy. To wrestle with the ultimate problems of existence was a task which both frightened and fascinated the young Rosenzweig. He was beginning to feel the stirrings of that religious intuition which was later to govern his life. Thus, trying like Jonah "to escape from God," he avoided the study of philosophy. For, to men of his deep honesty, philosophy could only mean the endeavor to render an account of his soul to his God. Significant in this connection is a letter which the twenty-two year old student wrote to his mother, containing this characteristic question, "Hast du mich nicht eigentlich zu lieb fur Philosophie?"[4] Philosophy is the self-revelation of a great soul, not a mere recitation of bare facts and arguments. And Rosenzweig was then not yet ready for the great ordeal.

Years later, when his thought was already fully matured, Franz wrote that he became a philosopher in 1913.[5] It was then, too, that he became a Jew by conviction. Up to that point, he was still wavering between atheism, Christianity and Judaism. When the above mentioned Hans Ehrenberg, who was later to become a Christian theologian of note, accepted Christianity, Franz wrote to his parents that it was at his advice that his cousin and life-long friend took this momentous step. It was only by degrees that his interest in

---

[3] "Briefe," p. 27.
[4] "Briefe," p. 36.
[5] "Briefe," p. 618.

and knowledge of Judaism grew. Caught in the mad whirl of intellectual currents at the opening of the century, Rosenzweig paid little heed to theology.

Before the outbreak of the first World War, materialism had lost its hold over the minds of the young intelligentsia, and in Germany, especially, a widely ramified neo-Romanticism arose, which had not yet run its course. Socialism, which at first was moored solidly to the bandwagon of dialectical materialism, at this time began to acquire a religious foundation, as is illustrated in the philosophies of H. Cohen and M. Buber. Mechanistic materialism was losing ground on the whole front. This tendency derived additional strength in the sphere of speculation from the impulse which Darwin's theory of evolution gave to European thought. As is the case with most scientific theories, this impulse was given in diverse and even opposite directions at once. We are here concerned chiefly with the biological view of the course of human history, which the theory of evolution stressed. Attention was thereby shifted from the battle of ideas on the scene of history to the struggle of races for survival, for power. This emphasis on the stream of life, which underlies and conditions the stream of thought in the course of the evolution of civilized mankind led, on the one hand, to the anti-moralistic outbursts of Wagner, Nietsche and the military exponents of Teutonic world supremacy. On the other hand, the same emphasis led to a renewed interest in religion, as the discipline which teaches man to feel at one with the stream of Life, that current of being, which reaches onward, beneath the dreary veil of the phenomenal world. Euken in Germany and Bergson in France are the best known exponents of this latter trend of thought.

Thus, the young Rosenzweig, who was keenly sensitive to the changes in his spiritual atmosphere was drawn to both nationalism and religion. As a Jew, the tension in his soul was, however, more complex than that which is described by indicating the two pairs of extremes—materialism and religion, nationalism and cosmopolitanism. If nationalism is a right ideal, then with which nationalism ought he to identify himself—the Jewish or the German? Patriotism is not here in question. One may be a Jewish nationalist, as Rosenzweig later became, and yet do one's duty to the German state with complete devotion, out of a sense of moral obligation and gratitude. This was in fact the final attitude of our philosopher. His work in the fields of philosophy and education, he regarded as his "rent-payment" to German culture and all his accomplishments outside the field of Judaism, he came to look upon as "Hand-langerarbeit"—the work of a craftsman, no more. His heart was, by then, devoted jealously and zealously to the Jewish religion only. However, in his twenties, he still hesitated between German and Jewish nationalism, uncertain of which group he belonged with, in his innermost being.

The question of religious allegiance was to Rosenzweig equally difficult to decide. Assuming that religion is true, shall he be a Jew or a Christian? To become a Jew in earnest would involve as much of a change in his life—nay, more than the adoption of Christianity. In the former religion he was born, but his entire spiritual development took place within the Christian intellectual atmosphere. To him, the question of becoming a believing Jew appeared in the following, clearly unfair guise, "is being a Jew justified from the Christian viewpoint?" or more concretely, "is the role of Jews as witnesses of God still required by Christianity?" Strangely enough, he finally answered this question in the affirmative. Judaism and Christianity should not only be tolerant of each other; they should recognize in each other their necessary complements. It follows, that those who are born Jews must deem it their God-given task to maintain the Jewish religion as an active, spiritual force in the world. The full implications of this view will become evident in the later sections. For the present, it need only be noted that Rosenzweig overcame the multiple spiritual crisis sketched herein and obtained a fixed viewpoint at the age of twenty-seven. His life thereafter was dedicated wholly to the deepening and clarification of that viewpoint. On all fronts, the one basic intuition of a living God Who loves men and redeems Himself thru them, compelled one and only one attitude.

In the second section, we shall endeavor to trace the different strands of thought which formed the raw material of Rosenzweig's philosophy. However, it must be understood at the outset that we are not here dealing with a nondescript, feebly eclectical philosopher. Rosenzweig was an intensely earnest thinker, and the ideas of his age were fused together in his mind, as in a furnace, to emerge again radically transformed. Thus, while we may record the circumstances attending Rosenzweig's decision to become a believing Jew, culminated in his letter to Rudolf Ehrenberg of the 31st of October, 1913, the ultimate grounds of that decision must remain a mystery to us.[6]

Once his mind was made up, the young philosopher determined to devote the rest of his life to the service of Judaism. With this end in view, he undertook a journey to Berlin, with the intentions of learning Hebrew more thoroughly and of meeting the two religious thinkers, Hermann Cohen and Martin Buber. The latter two philosophers seemed to Rosenzweig to be emphasizing different aspects of the one whole, which is Judaism. As is well known, Buber and Cohen were opponents in nearly all fields of thought. In philosophy, Cohen represented, or at least thought he represented, the extreme rationalistic position; whereas Buber was an anti-intellectual and a neo-mystic.[7] In the questions

---

[6] "Briefe," p. 71.

[7] It is the contention of the author, in this book, that Cohen's system rests upon an act of faith. Only in this manner, it is claimed, can Cohen's "basic law of truth" be understood.

of present day Judaism, Buber represented the view of Jewish nationalism and Zionism, whereas Cohen viewed Jewry as a religious group and was strenuously opposed to Zionism and to Jewish nationalism generally. Yet, when the gray-haired rationalist asked Rosenzweig how he could see anything of value in the writings of Buber, the young philosopher replied: "You and Herr Buber express together the ancient Jewish credo, 'Here, O Israel, the Lord our God, the Lord is One,' but, whereas you emphasize only the latter part of this sentence, Buber stresses only the first part." [8]

In Berlin, a close friendship developed between Cohen and Rosenzweig. To the eyes of the young philosopher, a thinking Jew at his best was revealed. It was not the ideas of the austere philosopher so much as his striking personality that enthralled the young "baal te'shuva." Here was not only a great mind, but a great heart, and ultimate truth, Rosenzweig felt, can be known only thru the wisdom of the heart. A few years earlier, the young student wrote to his parents,[9] "Truth is a sea in which only he is able to dive whose heart has a heavier specific gravity than it; otherwise, he can only splash impotently." In Cohen, the young Rosenzweig recognized the heart of a truly great philosopher. The admiration between the two men, so different in age, was mutual. Cohen came to Berlin with the avowed purpose of devoting the rest of his life to the task of revealing to Jews the inner brilliance of their faith. And he was sorely disappointed by the icy attitude of Berlin Jewry. In Rosenzweig, the sainted old thinker obtained his one real convert. And both of them knew it. "Mein Seelentrost" was the endearing title which Cohen bestowed upon his beloved disciple.

At the outbreak of the war, Rosenzweig enrolled as a volunteer in the Kaiser's army. A fervent patriotic spirit breathes in Rosenzweig's letters of the war era. Like Cohen,

---

[8] "Einleitung" to Cohen's "Judische Schriften."
[9] "Briefe," p. 154.

he believed in the justice of Germany's cause.[10]   In an essay written at the war front, which he published under a pseudonym, he advocated a revision of the German educational system in the direction of greater unity and centralized control. During his intermittent vacation periods, he completed his work on "Hegel and the State" and his treatise on a fragment of Schelling.   These undertakings did not diminish his interest in religion.   It suffices only to read his letters of this period to notice how strong his consciousness of Judaism had now become.

It was during those frightful years, that Rosenzweig's views on Judaism matured and assumed final shape.   In the exchange of letters with the Christian theologian, Eugen Rosenstock, Rosenzweig appears to us as an amazingly apt interpreter of Jewish signs and symbols.   In the third year of the war, he wrote an essay "Zeit Ist's" in which he advocated the establishment of a Jewish society of scholars. After its publication, he conducted a vast correspondence from the front with a number of important Jews with the purpose of putting his plan into operation.   As a result of his and Cohen's efforts, the "Akademie für die Winenschaft des Judentum" was finally established.

During the war, Rosenzweig pursued his study of Judaism and of Semitic languages with almost desperate energy. Often his comrades were awed by the sight of this curious officer studying an Aramaic grammar in the muddy trenches, while overhead the ominous sound of bursting shells threatened imminent death.   It was in the trenches, too, that the first part of his great self-revealing work, "Der Stern der Erlösung," was written.   Knowing that he had a new message to tell the world and fearing that he might be killed before he succeeded in expressing it on paper, Rosenzweig wrote the "Stern" on regulation army postcards which he

---

[10] In the "Einleiting," Rosenzweig quotes Cohen as saying of the German war motives, "unser Sache, ist rein engelrein."

then mailed to his mother. "What a correspondence this Rosenzweig has!" his comrades jeered. So intense was the author's concentration in writing the "Star" that, years later, when he had ample time, he refused to add or to change a word in his book. Everything that need be said in writing, he felt, he had put down in the "Star of Redemption." [11] It was with great reluctance that he later wrote the essay, "Das Neue Denken," and only after the difficulty of understanding his main work was brought home to him. Once the "Star of Redemption" was completed, Rosenzweig believed that his intellectual balance sheet was drawn up with complete finality and that his task thenceforth lay in the field of practical Jewish leadership.

Coming to Frankfurt after the war, Rosenzweig met the sainted Rabbi of that city, Dr. A. N. Nobel. On the first day of Passover, Rosenzweig listened to the rabbi's sermon and declared himself to be the captive of Nobel for all time.[12] Here, too, as in the case of Cohen, it was not the ideas of Nobel which so impressed Rosenzweig, as the deep earnestness, modernity and piety of the man. Nobel, it seemed to

---

[11] The following excerpt from a letter to Buber shows what this book meant to its author: "For I will never again write something of this sort (i.e. the "Stern"). ("Briefe," p. 371.) I have the inexpressible feeling that I have here drawn the sum of my spiritual existence and that all that may come later will only be addenda, occasioned by external momentary considerations. That which is most peculiarly myself (mein Eigentlichster) I have given here insofar as that can be conveyed in a book. Only in life, no more in writing, do I see a future for me." ("Briefe," p. 619.) In a letter which he wrote a year before his death, Rosenzweig reveals the full extent of his plan. He wanted to write the "Stern" as a complete commentary on the Torah and the Sabbath readings from the Prophets. Such a project, however, he felt he could not execute before the age of seventy. Therefore, he wrote the "Stern" as a "commentary without the text." ("Briefe," p. 497.) Four years later he wrote to Dr. Breuer that, upon completing the "Stern," he cherished for a time the idea of writing a book on Jewish Law, revealing the inner significance of Jewish practices. Unfortunately, the years of study and reflection which such an undertaking required were not granted to him.

[12] "Der Denker" (see note on next page).

him, was keenly conscious of all the questions which man perennially asks of God and, in the quiet of his study, he could not give the answers, at least not a systematic answer. But, while he stood on the pulpit, his words seemed to well out of a deeper source and to bear the stamp of truth. For three years Nobel and Rosenzweig studied and worked together. This companionship was not based upon a basic community of ideas or upon an exchange of ideas save as Rosenzweig learned Talmud from the rabbi. But, the genuine piety of Nobel served to reinforce Rosenzweig's own religious convictions.[13]

The intimate friendship which developed between the rabbi and the philosopher proved to be of great consequence not only in the life of the two friends, but to the entire community of Frankfurt. As a result of their collaboration, there was established in that ancient and splendid Jewish

---

[13] The influence which Rabbi Nobel exerted upon men like Rosenzweig, Joseph Prager, Ernst Simon and Richard Koch has often been misunderstood. It was thought that Nobel's reputed knowledge of Kabbala or his supposed great philosophical acumen was the cause of his veneration by the said thinkers. As a matter of fact, Rabbi Nobel's influence was due almost entirely to his natural piety and deep earnestness. It was despite his attainments in modern culture, not because of them, that Nobel appealed to the young intellectuals of his day. The letter of Rozenzweig to J. Prager, written in the year of Nobel's death, is most important in this connection. ("Briefe," p. 420.) He writes there in part, "I have respected only the Talmud Jew, not the humanist; only the poet, not the scientist; only the prophet, not the philosopher. The rejected qualities I have rejected because they were in his case deeply un-Jewish. At least, I have always found them so. . . . I have always endeavored to lure people away from his mostly shocking lectures to his sermons, where, in the decisive moments, the Jew in him broke thru. . . . Had I come to know him earlier, say about 10 years ago, he would possibly have driven me out of Judaism; in all probability, he would have spoiled me. . . . I was three years ago more orthodox, more anti-Christian, more anti-heretic than I am now. I have learned from Nobel that in the soul of a great Jew there is place for many things. False doctrines are dangerous only for the little ones. I could have learned that already from Hermann Cohen . . ." Still Rosenzweig revered Nobel as his teacher, and upon the latter's death he named his young son, Nehemiah, in honor of the deceased rabbi of Frankfurt.

community an extraordinary institution, perhaps the only one of its kind in the long and colorful array of Jewish houses of learning. "Der Freie Jüdishe Lehrhaus," established at Frankfurt in the summer of 1920 was by design a college for the instruction of those, who had become estranged from Judaism and who were groping for the way back to their spiritual home.

The "Lehrhaus" did not offer a complete description of this "way." Its program was built on the faith that honest soul-searching will lead every Jew back to the religion of his fathers. The high estimate of learning as a sacrament, which Judaism had long staunchly maintained was taken over by Rosenzweig and expanded by him to include not only the Torah, but all the manifold insights into the workings of nature which the modern world has acquired. Our time, Rosenzweig argued, calls for a "new Learning," just as central for the life of our people as the old learning, but oriented in the opposite direction—a learning which is no longer directed from the Torah outward into the wide ramifications of life, but which begins from the periphery of life, the life of the secular world, knowing nothing of the Law, and moves toward the center, toward Judaism. This learning is not to consist in apologetics, in uncovering "relations" between Judaism and some modern ideals, or in showing the "contributions" of Judaism to this or that present day institution. It is "to find the means of entering the heart of our life. And to have the faith that this heart is a Jewish heart. For we are Jews." [14] This new learning cannot of course be dogmatic or even capable of systematic expression. For the way to the center must be different to those who start out from the different points of the peripheral life. Yet, there is a center, where the light of Judaism glows eternally and there is a way to that center, open to all who seek it. "We must seek the

---

[14] "Neues Lernen," p. 97.

unity (of the ways to the center) and we must trust to find
it." Such was the ambitious program of the "Lehrhaus."

If ever an institution was the shadow of a man, the
Lehrhaus was indeed that of Rosenzweig. In his letter to
Rudolf Hallo, Rosenzweig gives a complete history of the
institution.[15] With his customary modesty, he credits other
men with taking the initiative to found the "Lehrhaus."
Nevertheless, there can be no doubt that it was his spirit,
which became flesh in that extraordinary "Beth-Midrash."
The student body was drawn from all walks of life, as was
noted above. But, what is far more remarkable, the teaching staff was also selected out of those who were not authorities in Jewish knowledge. The lecturers and discussion
leaders in the "Lehrhaus" were men whose greatness lay in
other fields of endeavor and who brought to the students not
a coldly catalogued knowledge of things Jewish, but a feeling for religion and the will to be a Jew. Thus, he writes in
the above-mentioned letter: "In every program there must
be at least one perfect Am Haaretz and, if at all possible,
every time a different one. Naturally being an Am Haaretz
cannot in itself be regarded as qualifying the man for the
position; he must possess renown in some other field; out of
this renown and the so called "Will to Judaism," it is possible
to create a "Lehrhaus" instructor, provided he be brought to
lecture as little as possible about Judaism and to speak
mostly about himself." [16]

With this unorthodox policy, which illustrates once again
Rosenzweig's basic conviction that it is the man, not his
philosophy, that truly matters and that religion is more a
matter of experience than of dogma, the director of the
Lehrhaus undertook to perform the gigantic task of awakening and directing an interest in religion and in Judaism
among his contemporary Jewish intellectuals. And he was

---

[15] "Briefe," p. 448.
[16] "Briefe," p. 458.

successful to an amazing extent. About him, there was gathered a group of highly educated men, who were determined to live as Jews and to reestablish their ties with their ancient faith. The extent of Jewish law, that they adopted varied; Rosenzweig himself was uncertain about this point. He married an Orthodox girl, and in his home the dietary laws were observed. But, he did not scruple to eat "trefah" when he visited a non-orthodox Jew or a Christian.[17] In a similar manner, he for some time maintained a distinction, which he later gave up regretfully, between writing business and personal letters on the Sabbath.

We cannot here give an account of those thinkers who looked up to Rosenzweig as their guide and mentor, though he, in his modesty, rarely conceived of the relation as being that of master and disciple. Suffice it to illustrate the methods and influence of this Jewish theologian, by the choice that he has made of his successor to the post of director of the Lehrhaus. Rudolf Hallo, whom he had recommended, and who indeed succeeded him as director, was converted to Christianity at the age of nineteen. Later, he met Rosenzweig and corresponded with him. The latter, with infinite patience, wrote long letters to his friend on the nature of Judaism, in particular on Jewish law, finally imbuing him with sufficient enthusiasm for the Jewish religion to be eager to take up the work of directing the Lehrhaus at the point where its founder was compelled to leave it.

Had Rosenzweig been able to maintain his leadership of the Lehrhaus, it is possible that a lasting school of Jewish theology would have developed in Frankfurt. The boon to Judaism of such a school would indeed have been vast. For, while we have scholars aplenty in every field of Judaism, we

---

[17] I say this on the strength of a letter Rosenzweig had written to his future wife, a short time before he was married. It appears, however, that he later became completely Orthodox in practice. In a letter to his cousin, he warns him not to phone on the Sabbath. This, too, is the testimony of some friends of his that I have met.

do not have modern Jewish theologians capable of pointing the way back to Judaism from the vantage point of the present intellectual scene. But God had willed it otherwise. Only a year and a half after the founding of the Lehrhaus, Rosenzweig was stricken with the terrible disease, amyotrophe lateralsklerose, a slow and creeping paralysis. The disease affected the muscles of the tongue first, rendering him slow of speech. With the progress of the sickness, he was gradually deprived of all power to move any part of his body. From the middle of 1922 to his death in 1929, he lay helpless like a stone on his bed. At first, he still retained the ability to write, then his muscles weakened to the extent of his being able to turn the pages of the book he was reading only with the greatest difficulty. By the end of May 1923, the spread of the paralysis deprived him virtually of all power of speech. By means of the grunts which he still could emit and thru a machine of his own invention, this persevering genius managed to keep in touch with the outside world in this tortuous fashion, aided only by the loving and uncanny understanding of his wife. Providence had willed it that the latter years of Rosenzweig should provide a concrete illustration of the deepest meaning of his philosophy—the stillness of death being overcome by the power of love. For it was only Mrs. Rosenzweig's intuition, born of love, that rescued the living thoughts of this brilliant thinker from total oblivion. In their relationship, the Biblical ideal of marriage "and they shall be one flesh" was realized.

With amazing tenacity the stricken philosopher clung to his task. Despite overwhelming odds, he even undertook a new type of work. At the end of the first year of his illness, he began to translate the poems of Jehuda Halevi. This work is more than just a translation. The poems and especially the comments which follow each poem were meant to be practical illustrations of the central thesis of the "Star of Redemption," the reality of the love of God and its expression in language.

Two and a half years later, he began to collaborate with Martin Buber in making a new German translation of the Bible. The principles governing the translation were explained by Rosenzweig in two lengthy essays. The translators aimed to translate the entire Bible, the narrative as well as the exhortative passages, in language which would convey the impression of the direct speaking of God. The Bible is the word of God to man. But, God addresses man directly as "Thou," not in the third person. It is the feeling of being in a dialogue with the Deity, of being face to face with the living voice of God that Rosenzweig and Buber aimed to express in their translation.

As an illustration of their method, we may take their rendering of the Name of God. Believing that it is not the abstract recognition of the existence of only one God, but the perceiving of this One God in our immediate consciousness, that constitutes true monotheism, Rosenzweig argued that the Name of God should be rendered as a pronoun, "I"—"He," or "Thou." Thus he wrote, "He who is immediate for that person existing for him, thus: He; He, who is immediate to an I, existing for me, thus—Thou. He, who is immediate to a Thou, existing for Thee, thus—I." [18]

---

[18] As another illustration of the method of Buber and Rosenzweig, we may take their translation of the sacrifice terminology. The word "Korban" they rendered—Darnahung, a coming near to God, since the root "Karov" means to approach. The words mincha and olah they translated as "Hinleiteopfer" and "Emporopfer" respectively. Thus, the religious significance of the sacrificial customs was made clear. In the process of translation, Buber and Rosenzweig "Hebraized" the German language, inventing new words and expressions. The reader of the translation finds himself compelled to rethink and relive the words of the Bible. In a very real sense, the authors succeeded in presenting the Bible, to which so many of our generation have become used and immune, in a new light, revealing it as indeed the Word of God.

The translation of Buber and Rosenzweig resembles the one made by

While engaged in this task of translating the Bible, Rosenzweig wrote small and brilliant essays on various Jewish subjects. He also kept up an active correspondence, writing long letters, which are really marvelously condensed treatises. Neither did he entirely cut off his relations with the community of Frankfurt. A religious service took place in his home on every Sabbath morning. And, often discussions among the prominent Jewish leaders in the community were held at his bedside—discussions to which this genius, entombed in a mummified body, could only react by a letter written after the guests were gone. In the last two years of his life, his efforts were exerted toward bringing about a working agreement between the Zionists and the non-Zionists. His own opposition to Zionism was motivated entirely by theoretical considerations, believing as he did that the Zionist program for the Diaspora was total secularization and eventual assimilation. Thus, he was ready to give unqualified support to the religious Jewish colonies in Palestine.[19] But Rosenzweig, even on his death-bed, was not one to be misled by abstractions. The actual effect of Zionism as a movement, he recognized, was to produce good Jews. And that is, after all, the final test. "Among the Zionists I find, whatever the theory may be, better Jews than among us," he wrote to a Reform rabbi.[20]

Down to the last day of his life, Rosenzweig continued to work in this fashion. Gradually, the halo of saintliness began to gather about him. The spectacle of a spirit, so bright and generous, triumphing over the tightening tentacles of

---

Samson Raphael Hirsh, more closely than it does any other translation. This fact is due, in the first place, to the reverence for tradition of all the three authors. In the second place, it may be noted that both Rosenzweig and Buber saw in the Hebrew language a key to the understanding of the Jewish religious genius. Hirsh's views are expressed in an essay entitled "Jüdische Welt und Lebensanschaungen" (Gesammelte Schriften, *V* volume).

[19] "Briefe," p. 572.
[20] "Briefe," p. 591.

death was indeed impressive. Rosenzweig himself endeavored to dispel the mist of holiness in which he was being enveloped. Grateful to God for having allowed him to write his great work, the "Star of Redemption," he felt that his life thenceforth was an undeserved gift. The steady approach of death held no terrors for him who had declared in his book that love was mightier than death. Perhaps he recalled, in his last hour, the lines he wrote years before in commenting on his monumental work, "but now, it is simply true, true for me: To die is even more beautiful than to live."

(b) The Philosophical Background of the "Star of Redemption"

The "star of redemption" comprises a complete system of thought, ranging from a theory of knowledge to a commentary on the Bible. In condensed sentences, at times passionate and poetical, Rosenzweig deals in his book with all branches of philosophy—ethics, esthetics, metaphysics, the history of culture and religion. In the arrangement of its chapters, as well as in their contents, the "Star of Redemption" is a most unconventional philosophical book—so much so that even professional philosophers must find it difficult to get at the basic ideas of Rosenzweig.

We shall do well to become acquainted at the outset with two doctrines, which are more implied than actually stated in the "Star." The first doctrine is a critique of absolute idealism and the second is a theory of knowledge.

The theory of absolute idealism as propounded by Hegel and Schelling, in his early period, held sway over German thought almost continuously down to the present day. In England and America, too, idealism was firmly entrenched in all the universities and regarded as the only respectable philosophy down to the rise of pragmatism in the first decade of the twentieth century. Rosenzweig regards absolute idealism as the logical culmination of the entire course of philosophic thought. Hegel was the last of the philosophers, he asserts, since in the Hegelian system the final anwser to the central question of philosophy is given—the only answer which philosophers, with their basic assumptions and their dialectical methods, are able to give.[1]

The one question which stands at the center of all philosophic thought, which, in fact, made a philosopher of the first man who asked it, is "What is Being?" or, alternatively phrased, "What is the essence of all things?" This question arises, whenever we contemplate the manifold changes which are constantly taking place in the world about us. Our immediate physical environment, the expanding universe of stars and galaxies, the thoughts racing within our minds—everything is constantly in flux. Nothing ever stands still. This fact we regard as perfectly proper, until someone inquires "What does it mean to change?" Obviously, it can only mean that thing "A" or quality "A" has disappeared into nothingness and thing "B" or quality "B" has come from nothingness in its place. But the imagination of man cannot conceive how that which exists could turn into absolute naught, and the reason of man cannot allow the validity of the proposition that a thing "B," which at one moment was nothing, could in the next moment have become a reality. Before it existed "B" quite obviously could not bring itself into existence. But, at the next moment "B" was already existent. How then can the fact of change be understood? [2]

The obvious answer is to say that change is only apparent. Basically, there is only a rearrangement of particles. When the flower, that once was blooming, lies wilted and dirty in the mud before us, we say that no particles of matter were

---

[1] "Briefe," pp. 81, 645.

[2] This paradoxical nature of change was recognized by the first Greek philosophers. It was left for Parmenides, however, to state the case for the perplexed logician in the classic words, "Being is and non-Being is not."

really lost. It was only that the molecules in the petals of the flower entered into a new combination with some molecules from the air. When the carpenter changes a table into a chair, we do not say that the table disappeared into nothingness and that the chair came from nothing at all. The material common to both of them, wood, merely assumed a different shape. This, in fact, is in effect the answer of the first philosophers, and it is obviously the most convenient, even if not the most profound, solution. All things have one underlying substance in common, which does not change in itself, and which is the substratum of all change.

It is at this point that the central question of metaphysics comes in. This substance, this *real* essence, behind the phenomena of nature, what is it? How or by what analogy can we envisage it? In accordance with their answers to this question, philosophers are divided into the time-honored classifications—materialists, idealists, spiritualists, pantheists, etc. Materialists say this final substance is physical matter, or force or energy. Idealists, on the other hand, point to the fact that all we know of the world are the contents of our mind.[3] Therefore, they insist, the substance of the world is the stuff of which our thoughts are made, is, in fact, Mind or Will, or Thought or Self or Reason.

The idealists have no difficulty in explaining the presence of spiritual elements in the universe, but they are faced with the problem of accounting for the obduracy and stubbornness of physical facts. How is it that we cannot sit down in our study and figure out in advance the entire course of world history? If the world is, in appearance only, composed of shapes and pressures, colors and sounds, and is in reality of the same nature as our own reason, why are we unable to

---

[3] The argument to which reference is here made is, of course, that of Berkeley, in his "Principles of Human Knowledge." The same line of reasoning is also found in Fichte's "The Vocation of Man," and it is mostly assumed by modern idealistic philosophers.

reason things out? To this question, the idealists reply that
the world is in essence an Infinite Intelligence or an Infinite
Self, whereas our own minds and wills are distinctly finite.
Thus, our own reason or own self is an integral part of world-
Reason or World-Self, but only a part. If we could but know
our own mind completely we should know, too, both God and
the world. For all things are one in essence. The absolute
or the All is at once myself, God and the world.

Rosenzweig, accepted wholeheartedly the idealistic criticism of the materialistic position, claiming that modern
philosophy contained a clear refutation of the materialistic
hypotheses. Nevertheless, he began his system with an attack on the idealistic theory of the One all-embracing Absolute. If absolute idealism were right, he argued, then men,
or rather philosophers, should have been free from the fear
of death. If our self is indeed in reality the World-Self, why
fear the approach of death? We should in death be exactly
what we are now, parts of the Infinite Intelligence, which
encompasses all things and which never dies. Yet, the
human soul is not calmed by the considerations of philosophy, and it longs to retain its earthly existence. Is this not
proof that the human individuality is different in essence
from the Absolute?

To refuse to recognize the fact of human individuality is
to deny the fact of life, Rosenzweig asserts. Philosophy
should have "the courage to hear that cry and not to close its
eyes to the terrible actuality." For it is with this cry, with
the fear of death, that all knowledge of the Absolute begins.[4] We learn from this fear that our own soul is not
simply a part of the phenomenal world, or of the underlying
Substance. We are justified, in fact, our author maintains,
in drawing the conclusion which breaks the entire tradition
of idealistic philosophy—to wit, that there is not one Absolute or Substance, but three different essences. Man and the

---

[4] Vol. I, p. 7.

world and God are not essentially one, but just as different in essence as in appearance.

This argument from the fear of death appears on the surface to be a mere argumentation ad hominem. It is as if Rosenzweig were taunting the philosophers with the charge of insincerity. As a matter of fact, Rosenzweig conceives the philosophers' solution to be the only "natural" one—natural, that is, in the sense that all men, who operate only with the resources of reason, turn perforce to that solution, whenever they are confronted with the fact of ceaseless change. The disillusionment of the "natural" man and his ever-present fear of death are therefore proof that the idealistic solution is only a mental contrivance, satisfying indeed to surface logic, but incompatible with the deeper realities of the human soul. Rosenzweig's argument is hence wholly empirical. "We do not feel at one with the world or with God, and we feel our individuality most when we should feel it least," he asserts, in effect, "ergo, we are not really, essentially, part of either God or the world."

Thus, from the ineradicable fear of death, we have learned that man and the world are two different substances. In a somewhat similar manner, Rosenzweig proceeds to prove that God and the world must not be identified. This argument, he bases upon the persistent conflict between religion and philosophy, the studies, respectively, of God and nature, a conflict which absolute idealism was never able to overcome.

Modern philosophers did not succeed in finding a place for religion in their systems, though they tried valiantly to do so. Here, too, Hegel's solution is the most rational one. Hegel, it will be recalled, conceived of philosophy as gradually discovering that which religion knew already. But, this solution, too, proved inadequate, for, as a result, the boundary lines between religion and philosophy were demolished and a struggle for the control of the human mind between the two attitudes was begun. The numerous and desperate

methods by which different thinkers have sought to demar-
cate the boundary lines between philosophy and religion in
the course of the nineteenth century, testify to the confusion
which the idealistic dogma of the one Absolute—at once God,
the world and Self—had introduced into the thought of the
Western World.

Yet, it was inevitable that philosophy should insist on the
concept of the one Absolute. Hegel was right in his claim
that the Absolute need not be proved, since it is the necessary assumption of all thought. Rosenzweig agrees with
Hegel in this assertion, maintaining that, if thought is to be
considered the sole measure of truth, the only answer to the
question, "What is Being?" is the necessarily time-honored
teaching of idealism, "Being is the Absolute." This answer
is already implicit in the question which brings together all
events and things in the one word "Being." But, this all-
inclusive "Being" is a false concept, hiding beneath its man-
tle of obscurity three distinct essences. Thus, taking into
consideration, man's feeling of his own individuality, his
fear of death, and the failure of philosophy to understand
religion, Rosenzweig breaks up the central question of metaphysics into its three components—what is the essence of
man? what is the essence of the world? what is the essence
of God? In other words, he sets himself the task of discovering separately what man means when he says "I," what
the ever-changing phenomenal world is at bottom, and, finally, he endeavors to get a glimpse of that sea of Being which
underlies all phenomena, the eternal God of truth.

It goes without saying that, were Rosenzweig to employ
the same method of reasoning as do the idealistic philosophers, he would have arrived at the same conclusions, even
though his starting point is so vastly different. Many of the
post-Kantian idealists have, in fact, started from the same
premise as Rosenzweig. Before proceeding to view Rosenzweig's picture of the Universe, it is, therefore, necessary

that we become acquainted with his theory of truth and with the nature of his method.

The term, "theory of truth," will no doubt strike the layman in philosophy as a strange aberration of unworldly dreamers. "Truth is truth, and that is all there is to it," he is likely to insist. No doubt, such an attitude is entirely justified so long as we deal with concrete objects, with things that we can feel and see. When we deal with the invisible and the intangible, however, we are forced to rely for our deductions on certain principles, in the validity of which we have implicit faith. Thus, we rely on the formulae of mathematics in undertakings where simple counting is impossible or too burdensome. The formulae and concepts of calculus, it will be remembered, defy the power of visualization. Yet, we regard the propositions of higher mathematics as true, beyond question. In fact, the simplest maxim of mathematics, "twice two equals four," has been taken to be the typical example of all truth. Only that is true, it has been asserted, which can be formulated in a series of propositions of this type. This minimal definition of truth, Rosenzweig rejects with passionate vigor, "From those unimportant truths of the type, 'twice two equals four' in which men lightly agree, without any other expenditure than a trifle brain-fat, a little less with the ordinary multiplication table, a little more with the theory of relativity—the road leads through the truths, for which a man is willing to pay something, on to those which he cannot prove true (bewahren) except with the sacrifice of his life, and finally to those (principles), the truth of which can be proved only by the staking of the lives of all the generations." [5]

Basically, Rosenzweig argues, truth is a matter *between* man and something else. The degree of truth is the measure of the strength of the bond, which, we feel, exists between us and that other thing. Instead of taking the mathematical

[5] "Das Neue Denken," K. S., p. 396.

proposition as the typical expression of truth, this daring thinker takes man's belief in and attachment to ideals as the proper form of truth.

Mathematical propositions are true, of course; but, despite their universal acceptance, they rank among the lowest in the hierarchy of truths. For it is the degree of earnestness and sincerity with which a belief is avowed that constitutes its ultimate value. Ultimately, all truth is based on the feeling of trust. Most thinkers define truth as "that which cannot be doubted." Rosenzweig argues that this view of truth is based on a supposed fact, the fact "that it cannot be doubted." But, if we are going to believe simply because of the fact that we do believe, how shall we discriminate between truth and error? For there are false beliefs we must agree, which hold the minds of multitudes captive. It is impossible, then, to eliminate the element of trust from truth. "The self-trust of reason which the masters of the school cultivate is entirely justified. But, it is only justified because it rests on a trust of the whole man, of whom reason is only a part; and this trust is not self-trust." [6] In all truth, there is an element of trust concerning that which is beyond the judgment itself. And in judgments concerning ultimate being, truth can only take the form of trust in the Eternal Being, in the God of truth.

Thus Rosenzweig maintains that all truth is from God, "Whatever shines brightly is true, receives its brilliance and illumination from Him." [7] All truth is such only because it comes from God, for the "Seal of God is truth," "*chosamo shel hakodosh boruch hu emeth.*" If truth be compared to light, then is God the source of that light.

The statements concerning God and truth are necessarily obscure at this point of our exposition. In the course of the discussion in the subsequent sections, this phase of Rosen-

---

[6] "S. d. E.," III Vol., p. 165.

[7] Ibid., p. 165.

zweig's thought will be further clarified. Here, we need only remember that knowledge concerning the final meaning of existence can, according to Rosenzweig, be obtained only when we assume a certain attitude toward the universe, an attitude in which it really matters to us whether things exist or not, an attitude, then, of love. Truth is closed to us so long as we seek to find it by the indifferent manipulations of formulae. The first insight upon which all deduction is based, is extra-logical, is discovered only through faith.

We know truth, to the extent that we may know it, only when in deepest earnestness we feel the power of trust welling up in us. All knowledge is based upon belief. In this position, Rosenzweig is not alone. After Kant, many thinkers have come to realize that discursive logic, unaided by other sources of truth, is incapable of comprehending the world. Logic teaches us how to deduce inferences when certain premises are given. But the first major premise, the premise upon which all our subsequent reasoning in the field of metaphysics is based—how shall it be obtained?

The only possible manner in which the first insight into the meaning of life may be gained is by direct intuition, by an act of faith. Even the propositions, "the real is the rational" or "thought and being are one" which the philosophic tradition culminating in Hegel had regarded as axiomatic, are, after all, no more than assumptions. It was on the basis of reasoning similar to that of Rosenzweig, that Fichte, Schopenhauer, Nietsche and Bergson had argued that philosophy must begin with a central truth, which is subjectively felt to be of supreme ontological value. These exponents of "Standpunkt Philosophie" all realize that, in strict logic, complete skepticism is possible and that the beginning of all wisdom is an act of faith.[8]

In the field of religious thought, it was the Danish philoso-

---

[8] G. Santyanna in his "Skepticism and Animal Faith" presents a completely up-to-date and lucid version of this line of reasoning.

pher, Kierkegaard, who had first pointed out that while reason could only deal with general terms, it was with man as an individual, in his most individual mood, that religion was born. Revelation of the nature of reality can come to man only, when, excluding all else from his mind, he is concerned solely with his relation to God. In present day German thought, this doctrine, which describes reality as communicable only to those who place themselves in a certain receptive mood, has come to be known as "existential" thinking. Heidegger, Heim, Buber, Rand and Berdyaev may roughly be characterized as belonging to this school.

To complete our picture of the background of Rosenzweig's thought, it is necessary to keep clearly in mind the general philosophical tradition upon which his view of the world was based. Philosophers think and write of the world in general, but what they mean by the term "world" is often difficult to tell. Since their knowledge of the world is derived more from books than from the incoherent bustle and the meaningless jumble of events which constitutes actual life, they tend to overemphasize certain aspects of existence. The data of experience are likely to be viewed by them as organized in certain patterns—the patterns, that is, which they find ready-made in certain books. A knowledge of these patterns is essential to the understanding of the thought of any philosopher.

This observation is particularly true in the case of our thinker, and it accounts in large measure for the difficulty of understanding his main work. Fortunately, he informs us in several places that his terminology is based upon the worldview which Schelling, in his later years, began to sketch.[9] Thus, a thorough presentation of Rosenzweig's thought would require a complete exposition of the late-Schellingian hypotheses. For our purpose here, a brief outline of the Natur-

---

[9] Letter to Hans Ehrenberg—"Briefe," p. 399.

philosophie found in Schelling's "Darstellung des Philoso-
phischen Empirismus" will suffice.

Schelling sees all of existence, the thoughts and ideals of
man as well as the course of physical events, as being a current which proceeds steadily onward from the objective to
the subjective pole of existence. The term subjective includes all the principles of logic, mathematics and ethics,
which man, on reflection, regards as being part of his own
reason. The term "objective" denotes all the physical phenomena, which transpire outside our own self. The gradual
conquest of the "objective" by the "subjective" can, therefore, be more simply expressed as the progressive extension
of the sphere of mind over that of physical nature. God is
at once this process of the world and the power outside it,
Who as a free being, creates the particular events of nature,
and determines their course. There are then, on this view,
three basic principles of existence—the world, or the mass
of physical events; man, or the reason of man; and God,
who, standing outside both man and the world, determines
the relation between them. Rosenzweig accepts this teaching
concerning the three elements of existence, though the manner in which he relates them differs, in some respects radically, from that of Schelling.

In the development of his method, Rosenzweig was greatly
influenced by Cohen's "Logic der Reinen Vernunft" especially by the latter's "Category of Source." [10]   Both maintain
that reality is at bottom a group of continuous processes,
which begin with an original affirmation, regarding elements
that appear to be sheer nothingness.[11]

(c) The Star of Redemption

THE CENTRAL FACT AROUND WHICH THE CURRENT OF ROSEN-
zweig's thought winds in ever-widening circles, is the one of

---

[10] See "Stern," p. 30.

[11] See sup. note 3 to section (c).

Divine revelation. That God speaks to man, on occasion,
he asserts, is a fact, which cannot be evaded or explained
away. Here then we have a modern thinker who instead
of elaborating on the possibility of prophecy, actually begins
with the experienced fact of revelation. Since revelation is
at best a rare phenomenon, we may presume that anyone
desiring to base his system of thought on revelation as a real
experience would begin by a description of that extraordinary event. Yet it is true that Rosenzweig never gives a
detailed account of the experience of revelation, as he had
known it.[1] In vain do we look for a description of the progress of feeling toward that state of mystical ecstasy when
the Divine Word is heard, or the assurance of His command
is felt. Mystics of all ages and faiths, as is well known,
never wearied of relating in fullest detail the various crises
through which they passed, before they attained the "State
of Illumination" or the final stage of ecstasy.

In contrast to the exponents of "grand mysticism," Rosenzweig asserts that the experience of the Divine is always of
an imperative command; "the indicative (experiences) of
mysticism and philosophy are indeed very problematical.[2]
This command is always in reference to a particular situation that is close at hand."

We are all familiar with the type of experience that goes
by the name of the "voice of conscience." What Rosenzweig
calls "the experience of revelation" may be classified as belonging under this general heading, since it is ethical in nature
and it is not a general principle, like the Categorical Imperative of Kant. However, it must not be simply identified with
the common phrase "the voice of conscience" for, in addition
to the ethical demand, it contains the following "moments"

---

[1] The single exception to this statement, is a single sentence in a letter
written to Edith Hahn, his future wife: "Ich habe Gottes ruttenstreiche
und seine sanften Hände unmittelbar auf meinem Leibe verspürt." "Briefe,"
p. 386.

[2] "Briefe," p. 611.

—the impression of truth, the sense of the presence of a personal Being, the feeling of being loved by that Being and the consciousness of responding in love to Him. Not all of these elements are clearly perceived in the glow of revelation, for it is the characteristic trait of this experience that it is not wholly expressible in clear language. The Divine is a unique quality, sui generis, which men may recognize and talk about, but which they cannot adequately describe in terms of other qualities. Being a most intimately personal experience, it is not wholly communicable to the objective observer.

"Just So," he writes in a letter, "is that which man experiences of God, indeed simply immediate, and whoever tells of it makes himself ridiculous; shame should envelope this two-loneliness, too; and yet everyone knows that this inexpressibility is not self-deceit . . ." Thus revelation is an objective fact, though once it is so stated, the psychologist is entitled to "analyze" it to the best of his ability.[3]

What is the content of this revelation? It is the assurance of God's love, Rosenzweig asserts, and the resolve "to love thy neighbor as thyself." None of the heart rending problems with which man, in moments of earnest reflection, confronts God is resolved by revelation. "The problem is for the seer of the Face not solved—only, faded away. . . . Out of a problem of thought a power of the heart has become. God has said "Thou" to man,[4] and man can respond only by saying "Thou"—that is, turn in love to another man." [5]

It is thus evident that Rosenzweig addresses himself only to those who had already become troubled at heart by the "voice of God." The average reader will part company with Rosenzweig at this point, concluding that the brilliant phi-

---

[3] "Briefe," p. 519.
[4] "Ereignis und Erlebnis," Jehuda Halevi, p. 174.
[5] See supplementary note 1 at end of book.

losopher had lived in a dream-world of his own making and that his thought is of no relevance to the "normal" mass of mankind. It must be conceded that the authenticity of the mystic's communion with the Deity is of necessity incapable of being proved. Yet, the state of mind to which Rosenzweig refers is not really as rare as it may appear. We have all experienced the feeling associated with the word "holy"— something akin to fear, awe, austerity, beauty, love, loyalty, containing withal an irreducible element of mystery. Now, the experience of revelation, as described by Rosenzweig, refers to a blend of this feeling of the "holy" with the "voice of conscience." Rudolf Otto's famous book "The Idea of the Holy" presents an analysis of the experience of sacredness containing little if any ethical connotations. Rosenzweig's incorporation of the central ethical command within the basic religious experience bears the stamp of traditional Jewish feeling. Revelation, in Rosenzweig's sense, is therefore not far removed from, if it is not actually, the typical religious feeling of the truly pious Jew.

Returning now to an analysis of the "Star of Redemption," we may take up the problem of the relation between the three elements, man, the world, and God. Clearly, the recognition of the reality of revelation must lead to certain inferences concerning this threefold relation.

We have seen before that if thought is made the sole process of reality, all existence is absorbed into one All and both God and man disappear into the darkness of formulae and concepts. It is inevitable that in the process of thought there should be no room for either a living man or a living God, for all that live, live in time, whereas thought is timeless. The fact of revelation can be understood, then, only if we realize that God, the world and man are united by a process which does not deny the reality of either time or life. Such a process is speech.

It is here that Rosenzweig's originality and extreme subtlety are most in evidence. God and man are united in and through speech. Spirit is speech. "The new thinking" is not thinking, but speaking. How are we to comprehend such statements? In the first place, it must be understood, that the term "speaking" as used by Rosenzweig means "speaking to a person in all earnestness and devotion." It is the characteristic of thought that it is not directed to any one in particular. It has no address and it prevails everywhere. But, it is just this universality of thinking, which renders it incapable of giving an account of God and man. "Speaking," on the other hand, is dependent on the hearer as well as on the speaker. Speech exists between two beings, not completely within either person.[6] "The difference between the old and the new, logical and grammatical thinking, lies . . . in the need of the other and, which is really the same, in taking time seriously. To think means here to think for no one, but to speak means to speak to some one and to think for some one; and this some one is always an entirely definite one and has not only ears like universality, but also a mouth." [7]

In replacing thought by speech, Rosenzweig does not intend to question the validity of ordinary logic by any means. He shows, in the "Star" how logic is itself derivable from true speech. Just as in the previous section the mathematical principles of the class, "Twice two equals four" were shown to fall within the limiting case of the yearning for truth, so now we recognize logic as a limiting form of true speech, as speech in the third person, to be exact. But, and here the revolutionary import of the new method is stated, Speech is more primary than a chain of syllogisms. Hence it is that in the attempt to understand man's place in the scheme of things, simple logic proves rudderless and useless, lacking the ground of a basic premise to stand on, whereas

---

[6] See supplementary note 2 at end of book.
[7] "Das Neue Denken" Kleine Schriften, p. 387.

the method of speaking proves capable of doing justice to God and man as well as to the world.

That logic or thinking cannot in itself render a full account of reality has been partly shown before. At this point, we may illustrate this fact by examining the teachings of philosophy regarding the three elements of existence—man, the world and God.

Of man, then, we know nothing. Introspection reveals a succession of thoughts, feelings and wishes—but where is the self of man? We say, "I," so often and so lightly, but what do we mean by this "I"? A little reflection shows this very simple question to be most baffling. We must admit that we don't know the answer. The more we look for this "I" the more it eludes us. Thus, Hume, after a diligent search, had announced that there was no soul, or self or "I." Idealistic philosophers, after Kant, were compelled to follow suit, so that we have today what may be termed "a negative psychology." We are told of various elements of the mental life, but of the self, we are told nothing at all. In looking for the self, we say of every idea that we find in introspection, "it is not the self," so that we are left only with the knowledge of what the self is not. Hence, the name, "negative psychology."

Of God, too, we have in philosophy only a "negative theology." The philosophers of the Middle Ages have already arrived at the conclusion that we can describe what we know of God only by saying what He is not. Maimonides, it will be recalled, even refused to accord to God the qualities of "life," "power" and "wisdom" in their human senses. God is perfect and no positive attribute that we can think of can be applied to God, without "materializing" Him. Thus, in different words, but all to the same effect, most philosophers have argued that of God we can know nothing.

Of the world, too, the method of thought yields us only a "negative cosmology." The world of colors and sounds, we are told, is only secondary. In "reality" there are atoms and electrons, whirling about dizzily at tremendous speeds. But, we do not stop at this point. Further analysis and study reveal that the atoms are not solid particles of matter at all, but combinations of electrons and protons, which elements in their turn are resolved by thought into centers of energy, appearing as particles at one moment and as multi-dimensional waves at the next moment. The world, in essence, is a mystery to us, then, even as man and God.

Thus, while the world and man, in contradistinction to God are actually always before us, in their essences, the world and man are equally as mysterious to us as the essence of God. To the questions, concerning the beings of God, of man, of the world, thought can offer only the same series of negative replies.

Are these conclusions of philosophy and science, then, to be regarded as erroneous? No, Rosenzweig replies. They are true, but only partly true. Logical thought can go no further. Only by the new method of language can we learn to see reality in a manner consistent with the healthy understanding, with common sense.

Now, though of man, of the world, and of God we know nothing, yet the "naught" that we know of each one of these essences is not simply nothingness. We know the manifestations of these three elements in life; we are acquainted with the qualities of the physical, the human and the divine. The problem, then, is to show the evolution of these elements out of the three "naughts" to which thought has reduced them.[8] This can be done through the analogy of language. In language, there are three primary words (Urworte) that accompany all spoken and written sentences. The words "yes," "no" and "and" are the silent partners of all speech.

Even when one word, like the word "red," is spoken, these three primary words are heard—"yes," denoting the being

---

[8] See supplementary note 3.

of that which is described, "redness"; "no," being the definition of "redness" by excluding all other things, which are not "redness"; the "and," representing the combination of quality and relation. Rosenzweig's meaning can be clarified still further by taking the briefest possible sentence as an example, "A" is "B." It is evident that in this sentence, "A" is the subject, representing continuous being, which may well be designated as "yes." "B" is a definite adjective, stating that only "B" is meant, "no" being said to all else. The copula "is" echoes the "and" of language, uniting the "A" and the "B," the subject and the predicate, the quality and the relation.

Clearly, then, all meaning is analyzable into the schema of "yes," "no" and "and." To be sure, these primary words offer us nothing but schema, mere shadows of real things. They can do no more if they are to apply to all sentences and words. Nevertheless, they provide us with a scaffolding, which may prove useful in the attempt to scale the ethereal heights of metaphysical entities. For at least we know that those entities will have to contain aspects corresponding to the threefold structure of language.[9]

Applying this method to the essence of God, we are enabled to reverse the course of negative theology and to evolve a living Being out of the quality-less Naught, to which speculation has reduced the idea of God. If language corresponds most closely to the relation, which actually obtains between man and God in moments of revelation, then is the basic structure of language, the exact analogy of the revealed nature of God. Now, then, the "yes" of language, when applied to God means an endless affirmation of Being. The "no" of language is as original as the primary word "yes." In the case of God, it expresses His freedom, as the primary word "no" guards against all relations which are "other" to the Being of God. As the "yes" in God represented Infinite

[9] See note 4 at end of book.

Being, so does the "no" represent infinity in terms of relation, an infinity of potentialities, or freedom. The "and" of language represents, in the case of God, the indissoluble unity of His Being and His freedom. God is both substance and cause, absolute necessity and absolute freedom. Thus, we obtain the notion of a living God, one who has definite character and who yet can be arbitrary in action. This combination may be inadmissible in strict logic, but it is a simple concept—indeed, the concept of a living being.

Have we obtained, then, in this simple manner, a clear idea of what God is like? Rosenzweig makes no such claim. In the above structure, we have only a shadow of God, so to speak, an outline of what His Being must contain if speech is really the one medium in which both God and man share. The preference of dialogue-speech to logic is based, it will be recalled, upon the fact of revelation. This scheme of the primary words is thus an attempt to project the glowing fact of revelation unto the dark, unknown reality. The significance of these constructions, accordingly, must not be dissociated from the central thesis of an actually experienced revelation.

The same primary words, when applied to the "naught," which is the net result of "negative cosmology" yield us the picture of a growing world. The "yes" of the world can only be interpreted as "always" and "everywhere," since pure being as such has already been defined as an attribute of God. We thus have, as the abiding quality of the world, the sum of logical principles, the mathematically expressible order, which prevails in the world. These principles constitute the framework, into which all things, which enter the world, are made to fit. The complementary aspect of the world is the fact of particularity. The world abounds in things which cannot be satisfactorily classified. Nothing in nature is perfectly uniform. Everything, like every man, has its own personality. This multitude of particular things and events which are constantly being born "out of the night of naught" represents the "no" aspect of the world, the aspect which baffles all comparisons and all generalizations. The world wears this double face of particularities and universals —the sign of the third primary word "and."

In conscious agreement with Plato and Schelling, Rosenzweig represents the progress of the world as being from the raw particular to the universal. With Schelling, he sees a constant incursion of the novel and the strange into the stream of phenomena, where they are destined to be gradually overcome by the principle of order. Things progress from the pole of objectivity to that of subjectivity, as described in the previous section.

In the case of man, the primary word "yes" can only mean individual being (Eigensein). The individuality of man differs from the mere particularity of all new-born events in that man is conscious of his own enduring discreteness and loneliness. The primary word "no" signifies the freedom of man. Of course, man is not free in the same sense in which God is free, for God's freedom is expressed in acts, whereas man is free only to will. The self of man is the expression of the "and" of language, being the union of man's character and arbitrary defiance. (Trotz)

In this manner, then, we obtain the notion of a God, whose Being stands outside the course of actual events, but Who enters into them thru creation and revelation, as we shall see later. Similarly, we see a world which is knowable, but in which new particulars are always added and we see that man is living in the world, but that he is, in essence, not of the world.

Rosenzweig calls these conceptions—the metaphysical, the metalogical, the metaethical, respectively. Each one of these three elements is in the same relation to its actual manifestation as a picture hung against the wall is to the wall on which it is hung. Other pictures may be hung on the same wall or a different picture might have been put in its place. While the picture could not have been attached if there had been no wall, the wall does not, thru any inner law of necessity, require the picture. Similarly the world is amenable to logic, its multitude of phenomena breaking in ever fresh waves upon the rational order, but it stands outside logic; man's self is expressed in ethics, though yet it dwells beyond mere acts and intentions and God's will is expressed in man and in the world, while yet He remains outside both.[10]

Thus, as a result of employing the analogy with "the language of language," to use a phrase of Rosenzweig's, we now possess a description of the basic three elements of existence. These elements, each dwelling in the isolation of its own essence, are not found as such in the world of our experience. In the actual world, man, the world, and God are in constant relation with each other. However, it is for the purpose of understanding this threefold relation, which is taken to be modelled after the architecture of language that the three elements were described in terms of the "primary words." The metaphysical, metalogical and metaethical essences occupy in Rosenzweig's system a position analogous to that of limit concepts in mathematics. With them knowledge must begin, but their real meaning is exhibited only in the deductions concerning the actual world, which are made thru the employment of them as methodological instruments. Rosenzweig calls them the elements of the Vorwelt.

What then are the relations of these three essences to each other in the actual world? In what manner do they subsist together? The scheme which Rosenzweig employs to exhibit the mutual relations of the three elements of the "pre-world" is the ancient Jewish symbol, the "Star of David." The three points of the upper triangle are the three beings of the "pre-world," while the second triangle shows the relations that obtain between these beings. The full meaning of this

---

[10] "S. d. E.," book I, p. 25.

symbol will become apparent in the course of our discussion of the nature of the currents that course between God, the world and man. We shall begin with an analysis of the functional relation obtaining between God and His world.

Of creation, then, God creates the world. What does this act of creation imply in reference to the being of God and that of the world? In the being of God, we noted the aspects of "yes," "no" and "and." Now, as we proceed to direct the process of thought back from the "naught" to reality, the way that we have followed before must be reversed. This observation applies with equal force to the other elements of the Vorwelt. Entering into reality, each "primary word" turns into its opposite. Thus, in God's creation of the actual world, it is the "no" of God's being, His power and freedom that are made manifest. But, to the world, the act of creation represents the reversal of its own being, its "yes." In this manner, the "no" of the Vorwelt is turned into a "yes" in the actual world.

This doctrine of "inversion" which declares that each "primary word" of the Vorwelt turns into its opposite in the

actual world, is one of the most abstruse points of Rosenzweig's philosophy. The author himself helps us little with
the analogy that he offers in the "Star of Redemption." He
suggests there the comparison with the acts of filling and
emptying a drawer—what we put in first, we take out last.
To understand his real meaning, we should recall first that
the problem of relation in philosophy contains some baffling
difficulties. Bradley's "Appearance and Reality" presents
this problem in its diverse aspects. How can two distinct
things be related? Is not the relation itself a third thing
which again needs to be related to the first two objects, and
so on ad infinitum? Starting as we do with three distinct
metaphysical elements, how can we ever hope to relate them?
Rosenzweig meets this problem by reverting again to his
basic thesis that speech and not logic is most akin to the
processes of reality. Now, dialogue speech is a directional
process; it proceeds from an "I" to a "Thou." In constructing the elements of the Vorwelt, we pursued to its culmination one direction of human thought, a tendency which
culminated historically in the Greek religion. Rosenzweig
labored hard to prove that the classical tradition operated exclusively with the concepts of the Vorwelt, because he was
convinced that no further evolution in a straight line was
possible. The Hellenic genius for impersonal thinking could
not do more than produce three self-contained essences.

When Judaism, or true revelation, superseded paganism,
a new process was begun, leading not into the elements of
existence, but from them into the actual world. The movement of metaphysical thought toward the Vorwelt has thus
been reversed. Since no new things or qualities were added to
the three essences by the Jewish tradition, these essences
themselves must have been turned inside out, as it were.
The "prime words" are all we know of the elements of existence; therefore, we must conceive of these "prime words"
as turning into their opposites.

Returning now to the problem of creation, we note that it is the whole of the world, its physical laws and its mathematical principles together with its myriad of particulars, that is maintained by the power of God. The world is a "many" consisting as it does of a multitude of diverse events and things. At the same time, it is a "one" in that all things are mutually related, connected by an interlacing maze of physical and mental "lines of influence." The question of relating the "one" and the "many" has been one of the most perplexing problems of philosophy. In Rosenzweig's scheme, the "one," the principle of unity, stands outside the world itself, contained as it is in the being of God.

The actual world, we may note at this stage, is always conceived as being in the past. Everything we see or feel or think "has been." So indeed it should be, for the world is "created," something already done. It bears no life of its own and is hence without "presentness." This creation is creatio ex nihilo, as the Jewish philosophers (except Ralbag) have always insisted. Rosenzweig traced the evolution of the pagan concept of chaos into the modern idealistic philosophy and showed that, in his theory of creation, there was no need of a chaos.[11] "The chaos is in, not before creation" —a creation, which, stemming from the Power of God, not from His Being, must be perpetually maintained by the same Power. Thus, creation is an endless process. God, "in His Goodness renews the world on every day."

This hypothesis of the creation of the world, it will be conceded, may be helpful in solving some riddles of philosophy. But, one is led to inquire how creation can be understood. Haven't we seen in the previous chapter that the driving force of philosophy has been the incomprehensibility of change? How much less, then, can creation out of nothing be understood? Here is where the replacement of traditional logic by the grammar of language proves its usefulness.

---

[11] S. d. E., Vol. II, p. 59.

Thought, being timeless, must be puzzled by the fact of change. Speech, however, includes time in its very essence, as we saw above. Accordingly, change, or creation, is not foreign to language. God created the world and He has been maintaining it since then in a manner analogous to speech. "He spoke and it was done." This analogy, it can hardly be overemphasized, is meant to be taken literally. The world is in truth the speech of God.

Pursuing this analogy still further, we learn that grammatical forms are not deducible from each other, in the same manner as are the elements of an ideal logical structure. Grammar is like a tree, with branches and leaves. So, too, is the created world, divisible into various classifications, but incapable of being reconstructed from any logical principle or group of principles. However, there must be a word which expresses creation as such. This word, echoed in every act of creation, Rosenzweig calls a stem-word. In looking for the stem-word of creation, we note that it must be a word denoting one meaning, which meaning may be understood without the need of knowing all that it is not. The only group of words that answers this requirement is the evaluating set of adjectives such as, the word "beautiful" or more generally "good." The positive evaluation is further nothing but the "primary yes" become audible. Thus, the adjective "good" or the phrase "it is good" is the stem-word of creation. How remarkable is it then, that, in the Biblical story of creation, God says of every stage of creation "and it was good." [12] "The word of creation, which thrills in us and speaks out of us, beginning with the stem-word, that rings immediately out of the stillness of the primary word up to the perfectly objective narrative form of the past—all this is also the word which God has spoken and which we find written in the book of Genesis." [13] Beginning in this manner,

---

[12] S. d. E., Vol. II, p. 51.
[13] S. d. E., Vol. II, p. 81.

Rosenzweig lists the various classes of words—adjectives, nouns, verbs, in order to complete the picture of the creation concept and to demonstrate the truth of the Biblical account.

Is this schematization of the world, proof of the correctness of the theory of creation? By no means, Rosenzweig admits. All that has been thus far demonstrated is the possibility of regarding the world as created. Nevertheless, he insists, we should have no right to accept the creation hypothesis as a scientific theory, if we had not possessed the proof of revelation. "Whoever has not yet been reached by the voice of revelation has no right to accept the thought of creation, as if it were a scientific hypothesis." Sheer human thinking cannot advance beyond the point reached by the speculation of the classical philosophers. Other old civilizations, like those of India and China have never advanced beyond the "yes" and the "no" stages respectively. Historically, it was Judaism which brought forth the doctrine of creatio ex nihilo, and, logically, this doctrine will be acceptable only to those who have themselves experienced the phenomenon of revelation. The alpha and omega of all the speculations of Rosenzweig is, as was remarked above, the fact of revelation.[14]

Revelation is the relation between God and man. As the "no" of God's essence was interpreted to be His creation of the world, so is the primary "yes" of God displayed in His relation to man. Here, too, an inversion of the primary word takes place. The stillness of God's Being, His "yes," is revealed as a moment of love, directed to a chosen, arbitrarily selected, definite man. Like an instantaneous "cosmic ray" it pierces the heart of different men at different times. God's love is directed not to all men at once, like the rays of the benevolent sun. Rather, like the proverbial thunderbolt from heaven, its aim is always unpredictable.

The common view of revelation is that a definite fact has

[14] S. d. E., Vol. II, p. 60.

been made known by God to man. Among the "enlightened" exponents of religion on the other hand, revelation has been steadily secularized, until it came to signify merely a sort of poetic inspiration. Rosenzweig's view of revelation stands midway between both conceptions. Revelation is a fact, not merely a poetic phrase; it is really the flow of God's love to the heart of man, but its immediate content is no more than love. Later, in the course of our discussion of Rosenzweig's views on Judaism and Christianity, the full implications of his theory of revelation will become apparent.

For the present, then, we have to remember that God loves men and that His love is spontaneous, arbitrary and discontinuous. Philosophers in the past, were constrained to deny that God loves anything but Himself, for love implies needfulness and God, who is perfect, needs nothing. But, God's love is love of the lover which is a "momentary self-transformation." The "I" which is the bearer of qualities is in the moment of love entirely gone. "God loves" is purest present, knowing nothing, in the intoxication of the love-filled moment, of other moments or of other people. This apparent narrowness of heart makes His love, truly love, even love as men know it, marked as it is by complete devotion in the momentary present.

Rosenzweig conceives of love as coming in two forms—love of the lover and love of the beloved. These terms are not to be taken as identical with the forms of love that obtain between men and women, though undoubtedly it is abstracted from the relations between the ideal or typical man and the typical woman. God is the lover and the soul of man is the beloved. While the love of the lover is arbitrary, momentary and unreflective, the love of the beloved is responsive, continuous and concerned with the future.

How does man receive the love of God? Defiance or pride, which is the "no" of man's self, is converted into humility which, too, is a form of pride, containing as it does the feeling of belonging to and being carried by a higher power. The rebellious pride of man is converted into humble devotion. Thus, man's love, in response to that of God, is the love of the beloved. As such it is an enduring quality of the soul. The love of God converts the defiant "no" of man's soul into a great "yes," thus making His love eternal.

Since love is self-revealing, its stem-word is "I." God's "no" is made audible in the Divine "Onochi-I." In contrast to the stem-word of creation "good," the stem-word of revelation attains its proper meaning only in a dialogue. The opposite of an "I" is in strictness not a mere thing or "it" but another "I," a "Thou." The love of God, streaming into the heart of man, awakens the soul to a consciousness of its own responsibility, in the presence of the Divine call "where art thou?" Man, after vain attempts at evasion, symbolized in Cain's reply to God, finally exclaims, "Here I am." The readiness of man to respond to the will of God marks the birth of the human "I." To this receptive soul, God makes the one command—"And thou shalt love the Lord, thy God." God, as the lover can do nothing but command. "Declarations of love" refer to the past, whereas the love of God, His revelation, is always in the present, always *hayom*. The substance of revelation is the peremptory order of the eternal lover, "love me."

How does the soul of man respond to this order? Man's reaction is carried out in two directions. In the first place, the love confession of the beloved wells up in response to the call of God, for only the beloved speaks in the form of confession. Since her love is constant, she exclaims, "I have sinned," on realizing that she was not loved before. With this confession she clings the more to the assurance of the Divine lover, "I have called thee by thy name; you are mine." The soul of man knows that it belongs to God, who created her. The lover, the Revealer, is also the Creator. Yet, though man knows that in his world of mud and distress,

God has stepped in; that his experience of Divine love is as much a part of this world as its rocks and mountains, an unfulfilled desire keeps him restless. The assurance felt by the beloved of the Divine Love rests upon only a moment of actual experience. Therefore, she prays for complete actualization. The God, who had once called her by her name—may He do so again in the future! "The soul prays for the coming repetition of this miracle, for the perfection of the once established relationship and for nothing more." [15] The beloved desires to be known as the beloved "in the eyes of all flesh"—a wish, which, in the pale of reflection of true love among men and women, finds expression in the institution of marriage. "That the soul has the courage, so to wish, so to ask, so to cry out—this perfection of the latent trust in God is the work of revelation." Thus the dialogue of love, which is revelation, ends in an anguished prayer for the perfect realization of the Kingdom of Heaven.

Pursuing our method of comprehending the three currents of reality by the analogy of language, we note that in revelation the present tense prevails. There is a looking back to the past and a longing to the future, but it is the present moment in which the dialogue of "I" and "thou" takes place. Characteristic of revelation is the proper name, since the individual is addressed by God, as an individual, not merely as a specimen of a general class. Thus, in the Holy Scriptures, God calls men by their names and He even reveals His own Name. Echoes of the dialogue of revelation, Rosenzweig finds thruout the Bible. Most remarkable, in his view, is the inclusion of the Song of Songs in Holy Writ, for there the simile of love between man and woman as the analogue of revelation is found in most explicit form, and not merely as an ordinary simile. "Love is like language itself, sensual-suprasensual." [16] The incoherence of the dia-

---

[15] S. d. E., Vol. II, p. 125.
[16] S. d. E., Vol. II, p. 146.

logue in the "Song of Songs," its apparently senseless repetition, its mingling of dream with reality, the frequent occurrence of the first person—all are proof of the lyrical nature of the relation between man and God. Moreover, there is one declaration concerning love in that book, which expresses its metaphysical value—"Strong as death is love." Death is the last word of creation, turning the living present into the lifeless past. ["very good—that is death" (Genesis, Rabbah I)]. Everything that we perceive about us has already been. But, Divine love, or revelation, generates the hope of redemption, which in turn, overcomes the universal reign of death. It is to the study of redemption, then, that we must next turn our attention.

In the analysis of the process of revelation we have seen the soul of man break out of its lonely isolation into direct relation to God. Thus far, however, the soul was open only to God. It might even have been thought that absolute devotion to God precluded any interest in the worldly affairs of men. This belief was, in fact, the rock, against which many ardent mystics have floundered and have, in consequence, lost sight of their fellow-men. Through his philosophy of language, Rosenzweig succeeded in showing how the love of God becomes fruitful in the lives of men.

In the soul of man there is the "yes" of character as well as the "no" of defiance, which latter quality had been turned into faithful devotion to God thru His revelation. Now, it is this "yes" of the pre-world that, turns into momentary flashes of love of neighbor, when it is energized by the power of revelation. The "yes" of man undergoes the same "conversion" as the other elements upon entering the actual world. Thus, love of neighbor is neither continuous, nor elicited by definite rules. Ethical laws, which stipulate precise actions and attitudes in every contingency, are in place only among those men in whose life the light of revelation has not yet entered.

The ethics of religion, or more clearly, the ethics of love, is both supplementary and superior to the ethics of law. Of moral laws, it was rightly said that man is "autonomous" and "free," the two ethical postulates which Kant had made famous. Not so of love, "for man is able to express himself in the deed of love only when his soul has been aroused by God." [17] All human, disinterested love, which is not biological in origin, is due to the momentary rays of love which God sends to men. "Love thy neighbor" is thus the direct result of "thou shalt love the Lord, thy God," and is therefore, as Rabbi Akiba had noted long ago, the essence of all the divine commandments.

It has been said that the feeling of love cannot be relied upon to function as a safe guide for ethical conduct, for love is essentially arbitrary. Often capricious, always unpredictable, aroused by the superficially impressive and the bizarre, love is apt to be directed to unworthy persons or to be restricted within the cramped confines of one's own circle. Rosenzweig recognizes these dangers. Nevertheless, he asserts that a deed of love, owing to its divine origin, never really misses its mark. Love is only in appearance directed by arbitrary caprice. In truth, "the law of growth, of which man himself is not conscious, determines the way of love and its object." [18] Man "knows only that he should love and always the next one and again the next one." In the divine plan all aimless and narrow-hearted acts are joined together in one scheme, the aim of which is to hasten the redemption of man and of the world.

For the world, too, needs to be redeemed. In comparison with both man and God the world bears the marks of incompleteness.[19] It has no enduring form, marked as it is by the incessant appearance of novel and surprising events.

---

[17] S. d. E., Vol. II, p. 163.
[18] S. d. E., Vol. II, p. 198.
[19] See note 5 at end of book.

Rosenzweig declares that, in the "Kingdom," the world will be "animated," transformed into enduring forms. In the ceaseless flux of nature, there are even now points where permanence of form triumphs over the dissolving effect of time, where a principle of preservation of form seems to be in action. Such points are, of course, all living beings. It is the very meaning of life, that the sameness of the organism is maintained despite multiple processes of change that go on within it. But life as we know it today exists only in spots, and is ephemeral in nature, subject as it is to the ubiquitous reign of death. To be completed, the world itself must become one living organism. "The world is destined from the beginning to be alive. (Zur Lebendigkeit) To be sure, the world was not completed in the beginning but it was endowed with this destiny, to be completed." [20] Again, he defines the Kingdom of God as the "verlebendigung," "vitalizing of existence," a process which the modern theories of evolution have abundantly illustrated. Life is growing in the world, evolving ever new, more efficient forms, and subduing dead matter in its triumphant march toward the goal when all that exists will be pulsating with the power of life. We have here a conception of world progress very similar to Bergron's concept of the elan vital, as expressed especially in the latter's book "Two Sources of Morality and Religion."

However, the growth of life in the world is not identical with the growth of the Kingdom. For life desires indeed to endure, but it fights a battle with an uncertain result. To be complete, the world must not only possess transitory living beings, but forms of life that are immortal.

Here is where the redemption of the world depends on the acts of men. Every deed of love performed by men, is directed to the world as a whole. The love of man to his fellow-man is, at bottom, directed in the first place to the

[20] S. d. E., Vol. II, p. 176.

abstract "next one," only secondarily to the one who happens to be the next one. This thought is now carried further. Though love is directed to the "next one," it is done so in anticipation of the organic unity of the world in the Kingdom of Heaven. Now, the love of man is directed to the next one as to a "thou" not as to a mere "it," and the bond of "I" and "Thou" is the bond that we noted before between man and God, is, therefore, the bond of eternity.

To Rosenzweig, eternity means the yearning anticipation in the present of the final attainment of the Kingdom. "Eternity is like the Dawn," being in the darkness of night, but containing the promise of day. He also seems to employ this term as identical with the term "beseelung," animating. His thought appears to be that the love of God is spirit (Geist), is eternal, and that all deeds of love are in consequence of their origin in Divine love, eternal, endowing things with living spirit.

The term eternal, as employed by Rosenzweig, is not to be taken as a mere rhetorical phrase—an interpretation which the above definition may seem to encourage. The definition is taken from Hermann Cohen, but the meaning which the word "eternal" assumed in the writings of Rosenzweig belongs to a realm of discourse, which his rationalistic teacher would have repudiated most angrily. Love and eternity occupy in the thought of Rosenzweig a role analogous to that of thought and timelessness in the Aristotelian philosophies. Whatever has become the recipient of true love has thru that very fact become eternal. To be eternal, means here to be a part of the redeemed world as it is envisioned by God. This redeemed world is even now in the mind of God; hence we may say that to be eternal means for Rosenzweig to be part of the Divine Order.

Coming back to the redemption of the world, then, we note that it is the human deeds of love which supplement the world's growth into an enduring organism. To the growing life of the world, love adds the quality of eternity. "Only and where the limbs of this growing organism are blown upon by the animating breath of love of the next one, do they gain in addition to their life, that which life in itself could not give animation, eternity." [21] The world, then, is daily being redeemed, becoming more and more of an enduring being. The powers of life and the animating force of man's love combine to produce a steadily evolving organic universe. Life and love are the two roads through which the world steadily advances toward the goal destined for it by the Creator. The work of love is something which remains obscure to man. It cannot be foreseen by the human agent, nor can it be calculated by an examination of the immediate results. Thus love animates the world, not essentially through what it does, but because it is love that does it.[22] A cosmic law regulates the harmony of love and the growth of the world. For love is a power which is indeed given to man to wield but not to direct; it streams forth from God to man and through man to the world.

Before gathering up the threads of the entire discussion thus far, we have to show, for the sake of completeness, how the category of redemption is expressed in human language. First, then, we turn our attention to the stem-word (Stammwort) of redemption. On reflection, we note that there is no stem-word for redemption, for the word "and" does not represent in Rosenzweig's method a creative act. In contrast to the term "Synthesis" in Hegel's philosophy, the primary word expresses merely the conjunction of the two creative forces, the primary words "yes" and "no." Accordingly, we should expect the process of redemption to be represented by a sentence, in which the two primary words of creation and of revelation are joined together. Thus, the stem-sentence we are looking for should contain the Divine "I" of revela-

---

[21] S. d. E., Vol. II, p. 197.
[22] S. d. E., Vol. II, p. 196.

tion and the term "good" of creation. However, since "I" can only be said by God, the stem-sentence of redemption is, "He is good."

This stem-sentence of redemption, Rosenzweig declares to be the basic sentence of all speech. It is even prior to speech for it is implied in the common song. Singing is primarily done by a group. And the common content, which welds a group together into a singing unit is this sentence "He is good," expressing the common feeling of gratitude and joy.

All creation, the blind elements of nature and the multitude of men, in their common perception of the process of redemption which carries them along on its irresistable onward course, join in offering praise and thanks to God, the Redeemer. This medley of diverse creatures is, in the prayer of redemption, joined by the common consciousness of "we." The union of man and the world in one eternal and living being is anticipated in this state of exultation. The prayer of redemption is thus oriented toward the future, enjoying, as it were, a foretaste of the coming Kingdom, in the present fleeting moment. While the prayer of revelation ends on a note of helpless yearning, the prayer of redemption begins with the anticipation of the final fulfillment.

The purest literary expression of the category of redemption is found in the Biblical psalms. Though in most of the psalms the authors speak in the first person, the psalms are really community songs, for the "I" of the psalms recognizes his own deepest nature in his concern for the entire community. The real subject of the psalms is "we," a "we" that often consciously includes the starry hosts of heaven and the green trees of the earth.

It is the live realization of this "we" that confers the crown of eternity on the fleeting moments of time. For it can be said truly only when men, filled with the power of love, anticipate, albeit dimly, the redeemed universe. In simpler words, the moments in which we say "we" in all earnestness are part of God's own Being, and, therefore, imperishable. "The we is eternal; before this triumphant yell of eternity, death is plunged into the naught. Life becomes immortal in the eternal chant of praise of redemption." [23]

And, here, the final meaning of redemption is made evident; not only are man and the world redeemed, but God Himself "Kbayochol," is redeemed in that He truly becomes, in the emerging Kingdom of Heaven, One and All. That which the philosophers assumed at the outset of their speculations, is now seen to become true only "in the end of days." God, in His love, draws the world and man ever closer to Himself, until, in the end they merge in His eternal essence.

We are now in a position to bring together the various points thus far discussed and to view with Rosenzweig the entire march of the cosmos through time. We note, then, to begin with, that the starting point of our thinker is an experience of God's love—the fact of revelaton. But, the love of God tells of creation, in that God as the lover says to the beloved soul of man, "Thou art mine." At the same time revelation points to redemption, for man's response to the love of God takes the two forms of yearning for the complete manifestation of Divine love in the actual world and of expressing the love of God through the love of the "next one." The basic insight, with which Rosenzweig begins his speculations, is thus seen to be the assertion that creation, revelation and redemption are categories of being—that is, basic lines of division within the current of reality. Since traditional logic does not take account of these categories, it is necessary to demonstrate that language, or rather "dialogue speaking," is a more real medium of expression than logic, which is the grammar of objective or third person narration. The primary words "yes," "no" and "and" are now seen to be the verbal expressions respectively of the basic categories, Revelation, Creation and Redemption. The elements of the

[23] S. d. E., Vol. II, p. 213.

pre-world, or the essences, were constructed by the employment of these three categories which later were demonstrated in their actual work throughout the real world in which we live. So much, then, for the method.

The results obtained by this method can best be surveyed by returning to that symbolic "Star" for which the book is named. In the upper triangle, we see the three elements, but of the three, God is supreme. He had created the world at a definite time in history, and, since, then, He has been re-creating it from day to day. The world is created, momentary existence consisting of a host of passing phenomena, but through the ever increasing current of life which courses

through it, it acquires more and more enduring being. Living in the world, yet in a sense outside it, is man, the recipient of divine revelation, who redeems himself and the world, through his love of his fellow-man. The three points of the second triangle, creation, revelation and redemption, do not lie, in our symbol, on the lines of the first triangle, in order to illustrate the fact that they are not necessary manifestations of the Being of God, who remains free to create or not to create, to reveal Himself or to remain hidden behind the veil of nature. Again, it is not only the world and man, but God too, who is redeemed in the process of being. For in the lowest point of the star, redemption, the world and man become one with the living God. The entire course of being, then, moves toward the goal of unity, the unity of God.

If God, too, is becoming, how can we speak of Him as the Eternal? We saw before that eternity means to Rosenzweig neither timelessness nor endless endurance—though these meanings form part of the significance of the term eternity —but the anticipation in the present of the final stage of redemption. Now, God Himself keeps His purpose and goal as part of His Being. Hence, He *is* eternal. Man *becomes* eternal only in the moment when, as the vessel of Divine love, he performs deeds of love in the actual world. In these moments, man is part of the Divine plan, part of the eternal will, for God's love is the revelation of His essential Being, of His eternity, and wherever it or the human love engendered by it, is manifested, an eternal moment has been formed. The world, in its turn, becomes eternal thru the acts of man.

With this picture of God and the universe in mind, we are prepared to begin the study of Rosenzweig's views on Judaism and Christianity.

(d) Philosophy of Religion

WE HAVE SEEN IN THE PREVIOUS CHAPTER HOW, ACCORDING to Rosenzweig, there courses through the universe the divine triangular process of creation, revelation and redemption. We know, too, that new acts of creation are quite rare; that a large proportion of mankind has never felt the call of revelation and that, in consequence, redeeming deeds of love are few and far between. The larger part of the observable flux of events flows outside these categories in the spheres which our author calls semi-real. So far, then, we have not yet shown how a positive religion, one that is lived in prayer and ceremonies, is possible. We have indeed the view of a God Who creates, and Who, through His love, causes man to redeem the world and make it eternal. A living religion requires in addition to these principles, however, a demonstration of the manner in which religious worship proves effective —that is, the religious man is not simply the one who believes on the basis of philosophical reasoning that there is a God who will in the course of time establish justice in the world, but the one who knows that through his prayer and devotion he aids in the consummation of the Divine intentions regarding the world and himself. The truly pious are partners of God, not merely believers in Him ("shutafim b'maasei b'reshith"). Also, the historical religions, such as Judaism and Christianity, require a theory of revelation which will justify their veneration of certain books and symbols. Both of these essential requirements of a living positive faith are often ignored by speculative theologians, with the result that their writings are of little relevance to the actual practice of their faith. The unique significance of Rosenzweig as a religious thinker consists in the fact that he propounded significant theories concerning the effectiveness of prayer and the historicity of revelation.

Turning our attention to the problem of worship, first, we note that, on the views of our author, Divine love of man is the source and the cause of man's love of God or of the "next one." God's love of man, we saw above was a free act and did not come as a response to anything that man did. What power, then, if any, does prayer possess?

In answer, Rosenzweig points out that individual prayer can have only the effect of "illumination." The worshipper cherishes the love of God which has come to him and concentrates on the resolve to perform deeds of love. After prayer he is, therefore, more likely to practice "love of neigh-

bor" than if he had not prayed. Personal prayer, consequently, is a method which man employs for the purpose of
rendering himself a better channel for the love of God. It
follows that people may well pray for all their physical needs,
since material things are needed by men for the practice of
philanthropy.

The essential point to remember is that not prayer as such,
but love is the effective force. Prayer may at times even
hinder the work of love. This happens when it deflects the
attention of the worshipper from the "next one" to the one
beyond. It will be recalled that, according to Rosenzweig,
all acts of love are Divine in origin and direction. In the
popular sense of the term, love is supernatural. When performed "blindly," in faithful reliance on the subconscious
drive of feeling, love finds its proper object—the object, that
is, which the growth of the world had prepared for it. If,
however, man in the enthusiasm of prayer, when the entire
road to redemption is anticipated by the yearning heart, directs his acts of love consciously to the distant goal, his work
proves useless. For the world grows slowly, in accordance
with the Will of God, and its hesitant advance toward redemption cannot be hastened by individual human effort.
Love, then, which is not blind is not divine, and the danger
which lurks in prayer is that dogmatism and sectarian interests may come to be the determining factors in the choice
of an object of love. If, however, these dangers are avoided
through scrupulous adherence to the principle that man must
love the "next one" and must trust that through the Providence of God, the world is so arranged that his love, if it be
true, inevitably finds the object which the course of life had
destined to be eternalized, then personal prayer serves the
purpose of strengthening man's resolution to be a good channel for the flow of Divine love.

The second way in which prayer is effective will become
clear to us only after we learn the answer to an ancient and

most curious question. "Can the advent of the Kingdom of God be hastened at all?" True, an individual must not attempt to direct the force of love in artificial channels. But, we may ask, is there a method whereby a group of people may accelerate the slow tempo of the process of redemption? This question, which formed the burning center of the speculations of the Kabbalists, Rosenzweig answers in the affirmative. At a time when "enlightened" proponents of religion vied with each other in toning down the claims of their respective faiths, Rosenzweig proclaimed the thesis that our human cults may have cosmic effects; that, through the institutions of religion, we not only help to redeem men from the slavery of selfishness, but that we hasten the process of the redemption of the material world as well.

It will be recalled that the moments when a man attains to the stage where feeling one with all creation, he is able to sing in all sincerity of the universal comradeship, of "we," are eternal. Such moments then, are part of the Divine process which abides forever in the mind of God. Those moments being, however, themselves the result of the love of God, were exceedingly rare even in the lives of religious geniuses. If now, a whole community orders its life so that at stated times, all its members know themselves as an eternal "we" and if, then, they all turn their attention to the final days, so that their individual wishes and views are forgotten in the light of the common goal, then God steps into the actual world and endows that community with the stamp of His eternity. In other words, while one man cannot draw down the love of God to himself, a "we," knowing itself to be an eternal entity, can accomplish this marvelous feat. Thus, he asserts, "The cult-prayer in which everything turns about the plea for the coming of the Kingdom and in which all other petitions, that are otherwise far closer are put forward only because of it, compels the redeeming entrance of the Eternal in time, in that it points to the love of the eternal as that of the "next one" and thereby directs to the eternal the irresistible power of the love of the next one. God cannot act otherwise; he must obey the invitation . . . this prayer, which rising beyond all particular things, looks only toward that which is common to all, pulls the Eternal with a powerful grasp in to the moment and endows the individual . . . with the sparks of the eternal light, which remain in him as Seed of the Eternal life." [1]

Thus, in picturesque and almost sacrilegious language, Rosenzweig asserts that the power of love, when freed from concentration on particular interests and severed from association with individual viewpoints, is capable of eternalizing situations and moments. This is indeed a radical doctrine, reminding us of the methods employed by the Kabbalists to bring down to earth the "emanation of grace." It must be added that this conclusion does not necessarily follow from the premise that love is a Divine force, for that premise has as its complement the assertion that the object of love has been pre-destined to that end by a Divine law. How, then, can human love, be it even that of any number of people, overcome the law of God and hasten the coming of the Kingdom?

The views of Rosenzweig concerning the power of public prayer become more plausible, however, after a close study of his doctrine of revelation. It appears, then, that the community which knows itself as a "we" and prays for the coming of the Kingdom is itself created through Divine Revelation. Just as love of neighbor is the result of the love of God, so too is the formation of a community of people who direct their love to the end of days, the result of a revelation of God. Hence, the devoted worship of that community is really one of the instruments through which God brings about the establishment of the Kingdom of God.

---

[1] S. d. E. Vol. III, p. 43.

It is the belief of Rosenzweig that Divine revelation is neither a subjective nor a transitory phenomenon. It is an event leaving objective traces and, wherever it has really become manifest, it endures eternally. Up to this point in our exposition of Rosenzweig's philosophy, we dealt with revelation merely as a subjective experience. Now, it is time to describe the signs whereby the fact of revelation in history may be recognized.

Two standards emerge, out of Rosenzweig's writings, as the means whereby authentic revelation may be established of which one is based on content, the other on effect. The nature of the content is evident from the entire discussion. God must be conceived as a living Being, Who reveals Himself to men that were chosen by His Will; Who stands outside of nature and is the Lord of nature or its Creator; Who loves men and redeems them through their practice of mutual love. The book, which alone can be regarded as the Holy Book must contain the language of the three Divine categories—creation, revelation and redemption. The standard of actual effectiveness requires, in addition, that the book or the idea which claims Divine origin, be shown to have been an active historical force. For whatever stems from the source of revelation is non-transitory, bearing as it does the mark of eternity.

On the basis of these standards, it obviously follows that the Bible is the revealed Word of God. Its content represents true revelation, as was indicated in passing, and its effect throughout the ages has been uniformly to awaken the soul of man to the call of its Creator. (The Koran, Rosenzweig claims, is merely an imitation of true religion, lacking inspiration and true ideas.)

Rosenzweig's view of "Torah min Hashamaim" comes close to the Orthodox view—perhaps as close as speculative thinking can ever come—but it does not actually coincide with it. In his view, the authors and editors of the Bible

gave expression to true religious feeling, which could stem
only from the actual experience of revelation. Again, in
their work as prophets and teachers, they were the chosen
agents of God in the propagation of His truth, for God reveals not only love as a blind force, but the proper recipients
of that power of love as well. This does not mean that every
word and letter of the Torah was dictated by God. Thus, in
a letter to Jacob Rosenheim, Rosenzweig writes, "our difference from Orthodoxy lies in that we cannot draw any conclusions concerning the literary process of the composition of
the Bible and the philological value of the traditional text out
of our belief in the sacredness and the peculiar value of the
Torah. (Sonderstellung.) If Wellhausen and all his theories were indeed right, and if the Samaritans really possessed
a better text, that would not touch our belief in the slightest." [2]

In spite of this critical objectivity, the translation of Buber
and Rosenzweig adhered almost uniformly to the traditional
interpretation and that because Rosenzweig refused to take
the letters [3] of the Bible as naked fetiches. The traditional
interpretations, the wealth of Midrashic material which in
the course of time was lovingly woven about every letter of
the scripture; all the ancient comments, which, born out of
the deepest yearnings of the Jewish people, were projected
backward through time against the background of the fiery
letters of the Law—all this mass of interpretative material,
Rosenzweig regarded as part of the Bible itself. For the
value of the Bible lies as much in its effectiveness as in its
content, more perhaps in the way it is heard than in the way
it is written. Thus, he wrote, "I believe that there is hardly
one element in the Bible that one could not with sufficiently
expanded knowledge show also elsewhere. The uniqueness
of the Bible can be indisputably proven not in the written,

---

[2] "Briefe," p. 581.
[3] "Briefe," p. 581.

but in the read book. The Bible, is not the most beautiful book in the world, not the deepest, the truest, the wisest, the most fascinating and whatever other superlatives there may be—at least no one can be convinced of these advantages who is not already prejudiced in its favor. But the Bible is the most important book. This one can prove, and even the most enraged Bible-hater too has to admit this at least for the past, and, through his inveterate hatred, he admits it also for the present. For here there is no question of personal taste or of disposition of the soul or of spiritual direction, but only a question of the hitherto transpired events of world history." [4]

If the Bible is God-given, it follows that both Israel and Christendom, which are based on the Bible, are divinely ordained religious communities; in both these groups there is an eternal "we," which through common prayer for the Kingdom, acquires eternity for its members and also hastens the final redemption of the world. Judaism and Christianity constitute together the "Überwelt"—that is, the stage of being which brings eternity into time and God in the world. True Jews and true Christians live at once in time with the world and in eternity with God. Both are, in a real sense, revealed religions and each one, in itself, is only part of the truth. To be sure, only part of the truth can ever fall within the lot of man, for, as we have seen in the second section, truth is the attraction with which we are pulled to the Divine Being. Truth is a noun only to God; to men, truth is really best known as an adverb, "truly," (wahrlich) as the measure of our inner faithfulness. Hence it must always remain partial.

In affirming the Divine origin of both Judaism and Christianity, Rosenzweig does not intend to be understood as implying that these religions are true, in toto, and that God has

---

[4] "Das Formgeheimniss der Biblischen Erzählungen," K. S., p. 178.

secluded himself from communion with those who stand outside the confines of these faiths. Revelation, it will be remembered is a general human experience and prayer, in all
languages, is still lyrical communion with God. The uniqueness of Judaism and Christianity consists in the fact that in
their liturgy and in their literature, true ideas are found
which cannot but foster the right religious attitudes. Nevertheless, it may be conceded that the revealed religions contain much dross, and that in pagan cults true religious feeling and insight occasionally burst forth.

Thus, he writes, "Just as there are no roads leading from
Sinai or Golgotha, upon which He may be reached with certainty, so too He could not have refused to meet also the persons who sought Him on the mule-tracks of the Olympic
mountains." Rosenzweig views paganism as a stage in the
gradual recognition by man of his relation to God. The
primary "yes" and the primary "no" found their respective
expressions in the religions of India and China, while the
complete exemplification of the elements of the "pre-world"
took place in the classical civilization of Greece. Judaism
began where the most developed form of paganism left off,
containing as it does the teachings of creation, revelation and
redemption. Thus, paganism is, in a sense, true, since revelation requires as its presupposition the existence of the elements of the pre-world.[5] (D. N. D. p. 382.)

Though we cannot here reproduce Rosenzweig's views on
the nature of Christianity in any detail, we have to indicate
at least the relations between Judaism and Christianity.
Now, in symbolic language, Rosenzweig calls Judaism "the
eternal fire" and Christianity "the eternal rays." While

---

[5] In his views on the history of culture, Rosenzweig follows, in part,
the theories of Oswald Spengler in his "Decline of the West." What
Spengler calls the Faustian spirit, the urge for infinite expansion, Rosenzweig,
it will be seen, calls the spirit of Christianity. Both find the essence of
the Classical spirit to be symbolized in a self-enclosed body. ("Das Neue
Denken" in "Kleine Schriften," p. 398.)

Israel stays with God, Christendom constantly marches toward Him, subduing the world on His behalf. Here, again, Rosenzweig, in line with his view of revelation, rationalizes the actual course of history.

Christianity contains within itself the tension between paganism and true religion. Therefore, it is suited to conquer the pagan world—a process which must continue endlessly, for even the Christian is born a pagan and he must forever battle with the pagan in himself. The Jew, on the other hand, is born a member of the eternal people. But, in order to remain eternal, the Jews have, as a people, forsworn any part in the life of the world. Hence, the Jew can bring the world to God, only through Christianity. Christianity, on the other hand, could not long remain an effective force for redemption, if Israel did not remain in its midst. The Jews are even yet required by Christianity as the "witnesses of God." For they are already at the goal to which Christians continually move. Borrowing the analogy of the medieval poet, Jehuda Halevi, Rosenzweig compares historical revelation to a seed, which falling to the ground, draws the necessary elements to itself, producing a tree, in the fruit of which it reappears again. The ground is the pagan world; the tree is Christianity; the seed is Judaism.

Remarkable indeed are the ways of Providence! Though both Christianity and Judaism are required in the Divine plan, God had set a wall between them, a wall which will not fall until the end of time. This wall consists of the twin phenomena—Jewish pride and antisemitism. The Christian recognizes dimly and unconsciously that Jewry is his "metaphysical enemy," in that the ancient People of the Book persists, and through persisting continues to be to him a reminder of his duty as a Christian. Whenever the pagan within the Christian soul rises in revolt against the yoke of the Cross, he vents his fury on the Jew. Thus, antisemitism cannot be understood simply by an examination of present-day conditions. It stems from the tension in the Christian mind between revelation and paganism. Following his theory that revelation is seen in the totality of its actual results, he regards antisemitism as a proof of revelation—a proof, that is, of the uniqueness and imperishability of Israel. Thus, he writes in a letter to his mother in reference to the "Bible-Babel" controversy, "My proof (of revelation) is not the uniqueness of the Shabbos, but that of 'Rishes.' The fact of antisemitism, age-old and ever present though totally groundless, can be understood only by the different functions which God had assigned to the two communities—Israel to represent in time the eternal Kingdom of God, Christendom to bring itself and the world toward that goal." [6]

(e) PHILOSOPHY OF JUDAISM

ROSENZWEIG'S PRESENTATION OF JUDAISM IN THE "STAR OF REDEMPTION" is admittedly one-sided. Interested as he is in showing Israel to be an eternal "we," he describes Jewry solely from the socio-religious standpoint, as an enduring social unit, built round the belief in a living and loving God. The manner in which Jewish life is blessed with eternity is the predominant consideration to him in his main work. In his smaller essays and in his letters, Rosenzweig displays a lively interest in all phases and problems of Judaism. We shall do well, therefore, to expound his views on Judaism in the form of answers given to these two questions—"What is Judaism as a living faith?" and "What does it mean to become a Jew?"

The first question is concerned with the meaning of Judaism to one who was born and raised in an intensely pious Jewish atmosphere.

The second question deals with the reasons why and the process whereby assimilated Jews may return to their ancient

---

[6] "Briefe," p. 100.

faith. The importance of the second question can hardly be exaggerated in the present time.

Educated Jews the world over are in need of knowing not only Judaism as it is in itself, but the road to Judaism from the outside, secular world in which we live. For every thinking Jew inevitably goes through a period when, placing himself in thought outside the fold, he judges Judaism from the viewpoint of an outsider.

Now, then, as to the first question, Rosenzweig declares that the central belief of the pious Jew is the selection of Israel by God to be the people of priests and a holy nation. So central is this belief in Judaism, he declares, that the systematizers of Jewish thought have never put it forward as an article of belief, taking it more or less for granted. Reflection hesitates to uncover the source of the nation's life. In contrast to the Christian, who feels that he must be converted in his own lifetime, the pious Jew believes that he has been converted already through Abraham. In his blood, the ancient blessing courses mightily; hence, the more Jewish he is, the closer he comes to God. The kinship of blood and family loyalty which unite the grandfather and the grandson are the basic feelings of the Jew. Conscious of the strength of these ties, the Jew knows himself to be part of an eternal people.

In the course of time, the Jews have had to give up all the external possessions of a nation; nevertheless, their faith in their eternity was, if anything, strengthened by this forced surrender. Attachment to a land, to a language, to an independent government—all these loyalties normally reenforce national feelings. But, it may also happen that these partial loyalties drag the nation down with them to oblivion. In identifying its nationhood with any of these external possessions, or even with all of them, a people bears the mark of mortality, since, in the course of world history, countries are apt to undergo changes in population, languages are prone to disappear, and independent sovereignties to be ground out of existence by superior forces. The Jew knows himself to be eternal, precisely because his land is the Holy Land, his language is the Holy Tongue, and his government is the Holy Law. The last named element of Judaism, the Holy Law, is particularly significant in this regard. It is through the constantly changing laws and customs of a people that its vitality is expressed. To obtain the gift of eternity, Israel renounced this privilege of flexibility and forced itself into the mold of an unchangeable Law.[1] These possessions, being spiritual, are not subject to the changes of fortune. The predominant feeling of the pious Jew is, therefore, the knowledge of being a member of the eternal people—a people made eternal by the combination of the physical ties of blood with the belief that this blood-stream is indeed "the holy seed."

In accordance with this supreme consciousness of eternity, the Jew feels that he lives in the world, but is not really of it. Like the philosopher of the school of Spinoza, he views everything "sub specie eternitatis." [2] The struggles of nations through peace and war for their "day" and their "place in the sun" do not really concern him. He does his duty to whatever country he happens to reside in, but in his innermost being he cannot regard any of those national aspirations as his own. It is not that the Jew lives in a secluded world and cares only for the destiny of his own people, but that perforce he views things from the standpoint of God, to whom national and tribalistic boundaries do not exist.

"Indeed, the Jew is really the one man in the Christian world who cannot take war seriously, and is, therefore, the one genuine pacifist!" [3] The Jew is, in the paradoxical position of being most loyal to all humanity in that he is most ardently Jewish. For to be Jewish means to regard with God all men as brothers.

---

[1] "Briefe," p. 113.
[2] S. d. E. Vol. III, p. 90.
[3] S. d. E. Vol. III, p. 88.

Living in eternity, the Jew arranges his calendar so as to represent the triangular process of Being in the annual cycle. Cutting through the year at regular, inflexible intervals, the Sabbath reflects the three categories of Being—creation, revelation and redemption. The Sabbath is primarily the holiday of creation, instituted as it was to remind us of the completion by God of the process of creating the world in six days. But the Sabbath is also the holiday of revelation, since the entire reading of the Law is completed during the Saturdays of the year. Again, the Sabbath represents the category of redemption, for the "Sabbath of the Future," the "Day which is wholly Sabbath," is the Kingdom of God. Thus, in the third Amidah of the Sabbath, we say, "Thou art one and Thy name is One." For though God is even now One, His Name will not be One until the End of Days, when all nations will learn to call upon Him in truth. The three pilgrimage holidays and the High Holidays all are interpreted by Rosenzweig to express different phases of the eternal process of being.

In this part of his work, our philosopher was greatly handicapped by his inadequate knowledge of Jewish laws—a defect which he intended to remedy by writing an exhaustive study of the legal expressions of Judaism. It is not therefore important to restate here his theories concerning Jewish customs. His conception of the nature of Jewish piety is clear enough. We have seen in the previous section the difference between personal prayer and group worship. The first is an expression of revelation as a personal experience. It is a yearning for the nearness of God that every individual in his solitariness can express. Such prayer, divine as it is in origin, is limited in its effectiveness. It cannot bestow eternity—that is, oneness with God's Being. When a group of people however, knowing themselves as an eternal "we," pray together for the Kingdom, God enters into their midst. Now, the Jew obtains his share of eternity, of the "world to

come," through his identification of his relation to God with
his relation to his people. Religion and nationalism, racial
memories and the command of God, the destiny of Israel and
of all mankind—all are inextricably woven together in the
Jewish consciousness. And so it should be for only through
the combination of biological and spiritual unity is the
"eternal we" formed.

Does it mean, then, that the piety of a Jew consists in the
proud announcement, "I am of the seed of Abraham?" By
no means. This basic declaration must needs be supplemented by the knowledge that to Abraham was given the
command to be a blessing to all the nations. The covenant
then concluded is binding upon all the descendants of Abraham and the career then begun is, in essence, to be the career
of his seed down to the end of time. Consciousness of blood,
of destiny and of obligation under the covenant are all
welded together in the mind of the Jew.

The question of racism is not at all involved in this attitude. The Jew does not necessarily believe that all the
descendants of Abraham are endowed with a special religious faculty, that they possess a "genius" for religion, as
the early teachers of the Reform movement have taught.
Nor has this consciousness of Jewish descent anything in
common with the Nazi theories concerning the "purity" of
blood as the foundation of true culture. Rosenzweig merely
calls attention to the fact that in nature there does exist a tie
of blood. The father lives again in the son and the son
knows that he is but a link between the generations preceding
him, that he reveres, and the generations, which he hopes and
trusts will follow him. This natural feeling of family unity
appears in all stages of culture. In nearly all cases, it serves
to engender a clannishness and a separatism that are distinctly undesirable. In early cultures, to be sure, this tie of
clan or tribe was joined with the worship of the tribal idol.
Thus, though religion and tribalism were conjoined, the re-

ligion was itself tribalistic and, therefore, from a cultural standpoint, the resulting union was altogether unfruitful and retrogressive.

In the case of the Jewish people, however, this natural bond was at an early age wedded to the true universalistic and revealed faith, so that a unique social unit emerged—a group in which that national consciousness, which is found at its strongest among primitive people, served as a base for the growth of a tree of faith, the leaves of which reach far into the Kingdom of Heaven. Thus, all the holidays of the Jewish people are connected with some event in their history, though their inner significance is always of a general human character, illustrating the peculiar combination of universalism and particularism in Jewish piety.

To prevent the spread of the conviction within Israel that descent from the seed of Abraham is the sole requisite of salvation, Judaism teaches the doctrine of "shearith yisroel" "the rest of Israel." Not all of Israel is eternal by any means. This distinction of eternity can be claimed only by those who adhere faithfully to Jewish law. Thus, a good life is made the chief requirement of membership in the eternal people. This emphasis on the good life as the proper criterion also serves to bridge the gap between Israel and the rest of mankind. Jew or Gentile—by the same door of good deeds shall they enter the Kingdom of heaven. The election of Israel is an opportunity and a responsibility to the Jew, not a free gift.

In brief summary, then, the believing Jew approaches God through the medium of his people. The basic element of Judaism is the consciousness of being a member of the eternal people of Israel. The eternity of Israel in turn is based, on the one hand, on the feeling of racial unity, and on the other hand, on the complex series of laws and judgments which makes Israel eternal. Through Jewish law, the Jewish people is lifted out of the history of the world. Holy Law is

not subject to the changes of time. It was in the mind of
God at the time of creation and it represents in the present
world the ideal order of the future Kingdom of God. Living
under the Law, the Jew knows himself to be a member of the
eternal "we," which is Israel—a partner with God in the
creation of the world of the future.

We are now prepared to understand fully the message
which Rosenzweig was able to bring to the Jews of his generation, who, like himself, have drifted far from the Jewish
fold. The first requirement in any program for "Baalei
Te'shuva" is to present a motive for the "return." Why
should comfortable men and women, at home in the wide
cosmopolitan world, bestir themselves out of their easy com-
placency and begin to make radical changes in their life?
Having become thoroughly acclimatized to the alien environment, what could Judaism offer them?

To be sure, sensitive Jews have never really felt at home
in the Christian world. No matter how far a Jew may have
strayed from the fold, there remained a "Kera," a rent in
his heart. He was torn between the knowledge that the
people to which he belonged are steadily disappearing
through such faithless conduct as his own and the attraction
of the outside world; between the urge to be part and parcel
of the nation among whom he lived and the realization forced
upon him by recurring unpleasant events that despite his efforts he was still an outsider; between the romantic longing
to maintain the religious ties which linked him with his fathers and the sorry fact that the ancient customs appeared to
him strange and outlandish. Thus, the assimilated Jew
found himself in a sort of No Man's Land, both socially and
spiritually. He could neither die as a Jew nor live as one.
Still, many people spend their entire lifetime in such an
atmosphere. The fact that a situation is spiritually not entirely satisfactory is not a sufficient inducement for a complete spiritual volte face, and oftentimes there are other

compensations in such a life. A stronger motive is needed for a return to Judaism. What then is that motive?

Ever since the emancipation, the main banner under which Jews, who have lost faith in the divine origin of the Torah, were able to reestablish spiritual contact with their people was that of nationalism. This was to be expected, since during this period nationalism had reached its apex in all the Western countries. However, Jewish nationalism was compelled from the beginning to tread a rather tortuous path. To other peoples, nationalism was primarily a political slogan. To emancipated home-seeking Jews, it had to serve as a justification for living a Jewish community life, for the acceptance of at least a measure of Judaism. For Jews live everywhere as a small minority and their cultural assimilation is, in consequence, fairly rapid. Now, it is obvious that nationalism is not a sufficiently strong incentive to prevent the assimilation of a dispersed group, such as Jewry is. This fact is clearly illustrated by the rapid assimilation of immigrant nationalities in the U. S. A. If Jewish nationalism was to serve as a basis for any form of Jewish life, a stronger motive had to be uncovered in it than is commonly seen in European nationalisms. Such attempts were, in fact, made by A'chad Ha'am, S. Dubnow, M. Buber, I. H. Brenner and in our own country, by M. M. Kaplan. None of these attempts can be pronounced satisfactory, for the obvious reason that nationalism does not contain any compelling motive for the observance of any laws or customs whatever. The fact that my nation observed certain laws does not make them true and cannot, therefore, make these laws binding upon me. Thus, the young Jew found himself unable to assent to the claim of the Jewish religion to be true. At the same time, he could not but remain indifferent to any appeals on behalf of his national culture.

Rosenzweig succeeded in effecting a combination between the national and religious motives. His view of revelation

as a gradual process allowed Judaism to be regarded as the
product of the "national spirit." On the other hand, Judaism
was true and hence obligatory upon all Jews. Thus, Rosenzweig was able to reenforce the national motive with the
religious seal of truth and to reestablish Judaism as an
organic unity of nationality and religion.

Considering the religious motive first, we say with Rosenzweig—"Judaism is truth." Every man should ever strive to
be true to himself, to do everything in a spirit of truth. To
think and live "truly" means again, as we have seen, to feel
one's relation to God. A Jew, who is religious, will find in
Judaism the means of living a truly religious life, a life that
is hallowed and commanded by God. His reward is the
knowledge of doing the will of God and of being a part of the
eternal course of Being. No longer does he suffer from the
fear of death, for his true self, the "I" which is aroused
through the saying of Thou by God, is now eternal in God.
More simply, Rosenzweig says, "religion is true and Judaism
to the Jew is the only true religion."

The latter part of the last statement is based upon Rosenzweig's philosophy of history and echoes the national motive.
Things do not merely happen at random. There is a unity in
the events of world-history which reflects the process of the
unfolding of ideas.

Applied to Jewish history, this theory implies that Judaism
and the Jewish destiny are one. In vain, do assimilationists
endeavor to escape Jewish destiny. It cannot be done, simply because history cannot be ignored. The ideals of a people and the history of a people are integrally united. The
actual situation in which modern Jews find themselves points
to the truth of the Jewish religion. The failure of assimilation proves the eternity of the Jewish people, which, in turn,
is the basis of Judaism. Hence, too, the Jewish religion is
more than truth to the Jew; it is his historically decreed fate
as well as the true faith. Thus, he wrote a year before he

began to write his "Star," "In the book will be written no
more than this, that the Jewish 'must' and the Jewish 'will'
('blood' and 'spirit,' 'race' and religion) are one, inconceiv-
ably one, for all that people call history happens so that a
'to will' rises above a 'to be compelled,' and thereby is finally
turned into a new 'must,' whereupon the song begins again
from the beginning." [4]

What does it mean to accept the Jewish religion? More
concretely, is it a matter of accepting certain principles, or
of undergoing certain religious experiences? It will be recalled that the philosophic versions of the Jewish religion
have nearly always been a series of specified beliefs. On the
other hand, in the various Protestant Sects, "conversion" or
a religious experience was regarded as the real entrance into
the fold. In Rosenzweig's view, the first step on the road to
Judaism is to know oneself to be part of the people of Israel,
to feel that the tribulations and the triumphs of the Jewish
people are indeed his own. "Every one should regard himself as if he had gone out of Egypt." [5] The Jew "experiences" religion by reliving the past of his people. Thus, he
writes, "(Judaism) we have only to know as our *own,* therefore not as something which puts demands to us, but as something which belongs to us. Really the entire praxis in this
connection lies in the decision (a decision it is, but an easy
one, because it is suitable for beginners . . .): nil Judaei a
me alienum puto. When this is once said, quietly for oneself—possession is suddenly taken of one's house. One is no
longer 'homeless.' " [6]

This method of arriving at the Jewish religion, by way of
feeling one's unity with the Jewish people, is not to be confused with the approach of the "national-culturists," who
revere the Jewish religion because it is an expression of the

---

[4] "Briefe," p. 200.
[5] "Briefe," p. 200.
[6] "Briefe," p. 380.

"national spirit." To Rosenzweig, the election of the people of Israel by God is a concrete fact. By self-identification with Israel, Rosenzweig means not a mere sympathetic feeling of unity with a mass of wanderers and traders, as Jewry may appear to an outsider, but an active affiliation with Israel, as it knows itself to be the chosen people of God. Thus, the first step is really the acceptance of a belief—the belief that Israel has been elected by God to spread His Name in the world. To those, however, who believe in a living God, who reveals His love and truth to men, this belief is simply historical fact, since Israel did indisputably produce and has long functioned as the agent of the dissemination of the true faith.

Having taken this step of acknowledging the Divine election of Israel, we are next confronted with the question, "how much of the Law is one obligated to observe?" That Jewish life cannot be equated with any sort of "feeling" or religious national consciousness, as Buber and his followers have asserted, seemed clear to Rosenzweig. His strong sense of realities revolted against any emphasis on sentimentalisms. Judaism can be an actual faith only through the observance of the Holy Law, which alone gives it form and brings its external character into concrete expression. In this attitude, he broke sharply with the Reformist approach to the problems of Judaism. Observance of the Mitzvoth, he insisted, must be prior to any mouthing of abstract principles. "Practice precedes theory for us," he wrote, "whereas, with the Reform movement, the contrary was true." [7]

Jewish piety requires that the formal observance of religious rites be supplemented by an inner response, by the proper spiritual attitude. There must be the doing of the Mitzvoth and the feeling of the Kavanah. It is the insistence of the Orthodox that even when the proper Kavanah for the performance of any religious ceremony cannot be summoned,

[7] "Briefe," p. 543.

it is obligatory to perform that ceremony just the same, as a formal observance of ritual is more likely to lead to the development of religious feeling than no observance at all. (Mitzvoth ain Ze'richot Kavanah). Rosenzweig accepts this principle of the Orthodox, though, as we have seen in the first section, he was not able to overcome entirely his previous habits. In letters to his friends, he urged that the deed must come before the inner response, that the Mitzvah be done even before the right Kavanah has welled up from the depths of the soul. In opposition to the neo-mystics, he wrote, "Your Hassid too did not begin with Kavanah. That will come one day, of course. But to desire to begin with that, as people tell us we must, is entirely un-Jewish." [8]

The acceptance of the Law must come first. But again the former question, how much of the Law should one accept? Rosenzweig was moved to ask this question since in his day there no longer existed one form of Judaism. He willingly granted that, had he lived a hundred years earlier, he would have advocated the outright return to the complete Torah-true life. Living, however, as he did in the twentieth century, he felt that the demand of all or nothing on the part of the Orthodox could only serve to slam the door in the face of the would be "baalei teshuva," with the spiritual plight of whom he had been primarily concerned.

Besides this argument from expediency, Rosenzweig was compelled to consider this question by the nature of his theory of revelation. It will be recalled that Rosenzweig's view of revelation did not accord a blanket certification of the entire Shulchan Aruch as coming from God. The Holy Law in general is a part of the Divine intention in the election of Israel, but the detailed minutiae of Jewish customs and tradition, may be largely human in origin. How, then, is one to separate the Divine from the human, the temporary from the eternal in Judaism?

---

[8] "Briefe," p. 356.

There is no definite answer to this question in Rosenzweig's writings. He insists that the "coming" to Judaism is the important point and that the "going" will somehow take care of itself.[9] Writing as he does from the standpoint of the dejudaized Jews, who seek to find the way home, he is concerned principally with the first steps—to know oneself part of the "Holy Nation," to study the Torah as the Word of God. In commenting on Buber's "Reden," Rosenzweig notes the basic defect to be the absence of emphasis on Jewish Law and he adds the thought that the nature of Jewish Law will be determined by those who in all earnestness accept the destiny of Israel. Recalling the Talmudic statement, "Do not say thy sons, but thy builders," he argues that those who know themselves to be the children of Israel will, through their actions and life, build the Judaism of the future. Divine revelation will be as effective in the present as it was in the past. As he put it rather succinctly, "Judaism is not Law. It creates Law, but is not it. It is to be a Jew."[10] The nature of future Judaism can confidently be left to the loving care of its devotees.

Nevertheless, he was not willing to concede that any part of Jewish Law is definitely to be discarded. In a letter which he wrote to the discussion leaders of the Lehrhaus, he expressed his concern over and disagreement with the following statement of his philosophy of Judaism, "only the election of the people itself is from God and every particular in the Law is only from men."[11] He explains in that letter that a series of ritual laws were implied in the Divine election of Israel, as was pointed out above. But, the extent to which the revealed Law coincides with the traditional system of laws must remain doubtful. Then, he offers the suggestion that there

---

[9] "Briefe," p. 384.
[10] "Briefe," p. 425.
[11] "Briefe," p. 518.

may not be any hard and fixed boundary lines between the human and the Divine laws.

As in the mystical experience of God, man is able to say only *that* he has experienced God, not *what* he is, so, too, there is a line of division between the expressible and the inexpressible in everyday religious experience. Only the unity of election and law need be postulated a priori as essential to Judaism. The numerous details of the Law must be proven to be Divine in actual life. If, then, any religious ceremony ever becomes an instrument through which man feels that he can say, "Praised art Thou, O Lord," then is that ceremony to be accepted as obligatory. The conclusions of the historical schools of Welhausen and Weber, and the psychology of Freud, Rosenzweig is willing to accept, if they can be shown to be scientifically valid, but he regards their findings as irrelevant to the question of the religious value of any ceremony. For the value of any religious ceremony can be known only in the moment of its performance and cannot later be retold. "People understand differently, when they understand in doing. Every day in the year, Bileam's speaking ass may be a legend to me; on the Sabbath Balaak, when it speaks to me out of the uplifted Torah, it is not." Then it comes as the Word of God. The proof of the authoritativeness of any law in Judaism is, therefore, the extent to which that law serves today to awaken the religious consciousness. Yet, all laws must be taken to begin with as God-given. As of old, Judaism must be accepted in the words with which the Israelites received it at Sinai—"Naaseh ve'-nishma." Thus, Rosenzweig concludes, "I would not dare to declare any law as human, because it has not yet been permitted to me to say through it in proper fashion, 'praised art Thou.'"

For all practical purposes, then, Rosenzweig advocated a return to Orthodox Judaism. His conception of an "eternal people," regulating its life by an unchangeable law, required even a larger measure of adherence to the "Shulchan Aruch" than he preached. Yet, he never identified himself with Orthodoxy, because he was repelled by the form which neo-Orthodoxy assumed in Germany in the last generation. In particular, he resented the complete change in emphasis from the People of Israel to the Torah of Israel, which S. R. Hirsch and his followers had brought about. Along with the Zionists who saw only nationalism in Judaism he classified as "little Jews" the neo-Orthodox who reduce Judaism to a dogmatic, ready-made "religion." [12]   Repelled, too, he was by the formalism and the legalism of so many men, who call themselves Orthodox. Despite these aversions, he felt a real kinship with the believing Jew of all ages. And he had the greatest right so to feel. For in modern times, there has not yet appeared one who was so completely modern and yet, in the best sense, so thoroughly Jewish. Some writers and leaders choose the easy way of effecting a "synthesis" between the ancient faith of the Jew and the modern way of thinking, in that they simply close their eyes to some one or several of the questions involved. Rosenzweig strove valiantly with basic issues and emerged victorious.

It may perhaps be expected that having completed the presentation of Rosenzweig's philosophy of Judaism, we should now offer a critical evaluation of it. Unfortunately, it is true that much of Rosenzweig's thought is built upon Hegelian and "existential" theories, which are little understood and less accepted in American circles. There is, therefore, the pressing and sacred task of extracting the seed from the shell in Rosenzweig's philosophy, that the permanent elements in his teaching may exert their proper weight of influence in our own country. While we intend to contribute toward this goal in later essays, we feel that to present such a critique in this chapter would prejudice the readers against taking the trouble to delve for themselves in the works

---

[12] "Briefe," p. 282.

of Rosenzweig. This, indeed, is the aim we set for ourselves in the writing of this essay, to acquaint the reader with the background and the pre-suppositions of Rosenzweig's thought, in order that he may then turn to the brilliant philosopher's own writings. We have been able to present in these pages only the dry bones of the great "baal teshuvah's" system. The spirit which permeates his work perforce escapes analysis. And that spirit is great and bright, glowing with the fire of God.

CHAPTER IV

MARTIN BUBER

(*a*) Early Religious Experiences and Intuitions

MARTIN BUBER HAS OFTEN BEEN CALLED THE ACHAD HA'AM of German Jewry. Like the great thinker of Odessa, he was an outstanding Zionist leader, concerned pre-eminently with the spiritual implications of Zionism. As editor of the Zionist periodical "Weg," Buber was the most outstanding exponent of Jewish national renaissance in Western Europe. His influence grew in the course of time far beyond the confines of the Zionist movement. His speeches on the nature of Judaism brought him a host of ardent disciples, who saw in him a veritable modern prophet, come to point the way to the distraught souls of our era. This circle of admirers includes great men in the fields of history and philosophy—such as, Hans Kohn, Hugo Bergmann and Max Brod.

As Buber turned his attention more and more to the problems of religion, his influence spread far beyond the sphere of Jewish life. He became one of the preachers of a new spiritual orientation to life, which, according to many writers, is of revolutionary importance in the progress of the philosophy of religion. His thoughts on the nature of the spiritual life, expressed with uncommon force and clarity, attracted world-wide attention. Wilhelm Michel, a Christian, wrote of him, "The German world-hour lives in him, though he may seem to be so exclusively preoccupied with the problems of Judaism." [1] Karl Heim, the great Protestant theologian, was most deeply influenced by Buber, as were also a number of less-known writers in the fields of sociology and religion. As Ronald Gregor Smith, an English writer, sums up the importance of his main work on religion, "In view of this in-

---

[1] Wilhelm Michel, "Martin Buber, Sein Gang in die Wirklichkeit" Frankfurt, 1926.

fluence alone, it may be affirmed that 'I and Thou' will rank as one of the epoch-making books of our generation." [2]

At present, Buber is on the faculty of the Hebrew University in Jerusalem, engaged in the study and the teaching of the religion of the Bible. Uprooted from the soil of German philosophy, Buber's influence has waned considerably in recent years. Still, his version of Judaism deserves most careful analysis and consideration.

1. The whole public and literary life of Martin Buber was dominated by one central motif—the feeling that true life can only be found by entering into personal relations with the environment. He did not always conceive this idea in the broad light of day. In the beginning, it appeared to him as through a cloud, giving some token of its presence, but not revealing its identity. It was not till 1924 that he was able to give a clear account of this experience and of its meaning for him.

2. However, even in the earlier period of his life, the marks of this conviction can be recognized in his active career. Buber lived his philosophy, long before he was able to express it. If we had attempted to learn his personal philosophy merely by observing his position on the various issues of the day, we should have been led to conclude that, to him, true life is a system of intimate relationships. To Buber, the central fact of life is love, the total and devoted orientation of one's will toward the needs of a fellow being. No erotic elements need enter into this attitude. It is a voluntary and conscious concentration of all one's energies and interests about one object that is conceived as returning this devotion.

To be self-centered, Buber believes, is to be uprooted from reality, is to rot in cold death, even if reveling in luxury. For life is not in man, but man is in life. Foolish indeed is the man who endeavors to hoard his life and interests for the

---

[2] See his introduction to English translation of "I and Thou."

sake of his self. He loses the very thing he is striving for
and is dead even when he thinks he is most alive, since life
is between persons and between things, not in them. "The
wicked even in their lifetime are called dead," remarks the
Talmud.[3] Those who wrest themselves forcefully from this
relation of love in order to enhance their personal happiness
are doomed to sterility and unreality. Like the man who
attempted to imprison the moon in a barrel of water, they
lose their own life by the endeavor to fence it off from the
rest of the world.

3. This conviction dominates Buber's career from the very
beginning of his appearance as a public figure. He tells us
in his little book, "Daniel," that as a lad of seventeen he first
had the experience, which he was later to interpret as the
"I-Thou" relation. He was then in deep sorrow over the
loss of a dear friend and, in the endeavor to regain his health,
was engaged in solitary contemplation in the mountains of
Switzerland. Chancing to peer from a great height into a
deep lake below, he was at first struck with the strangeness,
the total foreignness of the abyss below. But, as he continued to gaze at the dark surface beneath him, he suddenly
felt that the lake was no longer a stranger to him, that its
expression was indeed that of an animate visage, even as
"the face of a dog." [4]

4. This early experience illustrates another peculiarity of
Buber's thought. It is possible to enter into living relation
with all things, be they ever so humble. A stone, a lake, a
tree, even an institution can be turned into living reality by
the magic wand of intention. It is not at all necessary to
assume that these objects are animated with some kind of
soul. No panpsychism is implied in the experience, though
this conclusion is not definitely ruled out in the later writings
of Buber. It is sufficient to note that personality in the

---

[3] B'rachot, p. 18.
[4] Daniel, p. 37.

vaguest sense is imputed by man to the object of his attention.

5. It is interesting to observe that, according to Bergson, the removal of the horror of strangeness from the dark lake by the imputation of life to it is the manifestation of a characteristically religious reaction. It is the function of "static religion" to ascribe "intention" to crucial events in nature in order to counteract the solvent effect of intelligence and to make man feel at home in the world. It is in this instinctive reaction that Bergson claimed to find the source of primitive religion. As a modern instance of this phenomenon, Bergson cited a famous passage from William James' description of his impressions of the earthquake in California. James, taken by surprise at the elemental power of nature, apprehended the earthquake as a personal force, exclaiming, "go to it."

Though we note the resemblances between Bergson's instinctive reaction and the experience of Buber, we must not fail to observe the vital differences between the two descriptions. In the case of the supposed reaction of primitive man, the attribution of benevolent intentions to nature is made in reference to a certain definite impending action. The attitude of primitive man remains self-centered. The "power" his imagination conjures up will help him, he believes, to turn the course of events in his favor. In the case of Buber, there is not in the experience described above or in the similar experiences described in his writings, any reference to an action, favorable or not, that the imagined self would do. The author does not expect any favors from the self that he envisions. Rather, it is the case that he gives his devotion to that self which in turn gives itself to him. While primitive man says, "Help me to get this or that," Buber says, "I seek not thy goods, but thee alone."

6. The first movement in which Buber's basic conviction found expression was Zionism. Like most Jewish young men

at the end of the nineteenth century, Buber felt the claim
upon him of two rival cultures. Reared during his early
childhood in the religious and scholarly atmosphere of his
grandfather's home at Lemberg, he had a deep interest in the
customs and ceremonies of the Jewish religion. Though he
early ceased to abide by the laws of Judaism, he apparently
retained a sentimental attachment for them, which he could
not wholly explain to the satisfaction of his rationalistic
Western standards. Buber knew himself to be rooted in
both the East and the West and he was painfully uncertain
whether the twain could meet. The rising wave of nationalism at the turn of the century helped to increase the perplexity of Buber. Since it was no longer possible for men
to be regarded merely as members of the human race, where
did he belong? The emergence of Zionism under the leadership of Dr. Theodore Hertzl provided the answer. He was
a member of the Jewish nation and only as such would he
contribute to the advancement of general human culture. In
Zionism, he found an anchor for his soul. He now knew
that he belonged to his people and he set out to discover the
meaning of this new and exhilarating relationship.

There is nothing particularly striking about Buber's conversion to Zionism, as this movement enjoyed then a vogue
among his contemporaries, to many of whom it came as a
new revelation. But, his view of Zionism is somewhat original and it bears the marks of the dominant conviction of his
life: the belief that life is, in essence, a complex of personal
relationships.

Zionism, to him, was a movement, not a party. One must
be a Zionist; it cannot be lightly taken up. He early joined
the wing of Zionism led by Achad Ha'Am which saw in the
movement primarily a spiritual revival.[5] Through the return of a substantial number of Jews to Palestine, the vitality

---

[5] Jüd. Bewegung, 1, p. 12, 29.

of the Jewish spirit would be renewed. All Jews should even now live as Zionists. Caught in the current of the nationalistic movements in Europe, Buber maintained that one's nationality is the sole means by which one may become creative.[6] Nationalism means "to penetrate to one's own being, to discover oneself, to win oneself."[7] Through nationalism, one finds humanity and creativeness. Thus far, Buber follows in the footsteps of Achad Ha'Am.

He strikes a different and characteristic note with his emphasis on the joy and vitality of life which he thought Zionism would bring. We note here an echo of his basic conviction that the forces of life are more real than abstract reasoning and codes of moral obligation. The object of Zionism is not the realization of a special ideal, but the enhancement of all the vital forces of the nation. The Zionist was not to retire to the sombre atmosphere of the Jewish religion, nor even to cultivate exclusively the national spirit, Achad Ha'Am's "Torah Sheb'lev." His field was to be the totality of human relations and interests, and to this all-embracing task, he was to bring a characteristic approach.

Buber found the essence of the Jewish character to be displayed, in modern times, in Chassidism, in previous epochs, in the "suberranean religion," which at different times broke forth in revolt against the barrenness of legalism. Assuming with Achad Ha'Am the existence of a Jewish national soul, he differed from the latter in regarding the essence of the Jewish soul as being the discovery of the divine spirit in all phases of life. Spurning the logic of asceticism, Judaism undertakes to hallow even the impulses of the flesh, for all life is holy. Following this line of thought, Buber came to the conclusion that, nothing that breathes the spirit of life could be foreign to Judaism. In this expansion of the scope of Judaism, he aligned himself with the group led by

---

[6] Ibid., p. 37.
[7] Ibid., p. 37.

Berdichefsky, which revolted against the narrow moralism of Achad Ha'Am.

In Buber's view of Zionism, we note the influence of his basic conception in the following two beliefs: 1. That one's own deeper self is reached only when one relates himself to a larger group. 2. That this relationship is not restricted in significance to any one phase of life, but that it has meaning for the whole of life.

Naturally, these ideas were floating about in the circles in which Buber moved, but his selection of them illustrates the inner consistency of his views. The idea that one's deeper self can be reached only through identification of oneself with a group was particularly in vogue among the neo-Romantics of the first decades of this century. Anti-intellectualism was then gaining ground in all fields of speculation. In the field of political thinking, attention was concentrated upon the specific qualities of nationalities.

The feeling that the actual world of space and time was but the reflection of a deeper current of reality was also general among Buber's friends. "Die Neue Gemeinschaft," a group formed for the purpose of clarifying the conception of an ideal society was dominated by mystic tendencies. Gustav Landauer, its most brilliant representative at the time when Buber joined it, sought to find humanity by going inwards, feeling in one's own life the biologic unity of mankind. In this group, the distinction earlier made by Ferdinand Tönnies between "Gesellschaft" and "Gemeinschaft" was current. The former is an aggregate of individuals regulated by a set of reciprocal relations; the latter is an intuitive and free organic unity wherein every individual feels the whole. The "Gemeinschaft" was to be achieved by the cultivation of the instinctive forms of union—the family, the clan, the folk.

Among Jewish writers, the confidence and inner security attained by the feeling of community of blood is perhaps best expressed by Richard Beer Hoffman in his famous poem "Schlaflied an Miriam." While rocking the baby, the poet is overcome with sadness at the thought that the little child will have to go through life all alone, for in this world "Keiner kann keinem Gefährte nichte sein." Then, however, he is consoled as he realizes the biologic unity of the race, of past and future generations. "In uns sind alle, wer fühlt sich allein? Du bist ihr Leben, ihr Leben ist dein." This thought is expressed by the same author with greater detail in the drama "Yaakob's Traum," in which Jacob says that he cannot listen to reason but must hearken to the voice of his ancestors which comes through his veins.[8]

7. The second Jewish movement which effected a revolution in Buber's inner life is Chassidism. In the autobiographical essay, "Mein Weg zum Chassidimus," Buber describes the tremendous impression which this religious movement, then already far gone in its decline, exercised upon him.

He admired especially the following elements in Chassidism, elements which he later incorporated in his own philosophy:

a. The establishment of communal life on a basis of common reverence of the divine truth. The Chassidic community was oriented toward a "living center," the Tzaddik, who stands in direct personal relation with every disciple.

b. The view of Chassidism that "God can be seen in everything and can be reached through every act." For, nothing exists without a divine spark. Yet, this view does not identify God with the world. Rather is the whole world conceived as but "a word out of God's mouth." Hence, God can be served by every act of man.

---

[8] See Hans Kohn—Martin Buber pp. 96, 188, 200, 204. For Buber's comments on F. Tönnies' views on "Gemeinschaft" see his "Worte an die Zeit," first paper.

c. The idea that God is to be served through joy, especially through the bringing of joy into the lives of other people, and through the cultivation of the feeling of brotherhood.

d. The high emphasis laid upon the power of intention. The act alone is not as important as the intention of the act. The highest level of intention, enthusiasm, makes one God-like. (This is the thought which Buber wrote into his biography of Rabbi Israel Baal Shem).

e. It represents a form of mysticism which does not require seclusion from social life and which finds its most consummate expression in the believer's confrontation of the actual problems of life with a keen awareness of God.

f. The perpetual readiness of Chassidim for the coming of the Messiah and the feeling that every good action helps to hasten his coming. The Kingdom of God may, at any moment, become a present reality.

Not one of these aspects of Chassidism, taken by itself, could have seemed unique to Buber, who possessed even at that time a profound knowledge of the history of mysticism. The reason this movement obtained so powerful a hold on his imagination was the fact that it appeared to him to be a characteristic product of the creative Jewish spirit. Arising among the common people and bearing no marks of foreign influence, Chassidism appeared to him to be a revelation of his own deeper nature.

Buber spent many years studying the original documents of Chassidism. Later, he published translations of some Chassidic legends. He relates in the essay mentioned above that he endeavored to live through every episode that he translated. Indeed, the biographical stories collected by Buber are as much records of the spiritual life of the author as they are of the legendary personalities about whom they are woven. The stories are characterized by a strong note of mystery. The reader is filled with a haunting sense of

awe, as if the presence of God were hovering behind the veil
of phenomena, ready to break forth in splendor at any moment.[9]

In Buber's enthusiastic acceptance of Chassidism, we can
therefore note his basic conviction that a life of personal relationships with the universe is possible. Heaven is all about
us, if we would only see it.

8. The first views of Buber on the nature of the mystic
experience were set forth in the little volume "Die Rede, Die
Lehre und Das Lied." At that time, he still conceived of
ecstasy as attaining actual union with God. Later, he was
to reject this view most emphatically. In the introduction
to "Ecstatische Confessionen" he expounds the view that the
yearning for mystical ecstasy is due to the duality of the "I"
and the "world," which all men seek to overcome. This goal
is reached in ecstasy, but only those who have actually experienced an ecstasy are able to appreciate its nature, since
it is essentially inexpressible.

In the introduction to the sayings of Laotse, he confesses
the belief that "Die Lehre" hovers over and above the realms
of Being and Ought, descending to the latter, ever and anon,
to rejuvenate religion. The teaching is realized only in the
united life. Man's knowledge is no knowledge, for it is
achieved only by way of separation, of abstraction from the
whole. Man's action is no action, for it is generally expressive of only a part of oneself. True action is the action of
the whole being, is non-action. In the introduction to the
"kalewala," Buber claims that the song is prior to the word.
Men sang to men and to God before they were able to put
definite meaning into their noises. For, to employ Buber's
language of a later date, "in the beginning was 'Thou.'"

These essays do not reveal a consistent view of mysticism.

---

[9] See Note 1 at end of book.

They contain flashes of insight which were not yet coordinated in the author's mind at the time, and which were later to be merged in the "I-Thou" conception.

9. The same verdict must be pronounced on the book of "Daniel," which represents a far more sustained attempt to describe the mystical experience and its relevance to the problems of life. There is a loose connection between the five dialogues which compose the book, but no systematic unity. The author views the experience which is central to him from various angles. It is therefore best to examine the content of each dialogue separately, without attempting to expound the philosophy of the book as a whole.

a. The first dialogue deals with the concept of direction. The view is put forward that each person is endowed with a definite direction of consciousness. Most of us may be described as living in the realm of space, which consists of an infinity of directions. Our attention apprehends things and events from an objective viewpoint—that is, without reference to any particular line of direction. But, we possess, in addition, the faculty of viewing things as cutting across a kind of space which is formed by the radiation of lines of direction from our selves as the centers. Absolute space, Buber seems to argue, results from a particular human attitude; therefore, he sees nothing impossible in the assumption of a spaceless orientation of the soul along a line of direction peculiar to it. Strictly speaking, the apprehension of space is present also in the directed consciousness. The term "direction" can have meaning only in space. The difference meant by Buber is between a space in which all points are equally significant and one in which a particularly luminous core shines out.

Buber compares absolute space to a cross onto which man is nailed. It is possible, he declares, for the horizontal cross piece of the cross of space to fall down and for man to feel as standing in the perpendicular line, indeed, as being the perpendicular line.[10]   He relates an experience of looking into the dark night.   The sense of fear with which the darkness affected him was gradually lifted when he managed "to tear out of the infinity of directions" the one which corresponded to his own direction.   He was now a "brother," feeling the sorrow of the night and no longer frightened by it. This experience is but another example of the urge to enter into personal relationship with the universe that is so characteristic of Buber.   The word "brother" is extremely significant in this description, as it indicates the intimate nature of the connection involved.   The direction is the way from essence to essence, is without mediation, and therefore true.

Another example of the way the directional attitude can be attained is given in the same dialogue.   A man looks at a pine tree "with all his directed powers" and identifies himself so completely with it that he feels its bark as if it were his own skin and its cones as if they were his own children, while yet he remains conscious of his direction.   Then, and only then, he receives true knowledge; he is transplanted into the spiritual realm of direction, "from the earth of space" to "the earth of soul" (p. 15).[11]   In the realm of the "directional" spirit, true self is not dissolved, for the unity of the direction is still maintained.

This life of direction, Buber extols as blessed and he condemns as cowardly the flight into the ordered world of science. He asserts that the one necessity which truly matters in human life is the necessity of the soul to seek its own direction.

We find in this description of direction all the elements that were later described by Buber as inherent in the "I-Thou" relation.   The outstanding difference is the emphasis here placed on the person seeking to realize his own direc-

---

[10] Ibid., p. 9.
[11] Ibid., p. 15.

tion whereas in the "Thou" relation, as we shall see, the emphasis is placed on the response made to the apprehended object.

b. In the second dialogue, Buber deals with what he calls actuality. He asserts that there are two fundamental attitudes to life—those of orienting and of actualizing, respectively. The former is the attitude of both common sense and science; it consists in placing things in their spatial, temporal and causal contexts in accordance with set and invariable rules. The latter consists in meeting all things and events with the whole of one's being. The term "actuality" is referred to the latter mode of experiencing only, because things so apprehended are real in a unique sense, "as the higher meaning of a word is found in a poem." [12]

Buber advances the interesting hypothesis that both the primitive savage and the child are living in "actuality." Civilized man is a stranger to this realm, obtaining glimpses of it only from time to time. We also find in this dialogue the view which was later so masterfully elaborated, that "all actuality is filled connection; nothing individual is in itself actual." [13] He interprets the voice coming from eternity as commanding "be!" whereas later, he was to construe its message as being the imperative "do!" The false, unreal and unblessed reply of most men is here, as in the later book, described as "Ich weiss Bescheid."

c. The third dialogue deals with the concept of meaning (Sinn). The anecdote is told of a young man who, while peacefully rowing one evening, was suddenly overcome with a disquieting feeling that an abyss was yawning beneath him. When this hallucination passed away, there remained the feeling of unrest and the presentiment of imminent danger. The youth was obsessed with the doubleness of the "bright One" and the "dark Other"—that is, the cleft be-

---

[12] Ibid., p. 35.
[13] Ibid., p. 42.

tween subject and object. The various philosophic schemes
by which this contrast is overcome, he was forced to recognize as inadequate.

Buber assures the young man that his experience of the
abyss marked his entrance into the spiritual life.[14] For
security belongs to the attitude of orientation, whereas the
life of actualization is attended with the constant apprehension of danger. The laws of causality which prevail in the
physical universe form the basis of the confidence felt by
the orienting consciousness. The life of actualization, on the
other hand, is lived in freedom and hence involves the taking
of risks. In this form of life, every thing and every event
assumes new significance. In the experienced duality, man
finds his task: "to create unity out of his and all duality."[15]
He construes "all that happens to him as a message, he does
what is necessary as a task and a demonstration."[16] The
deed of man assumes cosmic significance. By his decision
he helps God to be realized, for even the Supreme Being can
be actualized only through man.

It cannot be said, that "a clear and distinct idea" is contained in this dialogue. It urges a kind of "universe loyalty."
The universe is vitiated by many dualities, which it is the
task of man to overcome by his deeds. The idea of receiving
all that comes to us as a message embodies the central conception of the "I-Thou" relation. That everything in the
universe calls to us is illustrated in the dialogue by the example of one who, looking up one evening, felt a star saying
to him "all the time I was turned toward you." This experience comes closest to the saying of "Thou" as described
in the next section.

d. The fourth dialogue is devoted to an attempt to clarify
the meaning of the duality or dualities which compose the

---

[14] Note 2 end of book.
[15] Ibid., p. 82.
[16] Ibid., p. 76.

world. The view is set forth that the "I" of the spirit is primarily two-fold (urzweiheit). Being consists of two poles, "Wesen" and "Gegenwesen." Unity between these poles never is, but always becomes. Our spiritual deeds are dominated by the desire "to express the world—these establish the rainbow bridge from pole to pole." [17] This theory is not offered as an intellectual hypothesis, but as an experienced insight or revelation.[18] Buber describes very eloquently the certainty and the force with which he felt that "the streams that ran from pole to pole ran through (his) heart." [19]

Buber does not explain the nature of the medium, in which the two poles form contrasting opposites. Is it to be understood as being simply space? Obviously not, for the life of the spirit is viewed as in a sense spaceless. This point therefore remains obscure for the present. It is important to note, however, that the concepts borrowed from the theory of magnetism with which Buber here operates accord perfectly with the interpretation given in this study at the end of the third section, of the "I-Thou" relation.

e. In the fifth and last dialogue, Buber deals with the task of unity. Man must first become conscious of duality. Then he is to overcome that duality by action. "Unity must be lived, must be capable of realization." [20]

The vagueness of this advice need not be stressed. We must not fail to note, however, the presence of the same general insight of Buber's beneath this misty view. That the world is dual means that the different parts of the world need each other and this need is somehow satisfied in action.

It should also be remembered that the different dialogues in "Daniel" are descriptions of different phases of an actual religious experience. The author, for instance, tells us that

---

[17] Ibid., p. 119.
[18] Note 3 end of book.
[19] Ibid., p. 97.
[20] Ibid., p. 145.

he found a two-foldness in himself—"one half of him became
life, the other half death." [21]   Currents and cross currents
agitated his innermost being. Then, by means of a supreme
effort, he achieved the concentration of power within himself
so that he was no longer inwardly separated. "I have torn
down within me," he writes, "the eternal wall, the wall
within me." [22]

In "Daniel" we have then a preliminary attempt to comprehend the nature of the religious experience, which was
powerfully real to Buber. No final and consistent formulation is arrived at. This task was left for the much later work,
"Ich und Du."

10. We can gain further insight into the development of
Buber's religious philosophy by an examination of his views
on Judaism. In a series of lectures to the Bar Kochba Society at Prague, Buber outlined his views on the meaning of
the Jewish problem and on the destiny of the Jewish people.
These lectures, later printed in book form, exercised con-
siderable influence in Jewish circles. The Bar Kochba Society consisted of Jewish students, mostly from Western
Europe, who had already become estranged from the ideas
and practices of the Jewish faith. The message of Buber,
expressed as it was with angelic fervor, had the effect of re-
kindling within many of them the sense of kinship with the
Jewish religion. From the ranks of these students, great
thinkers and writers arose who were later to extend and
to deepen the views of their master.[23]

An extended examination of these lectures does not belong
within the scope of this treatise, since we are here primarily
concerned with Buber's views on the nature of the religious
experience. Yet it is instructive to note his ideas on the

---

[21] Ibid., p. 137.

[22] Ibid., p. 138.

[23] For an enumeration of the men active in the Bar Kochba Society, who
were deeply influenced by Buber, see Hans Kohn's "Martin Buber" p. 314.

Jewish people, since they reflect the general tendency of his thought.

His analysis of the Jewish problem opens with the observation that the inner life of every individual Jew is the battleground of forces which provide the setting for the problem to be solved by Jews in all ages, and in all lands. Buber builds his thesis on the foundation of an extreme form of folkism. "Now, the folk is to him (man) a community of people, who were, are and will be a community of dead, living and yet unborn, who together constitute a unity; and this is the unity which he perceives as the ground of his own 'I,' his 'I' which is but a necessary link eternally determined to occupy a definite place in this great chain. What all the people in this great chain have created and will create, that he feels to be the work of his own inner life, what they have experienced and will experience, that he perceives to be his own inner fate. The past of his folk is his own personal memory, the future of his folk is his personal task. The way of his folk teaches him to understand his own self and to will his own self." [24] In this view, Buber reflected the mystic spirit of nationalism, which looks upon all nations as unchanging individuals.

Viewing the role of the Jewish people in world history in the light of this racial hypothesis, Buber concludes that the peculiar aptitude of the Jewish people lies in the field of religion. He was preceded in this belief by the founders of the Reform Movement in Germany, who argued that the Jewish people must be kept alive for the sake of maintaining the Jewish racial genius for religion. The description Buber offers of the typical Jewish character is really a mirror image of Buber's own spiritual experience. He claims that the Jewish soul is particularly sensitive to the tension between the two poles of Reality. The Jew is more apt to find him-

---

[24] "Reden uber das Judentum," first lecture.

self torn between the spirit and the flesh, the claims of the ideal and the temptations of the real. The "divided soul," which all students of the psychology of religion have described, Buber regards as peculiarly a Jewish phenomenon. Needless to say that the lack of emphasis on the experience of conversion in Jewish literature is an unanswerable refutation of this claim, quite apart from the absurdity of the racial theories on which it is based.

Since the characteristic Jewish trait is inner disunion, the urge to attain inner unity becomes the chief drive of the Jewish soul. This craving for unity may find expression in divers fields of research. But its main direction is in the field of the spirit. In religion, the call from God, which is the cause of the experienced feeling of duality, as indicated in "Daniel," spurs the Jews on to ever greater spiritual insights.

Buber thinks of the "unity" sought by the religious person as a kind of Hegelian synthesis, a unity which becomes the source of further dualities on a higher plane. The spiritual insights of the past, which have since been crystallized into institutions, become the matter which a new act of unity must imprint with fresh form. This "unity," Buber seems to regard as the goal of every Jew, great or humble; and he does not distinguish it clearly from the mystic quest for unity.

Along with this special sensitiveness to the duality of the universe, go certain limitations of the Jewish genius. The Jew is more ear-man than eye-man; he lives more in time than in space. He is hardly capable of contemplation, of seeing things as they are. But he is forever conscious of what ought to be done, of the claims of the future upon the present. He is a motor being, anxious to realize the ideal within the actual. Hence, not "unity," the creative insight into new value, but the "deed," the endeavor to actualize the ideal in the real world, is the ultimate goal of Jewish striving.

For, the unity meant by Buber is not alone within the self and within thought, but between the self and the world and between thought and action.

Thus, the Jew can find peace with himself only by accepting in complete earnestness his task as a "servant of God." He must study the history, life and ideals of his people, feeling himself to be but a drop in the eternal current of his people's life. Then he will hear the call of God and become spiritually creative, for, "only the one truly bound to his people can answer with his whole being." [25] It is not necessary to adopt the outward forms of the faith. For, the inner growth of the spirit, unperceivable by the naked eye, is all that truly matters. "All religious creation, all genuine personal religion is a discovery and a taking up of an ancient treasure, a development and a liberation of the grown subterranean folk religion." [26]

In the seventh address of this group, printed under the title "Der Heilige Weg," Buber carries his thought about the "urjüdischer Geist" still further. The Jewish spirit, he declares, is attuned to the essential message of religion: human life is to be dominated by the consciousness of the presence of the Deity. To live in this spirit of piety does not involve the necessity of turning one's back upon the world; on the contrary, the aim of religion is to infuse the light of God into the actual living world.

Buber compares God to the sun and explains that He is to be found not so much in things as between them, in the lines of connection which mold the world into one system. In every essence is laid the Allbeing, but it cannot develop except in the essence's connection with all else. The Divine can and does arise in the individual, but it is fully manifested only in the relation between individuals. It follows that the true place of the realization of the Divine is the community,

---

[25] Cheruth, p. 8.
[26] Cheruth, p. 10

and "the true community is the one which realizes the Divine."

We note in this essay important modifications of the ideas contained in "Daniel." The lines of direction and the currents streaming from Pole to Pole described in that book are now conceived as being rays of God's presence. Also, instead of mere universe loyalty, we now have the concept of loyalty to the ideal human society. The whole complex of ideas, furthermore, is regarded as peculiar to Judaism. Buber agrees that Judaism was never formulated in these terms, but, he claims that it was expressed in the living ideals of the Jew. He interprets the Jewish longing for God as being the yearning for the Kingdom of God. The consciousness of Israel's election means the resolution to begin immediately the task of redeeming the universe—that is, we should not withhold our endeavors until the day when all other nations are similarly minded. The Jewish soul looks for God in the processes that make for the perfection of existence.[27] In the last analysis, salvation must come from man, for it is man's special task to establish God's power on earth.

Buber finds the uniqueness of Judaism to lie in the unity within it of both the religious and the ethical elements. To be religious means to help bring about the perfection of human society, the attainment of the Messianic Age. Thus, he interprets the threefold covenant in the Pentateuch as symbolic of the three basic ideas of religion. Adam was made in the image of God for it is the task of man to become Godlike; Abraham was taught that this task involves sacrifice. Israel, molded at Mt. Sinai as "a people of priests," learned that God is revealed not in the individual, but in the group.

In the course of reviewing the fortunes of this "urjüdischer Geist" in the history of the Jewish people, Buber represents

---

[27] See Note 4 at end of book.

the mystical societies as alone dedicated to this ideal. Throughout the greater part of Jewish history, official Judaism, being the crystallization of early insights, dammed the stream of the creative Jewish spirit and compelled it to flow along subterranean channels. Thus the Essenes, Jesus and the early Christians, and the Chassidim are described as exponents of the authentic expressions of the Jewish soul. These groups attempted to realize in their life the basic insight of Judaism.

In outlining the program for the future of Israel, Buber points to a blend of nationalism and religion. It is not necessary, he declares, to study the Law in order to know the commands of God. But it is imperative to live with a constant awareness of our duty to God. The nature of our duty, in every situation, will then come to us with clarity and force, in accordance with an inner necessity.

Out of our actions, directed by this Divine intuition, we shall learn the "Truth." The task of building an ideal community in Palestine he regards as offering an opportunity for the revival of the ancient Jewish spirit. In a co-operative community, every act is a "true service of God."

In this program, there is implied the dogma that every man knows his duty in the actual situation in which he finds himself. This dogma, later explicitly stated in the book "Ich und Du," seems to be contradicted by experience. Honest ethical doubt is by no means rare. We can note in this belief a modern version of the Pauline conception of living with the Holy Spirit. The religious man, both Paul and Buber agree, needs no laws to guide his actions. The decision is made by the Spirit, according to the former; by man in mystical response to the situation, according to the latter.

In several places, Buber writes in conscious contrast to the ideas of K. Barth and the "Theology of Crisis." The idea that life in the spirit is wholly unrelated to the actual life of men seems to Buber the height of irreligion. At least in part by way of reaction against the consequences of viewing God as "wholly other," Buber seeks to find God as immanent in the actual processes of communal life.

The question whether Buber's interpretation of Judaism is historically justified cannot be considered here, as it would take us far beyond the scope of our inquiry.

11. "Zwiesprache" was published eight years after "Ich und Du." In the brief epilogue, the author states that the work is to be regarded as a completion, not as a sequel of "Ich und Du." It does in fact add little that is new to the earlier work. But, it serves as a valuable commentary on the "I-Thou" conception.

No doubt is left in our mind after reading this book that, in the "Thou" relation, the author reveals to us a profound psychic experience. Buber tells us of a dream which, with few modifications, recurred to him over a number of years. "I call it the dream of Double Call." It would always begin with an unusual occurrence of a frightening nature. Then, as a multitude of events followed each other in rapid succession, the climax was reached when a call, rhythmic and melodious, would issue from his own mouth and an opposite call, not an echo, would respond thereto. This call was always followed by the sense of certainty and of profound significance; "now, it has happened," he felt. Once it happened (1930) during a recurrence of this dream, that he called out and waited for an audible response; none came. Yet, strange to relate, he felt the silence itself respond and a final sense of certitude came to him at the end of this dream, as at previous occasions.[28] Buber relates this story in order to show how the realization came to him, that a dialogue can take place without words. Two men, who may never have known one another before, may enter into a speechless dia-

---

[28] Note 5 end of book.

logue. "Mitteilung" streams out of one and the other receives it; "the silence carried it." "For where mutual frank-
ness prevails among men, be it even wordless, there the dialogue word is sacramentally become." [29]

This speechless dialogue serves to bind men together and
it may unexpectedly serve as a means of reconciliation. He
urges the cultivation of the power to assume that attitude as a
means of lessening social tension and of helping fellow-men
to an understanding of their own difficulties. This dialogue
attitude can be maintained as a constant quality of our personality. In his youth, he confesses, he used to have "religious hours" when the realm of space-time seemed to have
been broken through. But there was then no relation between those hours and everyday life. At a riper age, he
learned to find religion "in the lived All, in its possibility of
dialogue." He has learned to exchange the fullness of ecstasy for "the fullness of the mortal hour in its call and response." [30]

Who speaks to us in our dialogue moments?—God Himself, Buber asserts, employing as His mouthpiece different
men and even inanimate objects. Every time we receive a
message, God is apprehended in a new sense. Thus, we are
really dealing with moment-gods (Augenblickgötter). But
just as we compound our knowledge of a poet from the impressions we receive by the reading of many of his poems,
so we know Him as the One Speaker of the manifold voices
in our life. We are to be ever on the alert that we may perceive God's Voice in all the events of our daily life.

In this work, the terms dialogue-life and monologue-life
are explained and described. By dialogue living is meant the
readiness to receive the other into one's being. Erotic love
does not always rise to this standard, though it may provide
pure instances of dialogue-living at its best. "Only when two

---

[29] Ibid., p. 15.
[30] Ibid., p. 40.

say to each other with all their being, 'You are it!' does the
Eternal dwell among them." [31]

Buber refuses to reply to those of his critics who argue on
ideological grounds. To those critics, however, who maintain that his philosophy is irrelevant to the actual situations
in life, Buber replies that, while the saying of "Thou" is not
applicable in its purity in all circumstances, it applies in a
crude and impure form to all situations. He cites the case of
a working girl, who learned to speak to her machine as if it
were a person. In general, he insists that all institutions of
public life must be approached in the same personal spirit,
if they are not to weigh as dead matter on the spirits of men.

There is an extension of the "Thou" relation in this book
which does not accord with the argument in "Ich und Du."
Thought, too, is described as being of a dialogue nature. It
is difficult to see how discursive thought, which necessarily
operates with homogeneous space and time can be brought
under one heading with the experience of the "Thou." Buber
seems to make the following distinction between the dialogue
of thought and of experience. Whereas the "Thou" is immediately apprehended in experience, thought forever moves
toward it as an ideal. Still, it is the case that in "Ich und
Du," Buber steers clear of dialectic entanglements.

12. With this outline of the development of his thought in
mind, we recognize Buber as a true child of his age. His
fundamental and lifelong conviction that reality is apprehended more profoundly through a personal relationship
than by any categories of the intellect is a reflection of the
anti-intellectualism which gained momentum at the turn of
the century. The impact of the theory of evolution on men's
minds had the effect of undermining the belief in reason as
the source of ultimate truth. The intellect was seen to be
itself a product of the non-intellectual process of life. Thus
biology came to be viewed as a more fundamental science

[31] Ibid., p. 79.

than physics. Both Bergson and James interpret this world in terms borrowed from the former science and both regard the conclusions of logic as relative to the attitudes of living being. Schopenhauer, Nietsche, and Euken join in assuming a fundamental current of life beneath the physical veil of phenomena. The indebtedness of Buber to Bergson is evident in almost every one of the former's works. In dealing with the problems of the individual, of society, or of Judaism, Buber consistently finds all evil to be due to the hardening of life in thought and he accordingly recommends the cultivation and the strengthening of the essential attitude of life. His advice on current problems abounds in such phrases as "bring in life," "rejuvenate," or "vivify."

Another characteristic of modern thought which finds expression in Buber's philosophy is this-worldliness. Buber is this-worldly in two senses; he does not look for salvation in any but the present physical world and in this world he finds the ultimate human good to lie not in solitary contemplation, but in an active participation in the melée of social forces. This-worldliness as a common attitude, especially in the better sense, is a distinctly modern phenomenon. It became the prevailing modern attitude partly by the confidence gained from the progress of science and partly by the rise of democracy. Whatever its source, the social interest in Buber's philosophy is paramount.

We can also notice in Buber a profound feeling of disappointment in the principles of socialism. In the nineteenth and early twentieth centuries, socialism shone as a bright beacon of hope to the idealistic youth of Europe. By the outbreak of the World War, it became apparent that the ideals of socialism could not withstand the stress of nationalistic forces. The Bolshevik Revolution in Russia proved that theories alone, be they ever so nicely systematic, cannot solve the social problem, nor can they bring happiness to men. Something more was needed if men were ever to become the masters of their own economic system. A fundamental change in the attitude of men toward each other and toward institutions must take place. "I-it" must give way to "I-Thou." Unless that change becomes general no system will work. For only religious men can live together.

But wherein does the essence of religion consist? In Buber's answer to this question, we recognize another trend of modern thought, especially in Germany. The challenge of modern science and philosophy left no basis for religion other than that of actual experience. Conceived as a psychic event, religion is as real as the data of science itself. Our age, therefore, witnessed a renewal of interest in the study of the "Varieties of Religious Experience." James, Bergson, Royce, Hocking, Maeterlink and, in Germany, Dilthey reflect this attitude.

(b) I and Thou

1. IN THE BOOK, "I AND THOU," MARTIN BUBER PRESENTS the basic outlines of a system of metaphysics. His argument consists of two parts: the description of a unique realm of experience and the conclusions inferred from that fact. Though the author does not clearly distinguish between these two phases in the exposition of his thought, we must not lose sight of this distinction if we are to evaluate correctly his contribution to the philosophy of religion.

2. The fact to which Buber calls our attention is the existence of two attitudes with which we may confront the external world. We may adopt the "I-It" attitude—that is, we may look at things as so many tools capable of being employed to further our interests, or as so many obstacles to the achievement of our self-centered aims. This is the attitude which is characteristic of both common sense and physical science—the attitude which enables us to construct an ordered view of the world. In order to use things, we must be

able to locate them. Therefore, we place them in the context of space and time. Similarly, that we may be enabled to form a reasonable plan for dealing with things, we ascribe fixed laws of causality to the march of events. Thus, when we speak of the physical world, of the framework of Space and Time which characterizes it and of the inexorable laws of causation which pervade it, we are under the spell of the "I-It" mentality, employing the corresponding language.

3. But another attitude is possible—an attitude to which the concepts of Space, Time and Causality are wholly irrelevant. We may address things as "Thou," as if a living person were standing over against us. The world then appears to us as wholly different from the ordered "it" world and entirely incommensurate with it. Instead of dealing with things conjoined in a Space-Time continuum, we then face a person.[1]

4. When we ask wherein the uniqueness of the "I-Thou" relation is manifested, we enter the most delicate field of our investigation. The author obviously appeals to us to find an echo to his words in our own life. The power of analysis and of discernment of special characteristics belongs to the scientific attitude. The moment we propose to study two beings that stand in the "I-Thou" relation to each other, we bring them down to our world of "it." It follows that the description of the "I-Thou" attitude must be subjective. We must at the very outset agree to take Buber's description of what he felt when "addressing his Thou" as a fact of experience, though, of course, we shall have to examine critically his deductions from that fact.

5. Buber describes the following qualities as characteristics of the "I-Thou" relation: (a) *wholeness*—Buber insists that in the "I-Thou" relation, the whole of one's being is taken up. One feels then so wholly absorbed by the con-

---

[1] See note 1 at end of book.

frontation with the other person, that no part of one can possibly remain aloof as an observer. "The primary word 'I-Thou' can only be spoken with the whole being."[2] "Power is concentrated, everything that tries to divert it is drawn in the orbit of its mastery, the being is alone in itself and rejoices, as Paracelsus says, in its exaltation."[3] This stage is a necessary preparation for the saying of Thou. From it one may rise to confront a Thou, or through lack of decision, "fall back into dissipation of being."

Thus the "I" that says "it" is not the same "I" that says "thou." "The primary word 'I-It' can never be spoken with the whole being."[4] The former is felt as an individuality and "becomes conscious of itself as a subject of experiencing and using." The latter is felt as a person and is conscious of itself as subjectivity. The former feels itself as distinct from the world, separated from other beings and concerned with their possession. The latter feels himself to "be sharing in being," "possessing being as such" and aiming to meet other persons.

Striving to separate facts from their interpretation we can sum up the author's distinction of person from individuality as meaning that in the saying of "thou," one feels his self as charged with peculiar value and as being in direct rapport with reality. Whatever that feeling may be worth as a means of cognition, we have to assume for the present that it forms part of one's experience in meeting "his Thou."

(b) *Exclusiveness.* Not only is one's self become whole in the "I-Thou" relation, but the Thou, too, must be conceived as a whole. By this condition, Buber means more than that the Thou is conceived as a unity. He insists that Thou cannot be spoken to "a thing among things." All that one is conscious of in the relation that is not self must some-

---

[2] Ibid., p. 3.
[3] Ibid., p. 86.
[4] Ibid., p. 3.

how belong to the Thou. And belong too it must not as a separable component, but as a living part. "But with no neighbor and whole in himself, he is Thou and fills the heavens. This does not mean that nothing exists except himself. But all else lives in his light." [5] "As long as the presence of the relation continues, this, its cosmic range, is inviolable." [6]

While we are in the "It" world, we are conscious of experiencing only parts of the world. But when we say "Thou," we are conscious of meeting the whole.

(c) *Presentness*—Buber claims that the quality of presentness belongs to the "Thou" relation only. "The real, filled present," in contra-distinction to the mathematical instant of "now," is felt only when Thou is truly spoken. "The 'I' of the primary word, I-It . . . has no present, only the past." [7] So long as man is content to experience and to use, he has nothing but objects. "But objects subsist in time that has been." [8] Buber understands by present that "which is continually present and enduring." An object is perceived only when duration has ceased. It is a "breaking off and cutting clear and hardening." The meaning of those terms is understood only when placed in the context of Bergson's thought. Buber evidently accepts Bergson's analysis of time. He adds the claim, however, that duration is felt only in the Thou relation.

(d) *Centrality*—Just as the "I-Thou" relation transcends mathematical time to endure in presentness, so is the same relation exempt from the context of absolute Space. This relation endures about a center, "where the extended lines of relation meet—in the eternal Thou." [9] The bare

---

[5] Ibid., p. 8.
[6] Ibid., p. 78.
[7] Ibid., p. 12.
[8] Ibid., p. 13.
[9] Ibid., p. 100.

fact to which the author here alludes is that in the "I-Thou" relation the coordinates of space and time fade in the background. "And just as prayer is not in time but time in prayer, sacrifice not in space but space in sacrifice and to reverse the relation is to abolish the reality, so with the man to whom I say Thou." [10] The person who truly speaks Thou is not conscious of Space and Time.

(e) *Freedom*—In addressing oneself to a Thou, one feels free from the shackles of causality. "So long as the heaven of Thou is spread out over one, the winds of causality cower at his heels and the whirlpool of fate stays its course." [11] He echoes Bergson again in arguing that belief in determinism is due to the ordering of things that have already become. "Prediction from objectivity is valid only for the man who does not know presentness." [12] He who is capable of entering into relation, his personality having become concentrated, is also aware of freedom. By freedom arbitrary self-will is not meant but its very opposite. Freedom is like a semicircle the complement of which is destiny. Along with freedom goes the feeling of responsibility for "the course of being in the world," which needs him that he may help "bring it to reality as it desires." But the person always feels that the power of decision rests with him.

(f) *Directness*—The "I-Thou" relation is direct. It suffers no mediation. He who meets his Thou is not conscious of any intervening bridges, physical or mental. It is not as if he were trying to pierce to the soul behind the veil of the body. Rather, the reality he sees and feels appears to him as a living person. Buber is here trying to dispel the notion that in saying "Thou" we look for the noumenon behind the phenomenon, or that, after the manner of Plato, we discern the ideal form in the real appearance. He insists

---

[10] Ibid., p. 9.
[11] Ibid., p. 9.
[12] Ibid., p. 58.

that what is actually felt is that the common phenomenal reality which is perceived by our physical sense is apprehended directly as a person. Buber does not say what indirectness he has discovered in the "I-It" relation, nor does he imply the existence of any. His point is that in considering objects as "it" we aim beyond them and through them, whereas in the realm of relation, the Thou is felt as the end in itself.

(g) *Non-orderability*—The various moments in which we enter into relation with a Thou do not complement each other to form a definite order. Each moment is forever unique, ephemeral and isolated. "The Thou knows no system of coordination." [13]

(h) *Love*—Love accompanies the "I-Thou" relation. Buber defines love as the "responsibility of an 'I' for a 'Thou,'" the feeling that they are needed by each other. Hate is described by Buber as being closer to the Thou relation than indifference. He asserts that love is experienced in a radically different manner than any feeling. We have feelings, whereas we are in love. "Feelings dwell in man; but man dwells in his love." [14] In less flowery language, his meaning is that it is of the essence of love to feel that one's entire individuality is caught up in the sway of a larger relationship.

(i) *Effect of the Relation*—The moments in which we enter the "Thou" relation do not yield a definite increase either of knoweldge or of material objects. But they leave a residue of creative energy which in time crystallizes into new works of art. ". . . beams of their power stream into the ordered world and dissolve it again and again." [15] Every work of art is the result of the artist's having met a Thou. An object can be called a work of art only when it possesses

[13] Ibid., p. 31.
[14] Ibid., p. 14.
[15] Ibid., p. 31.

the capacity of becoming a "Thou" again to a human observer.[16] Knowledge, too, may later crystallize in the "It" world from the original moment of the "I-Thou" relation. "Every culture rests on an original relational incident, on a response to the Thou made at its source." But the highest effect of the relation is in the domain of practical life. The person who has had the relation is capable of "opening up the world of Thou" to other men. His own life then becomes "teaching" to his contemporaries.

When a person has once reached the height of entering into relation with the eternal Thou, God, the creative energy that he brings back with him from the meeting is termed revelation.[17] He to whom a revelation has come is veritably a new man. (Buber insists that revelation is not an experience. As he describes it, "something happens to the man." [18] In this paper, the term experience is used to denote every event of which a person may become aware.) He now possesses "Presence of Power," [19] which means:

1. That he feels life to be laden "heavy with meaning."
2. That he feels more assured of the values he has previously entertained. This added certainty is inexpressible and alogical. "It does not seek to be explained but only to be done by us." [20]
3. That this accretion of meaning and certainty refer not to another life, but to this life of ours.

Revelation issues in no definite command. The meaning received must be proved true by each man in his own life and in his own way.

(j) *Antinomies*—In the relation of man to God, there is an ineluctable antinomy. God comprises man's self; yet the

---

[16] Ibid., p. 41.
[17] See note 2 at end of book.
[18] Ibid., p. 109.
[19] Ibid., p. 110.
[20] Ibid., p. 110.

self remains distinct. Man is both in God and outside of
him. This felt antinomy should not be resolved otherwise
than with one's life. It is significant that, in contrast to all
classical mystics, Buber does not claim that in the state of
ecstatic union, all intellectual doubts and difficulties are overcome. He makes the contrary assertion that man brings
back with him from the supreme meeting at least two antinomies, which he then must resolve through his life.

The other antinomy which the moment of relation with
God bequeathes to man is the one of destiny and freedom.
Man feels that he is completely at the mercy of the Deity;
yet he also feels that he is free to make his own decisions.
This antinomy, too, is meant to be overcome by life. The
presence of antinomies in the physical universe is, to the
contemplative mystic, a proof of its unreality. To Buber,
the actual world remains real, the tension of contradictions
indicating to man his function as the agent of reconciliation.
The contradictions in the world show that man's true end is
action, not thought.

6. There are three spheres in which the "I-Thou" relation may be found.

1. A man may address another human being as his Thou.
   Then the relation naturally takes the form of the
   spoken word.
2. A man may address an inanimate object as Thou. The
   relation in that case is below the level of speech.
3. We may consider ideal essences as our Thou and address our whole being to them.

In each case, though we say Thou to a definite object, we
are really addressing the eternal Thou, thru it.

7. The primary word "I-Thou" precedes the primary
word "I-It" both in the history of the individual and of
the race. In the former case, Buber points out that the ante-
natal life of the child is one of constant bodily inter-action
with its mother. As the child grows, the yearning for con-

nection is gradually translated into spiritual terms as the longing to meet its Thou. Buber calls this theory the "a priori of relation," or "the inborn Thou." In the childhood of the human race, too, the "I-Thou" relation predominated. Savages personalize many things and events. The progress of civilization as of the growth of the individual is characterized by the consistent enlargement of the world of "It" at the expense of the power to enter into relation.

8. On the basis of the preceding description of the "I-Thou" relation, Buber suggests the following theses:

(a) The I-Thou relation introduces us to a different realm of being. Buber begins the book with the dogmatic declaration, "To man, the world is two-fold in accordance with his two-fold nature." When we say Thou, we transcend the world of experience and enter the world of relation. Leaving behind us the categories of Space, Time and Causality, we face a "person" exclusively and in freedom. Buber mentions once the phrase "dimension of Thou" [21] which suggests his conception of how the world of relation is contrasted with the world of experience.

(b) Buber claims that only in the state of relation is one real, though, he asserts, the physical world is not to be taken as illusory. So long as we look upon the world as "It," we are still unreal. The test of a person's reality is his ability to say "Thou."

(c) The reality which one finds in the saying of Thou is of a personal nature, whatever that may mean. Buber does not state wherein the difference between object and person consists. He disavows the common distinction between body and soul, though he fails to explain his own interpretation of the term "person." The qualities he evidently ascribes to a person are unity, purpose, desire to be expressed, and, above all, a certain incommunicable essence.

---

[21] Ibid., p. 67.

(d) By entering in the Thou relation, we receive a revelation from God. Through saying Thou to any object, we aim at God, and at times reach Him. Since the revelation thus received consists only of the assurance of the possession of meaning, its final result is, therefore, the confirmation of the value of the object through which God was addressed.

9. The religion which Buber bases upon the discovery of the "I-Thou" relation is a very practical one. "With the Thou on our lips" we go out into the world—that is, we are prepared to approach all things and persons in love and in humble readiness to serve. The man who has been in relation, refuses to turn his back upon the world in order to cultivate the purity of his soul in splendid isolation, except as a preparation for greater usefulness. Living amidst the "madding crowd," he will ever strive to know his duty to the "grand will" which works through the Universe. All things and phenomena he will regard as being the signs through which God addresses him, asking for his aid in advancing the course of history. God does not ask to be described or to be contemplated. He wants only to be obeyed by men. Thus, the men of relation know themselves to be free agents, partners of the Lord, ever ready to serve in love and in humility and assured of the ultimate value of their devoted labors. The rewards of heaven and the punishments of hell they see not in the distant future, but in the living immediate present, in the respective forms of success and failure in the adventure of being real.

In the field of social relations, the Thou relation is of particular importance. Evil, to Buber, is the exclusive domination of the world of "It." Whatever economic system may happen to prevail, mankind will be its slave, not its master, so long as most men persist in the "I-It" attitude. Genuine communal life can only be built around a "living center." Men should learn to pursue their vocations, in whichever nook of the economic machine it may happen to be, not as an irksome necessity, nor yet as a harsh moral obligation, but as a free response to the central authority which they address as their Thou.

In attempting to evaluate the significance of the "I-Thou" relation, as described by Buber, for the philosophy of religion, we propose to discuss it in reference to the following questions:

1. Can the "I-Thou" relation serve as the basis for a metaphysics?
2. How does the saying of "Thou" to God compare with the description by the classical mystics of their highest experiences?
3. Of what value is the "I-Thou" relation to the practice of religion?

(c) ANALYSIS OF THE THOU RELATION

ASSUMING THE ACCURACY OF BUBER'S DESCRIPTION OF THE experience of relation, we now proceed to examine the validity of the metaphysical inferences that he draws from that fact. In undertaking this task, we are conscious of the objection that criticism belongs to the realm of "It" and that we are therefore causing the relation to vanish by the mere attempt to examine and to place it within the context of human experience. The relation of "Thou" bears its own marks of overwhelming certainty, it may be argued. The person who is in that relation can no more question the reality of what he feels than the reflective thinker can doubt the principle of contradiction or the law of excluded middle. We wish to point out in reply that, as rational beings, we necessarily start out with the assumption that feeling certainty is not to be identified with possessing it. The feeling of certainty generally precedes logical analysis and is rarely absent from fools and fanatics. The man of relation is certain of his truth only so long as he is in relation. When he returns to the world of "It," he must assume, as we do, that feelings are not to be taken at face value. It belongs to the most elemental experience of civilized mankind that judgments made under great emotional stress are nearly always deceiving. Neither Buber, nor anyone of the classical mystics, is ignorant of this fact. Did not many great mystics, like Julian of Norwich and Mohammed doubt whether they communed with God or with the devil?

When one experience is singled out as furnishing the sole clue to the nature of reality, it must be shown that that experience is alone possessed of such characteristics as bear upon them the prima facie stamp of reality. This task consists clearly in the proving of two propositions: that the one experience is uniquely endowed with the qualities claimed for it and that these qualities are what we should expect in a direct experience of the real.

Buber does in fact claim that the experience of relation is irreducibly unique. The common distinctions between body and soul, mind and matter, idea and object fade into insignificance beside the profound cleavage that obtains between the world of "Thou" and the world of "It."

In the attempt to establish this claim to the uniqueness of the fact of relation, Buber faces a more difficult task than most mystics. For he claims that this relation can be found in different spheres of experience. We may say "Thou" to a tree, a person, an idea, God. Moreover, as children, we have all lived in this relation, though we were not aware of it at the time. Since the saying of Thou is not removed from ordinary experience by a long road of stringent discipline, we are in a better position to test the validity of the author's conclusions.

To indicate the uniqueness of the Thou relation, Buber, as we have shown in the previous chapter, cites the following characteristics by which it is distinguished—wholeness, exclusiveness, presentness, centrality, freedom, directness, non-orderability, love, the resultant creative energy and the resolution of antinomies.

It should be noted at this point that in order to realize fully the contrast between the realm of relation, as described by these adjectives, and the realm of ordinary experience, we have to accept Buber's description of the latter realm—that it is in fact dominated by the self-centered desire to possess and to use. I believe most men would reject this description of everyday experience as a false caricature, since men are not conscious of this desire as determining the larger number of their reactions. It must be borne in mind that Buber's distinction between the "I-It" and the "I-Thou" attitudes moves on the level of conscious experience. Buber evidently shares Bergson's view of the pragmatic meaning of perception as well as of conception.[1] He would probably have met the objection that in ordinary experience we are not conscious of the intention to appropriate and to employ by the assertion that this intention is taken for granted in most situations and that it can be discovered by analysis.

But even if we accept Buber's description of the nature of common experience, it is difficult to see how the qualities cited by Buber as characteristic of the "I-Thou" relation are really peculiar to it. The passion to possess or to use a definite object may reach the point when the whole energy of a person is concentrated about that object. Persons that are dominated by a passion of this kind may well feel that their whole personality is concentrated about one desire; that one object occupies their attention, everything else being seen in the light of that object; that the duration of their absorbing passion is not to be coldly measured by a clock; that all space is drawn around the object of their desire; and later, when the passion was dissipated, they may well conclude that that

[1] See H. Bergson's *Matter and Memory*.

passion was not to be ordered in the context of simple experience. Freedom, love, the feeling of certainty and the
consciousness of a message received cannot, it is true, be
found in any ordinary passion. The uniqueness of the experience then is not to be sought in the feeling of the transcendence of Space-Time and Causality, for that feeling accompanies also the powerful passion of lust for money or
sexual pleasure. For one object to become the center of our
universe for a brief duration, for the coordinates of Space
and of Time to sink into the background, for mathematics to
appear worse than false, for all logical antinomies to become
supremely irrelevant—for the purpose of accomplishing all
these results the experience of relation is not needed. Any
absorbing passion will bring about the same reactions.[2]

Our author takes partial cognizance of this objection in
his discussion of the nature of hate. He agrees that violent
hate may be described largely in the same terms which are
true for the "I-Thou" relation. But, he argues, whereas
love may be blind on occasion hate is always blind for only
when a person is partly known can he be hated. This argument is not quite to the point, since he who hates feels he is
hating the whole person, root and branch. He sees everything in the light of that which he hates, even as the lover
sees all in the light of his Thou. It must be remembered
that, for Buber, it is the conscious content of any experience
that alone determines its validity. Moreover, his concession
that more reality is attained by the one who passionately
hates than by the indifferent person is a dangerous view for
the religion which he intends to build upon this insight of
relation. For, if hate and love may be closely related in
terms of reality, they are certainly extreme opposites in
terms of conduct.

Furthermore, the concession in regard to the reality of

------

[2] See note 1 at end of book.

hate should apply with greater force to such impulses as sexual desires and the lust for power. These passions which are notorious for their power to obtain at moments exclusive domination of the human personality, may refer to a definite person even as the emotions of love and hate do. In brief, if we examine the list of characteristics which Buber claims for the "I-Thou" relation and discount those which enter into every state of high emotional tension, we find only the following two marks of the "I-Thou" relation which alone can be correctly said to be distinctive of it:

1. Love or the freedom-destiny couple, characterized by the feeling of belonging together and needing each other.
2. The feeling of a message received and the energy resulting therefrom. Since the second characteristic is felt only when the experience of relation is over, we can only consider the first one as being the special content of the "I-Thou" relation.[3]

We are thus left with the question whether or not the case of uniqueness can be established by this sole contrast of the independent ego with the "I" of relation, which points towards its "better half." In one sense, every experience is unique. For the purpose of establishing a prima facie presumption, that this experience of relation comes closer to attaining knowledge of ultimate reality, we have to show that the unique quality possesses a knowledge-seeking or reality-seeking character.

The experience of relation, as it is described by Buber, possesses this noetic quality in an eminent degree. One seeks, thru the saying of "Thou," to find the very meaning of one's own and the "Thou's" life, one's duty to the Thou, one's destiny. Again, one seeks to meet the unity, the center of the object which confronts him—in a word, the Being of

---

[3] See note 2 at end of book.

the object. Thru the Thou relation, one does not find the nature of the Thou, to be sure, but the significant aspect of the Thou is found in his message, his aim to be realized in life. This message is received at the meeting point of two beings in relation.

We conclude therefore that Buber had made good his claim, that the "I-Thou" relation is uniquely significant for the understanding of reality.[4] Our next task is to inquire whether the experience of mutual relation may legitimately be regarded as an ultimate metaphysical insight. We have stated previously the claim of Buber that only through the saying of Thou does one meet reality. This claim can be regarded as a rational hypothesis only if it can be shown that the "I-Thou" relation is expressible in ultimate metaphysical terms—that is, in terms which do not involve simpler more fundamental entities.[5] Reality may have many and diverse meanings; we shall examine later Buber's notion of reality. But whatever reality may mean, it must not require for its expression terms that are themselves borrowed from that which is unreal, unless it be described in negative adjectives only.

Some philosophers who, like Buber, built their metaphysical view on an insight which they could not adequately describe without the employment of terms extraneous to their view of reality, have put forth the claim that reality is essentially One. To know reality is to become part of it. By this assertion they have escaped the necessity of qualifying it any further, since any qualification is necessarily a limitation and a breaking up. Thus, ineffability was claimed for the experience of the One. Buber, however, asserts that the apprehension of the real involves two entities, that it is a form of speech, a dialogue. It, therefore, should be expressible.

---

[4] See note 3 at end of book.
[5] See note 4 at end of book.

Applying this criterion to the "I-Thou" relation, we ask whether it can be stated or even conceived without the employment of "it" terminology.[6] Now, relations may be of many sorts. (The German word "Beziehung" means reference as well as relation.) Taken by itself the term relation is so general as to refer to well-nigh every situation. It ranges in possibility of signification from complete externality to total unity. In Buber's view, the "I-Thou" relation is just one step this side of perfect unity. He seems to think of relation as belonging together. But the phrase belonging together, too, is capable of bearing a host of possible meanings.

From a metaphysical standpoint, "belonging together" involves a contradiction in terms: if the essence of the relation is togetherness, how is the separateness to be understood? To explain the meaning of belonging together, it is necessary to show how they are separated and in what way the togetherness comes to pass. Logically, the elements involved are a field "A" wherein "x" and "y" are differentiated and a crossing field "B" wherein they both belong. In Buber's description, field "A" is the ordered world of space-time, and field "B" is the spirit. When two beings are united in the field of spirit, they are still separated in the world of space-time.

This interpretation of the meaning of reality as being the consciousness of "belonging together," Buber seems to have in mind when he writes of the "dimension of Thou." As long as people live in the ordinary four-dimensional space-time world, they still lack reality. Only by entering the fifth dimension of spirit does one become fully real. Much of Buber's writings accords perfectly with this conception. We can especially understand why the physical world still exists for the spiritual person and why real life is expressed in this-worldly activity.

---

[6] See note 5 at end of book.

But, the term dimension has to be given wholly new meaning in order to serve Buber's purpose. For, to add a dimension to reality is to add another means of differentiation. What Buber is looking for, on the other hand, is a means of unification. We can speak of spiritual people as persons living in the fifth dimension, but in doing so, we introduce a scheme by which we are enabled to make additional distinctions among human beings. To go from separateness to unity is to decrease the number of dimensions that are to be taken account of in a situation, not the reverse.

Buber's meaning is better conveyed by the term, field, as he thinks of the realm of spirit as being a kind of magnetic field. In the world of "it," the magnetic lines of force are neutralized or blocked. When Thou is spoken, two centers of force bring about a magnetic field. Thus, spirit is the analogue of a magnetic line of force. To believe that "spirit exists in man" is a colossal "illusion." Actually, spirit exists with man as the starting point—"between man and that which is not man." [7] When Thou is spoken to any object, connection or agreement is established with the flow of spirit that extends from man to God. "God and man, alike in being, are the individually real pair, the two bearers of the primal relation." [8]

It may be doubted whether the term magnetic field is anything more than an abstraction. Buber does not in fact employ it. But his thought is incomprehensible except on the basis of this analogy.

Since, in the realm of spirit, when the "I" and the "Thou" are connected, they are still not one, we have to think of the world as consisting of three realms—the realm of things in themselves, the realm of absolute Space and abstract Time, and the realm of spirit. Things may appear in either the physical world or the spiritual one of relation depending upon

[7] I-and-Thou, p. 93.
[8] Ibid., p. 85.

the attitude of the human observer. To Kant's Transcendental Categories which necessarily order the phenomena in accordance with certain rules, Buber adds another faculty which views this world as a wholly different kind of order—unordered in fact and oriented toward a Center. Intention is the key which locks one faculty and opens the other. In that real or spiritual world, the lines of force which run from the various beings to the center are compounded of intention. This interpretation is not given by Buber himself. We suggest it only to prove that it is possible to order Buber's views in a rational setting. The I-Thou relation is capable of being developed into a consistent metaphysics.[9]

(d) Comparative Study of the Thou Relation

It is a fundamental hypothesis in buber's thought that the "relational" attitude is historically prior to the "experiential" attitude. "In the beginning is relation."[1] With the progress of civilization the "It" world grows. Things are multiplied and consequently the power to use reality for human ends increases. But this power grows in inverse ratio to the power to enter into relation, "for the development of the ability to experience and to use comes about mostly through the decrease of man's power to enter into relation— the power in virtue of which alone man can live the life of the spirit."[2] Accordingly, he asserts that the relational attitude is predominant in the life of the child and in that of primitive man.

This assertion, insofar as it refers to the psychology of a child, in its ante-natal and early post-natal life, cannot be verified. The babblings of an infant and its gestures can be

---

[9] See note 6 at end of book.
[1] "I-and-Thou," p. 18.
[2] Ibid., p. 39.

easily explained without recourse to the hypothesis of a relational attitude. The child undoubtedly does not order the data of its experience in a hard framework of Space and Time. But, then, the negation of a completely ordered world is not yet equivalent to the apprehension of the "Thou." [3]

We face the same difficulty when we attempt to verify Buber's contention that the mentality of primitive man is dominated by the relational attitude. The term "primitive man" in this connection can only refer to the tribes who lived in the dim prehistoric past, before the beginning of civilization. It cannot refer to the savages now living, since they, too, possess a complex civilization. Possessing no data whatever concerning the mental life of the Cro-Magnon or the Neanderthal man, we can neither prove nor disprove the theory that his life was largely lived in the "Thou" relation.

However, Buber himself refers to the language of the existing primitive tribes in order to corroborate his hypothesis, presumably on the supposition that present day savage mentality corresponds more closely to the psychic life of primeval man than the mind of civilized man does. Accepting the supposition, we ask whether the habits of thought and perception observed among present day savages are in fact consonant with Buber's theory of the "inborn Thou."

Two major schools are radically divided in their views concerning the nature of the primitive mentality. The English School, of which the most notable representatives are Tylor and Fraser, is committed to the animistic hypothesis. This theory assumes that the inferences of the savage run along the same logical tracks, that our own deductions follow. The savage view of life and of the universe is what we should expect people with little experience and still less reflection to hold. It is the *Weltanschauung* which we should have held had we been deprived of the lore and the achieve-

---

[3] See note 1 at end of book.

ments of past generations. The concept of accident is a difficult abstraction, wholly beyond the analytic power of primitive man. Since nothing merely happens, all events have some significance to man's life. Hence, "powers" or "intentions" are supposed to lurk within phenomena. The experience of dreams provided the means to the primitive philosopher, by which to visualize these "powers" as "spirits." Thus, Tylor writes, "It was no spontaneous fancy, but the reasonable inference that effects are due to causes, which led the rude men of old days to people with such ethereal phantoms their own homes and haunts and the vast earth and sky beyond." [4]

Obviously, this theory of the evolution of primitive mentality offers little support to Buber's philosophy. Insofar as primitive man apprehends personal forces in the world, he does it on the basis of definite reasoning. Freedom and destiny do not form the poles of his thought, but the same old determinism and bare logic of the "It" world, only more confused and misdirected. The basic operations of the savage mind are the same as those of the most advanced civilized mind.

The second school, headed by M. Levy-Brühl, declares that the laws and processes of the primitive mind are in no way commensurate with those of the cultivated European. Their consciousness is not a less developed form of our consciousness, but a generically different one.

The difference is due to the apperceptive mass which conditions the thinking of primitive man. He does not operate with concepts, but with "collective representations." The latter are not molds of the intellect alone but complexes of many elements, intellectual as well as emotional and motor. Hope and fear hover about them and their boundaries are

---

[4] "Primitive Culture" II, 4th edition, p. 108.

never distinct. Thus, the perceptions of primitive man, colored as they are by these "collective representations," are unlike our own. Levy-Brühl calls their perception "mystical," in the sense of an occult virtue being associated with the content of each perception. "Primitive perception is fundamentally mystic on account of the mystic virtue of the collective representations which form an integral part of every perception." [5] "It is not a question of association. The mystic properties with which things and beings are imbued form an integral part of the idea to the primitive, who views it as a synthetic whole." In their perceptions, the subjective elements stand out preeminently.

Far from possessing the notion of freedom, the primitive mind is dominated by a determinism as rigid as our own. But, whereas we look for the connections between phenomena, they seek the cause in the relation between the world of phenomena and the extra-spatial occult power. This form of mystic causality appears to them as imperative and intuitive as physical causality appears to us.

Primitive mentality is singularly indifferent to the principle of contradiction. Their reasoning, such as it is, follows the "law of participation," which states "that things can be both themselves and something other than themselves." [6] "The opposition between one and many, the same and another, etc., does not impose upon this mentality the necessity of affirming one of the terms if the other is denied, or vice versa." [7] This "law of participation" is relegated into the background when the primitive deals with his own individual problems and it comes to the fore whenever the collective actions or reactions of the group are concerned. It is on the basis of this law, termed "prelogical," that Levy-Bruhl ex-

---

[5] "How Natives Think." P. 44.
[6] Ibid., p. 76.
[7] Ibid., p. 77.

plains the phenomena of the belief in multiple souls and in the contradictory relations of the individual to his ancestral spirit, to the totem animal and to himself.

The thought of the primitive rarely soars above the level of the concrete, as is indicated by the extreme poverty of primitive languages in abstract terms. Money, to cite one instance, is not a general concept, but only a thing used at certain definite occasions and meant for certain specific purposes.

Their idea of time is not intimately connected with the ideal of a causal nexus and is more like a perception of quality. "It (the idea of time) rather resembles a subjective feeling of duration, not wholly unlike the duree reale described by Bergson.[8]

Space, too, is not conceived by them as a homogeneous container. In their mind, space is never abstracted from the concrete whole. "Space will not be so much imagined as felt and its various directions and positions will be qualitatively differentiated from one another."[9]

What support does Buber's hypothesis of two forms of consciousness corresponding to the two primary attitudes of man derive from Levy-Brühl's description of the primitive mind? Since Levy-Brühl describes the primitive mind as differing in kind, not merely in degree, from our mind, we are justified in concluding that our form of consciousness is not the only possible form in which reality can be apprehended. Kant's claim of the absoluteness of our forms of perception and laws of reasoning is thus rejected and his transcendental intuitions and categories of the understanding are now seen to be true only of a particular form of consciousness, which, as it happens, prevails generally and almost exclusively among civilized men today. Added plausibility is thus obtained for a theory, like Buber's, which postulates

---

[8] "Primitive Mentality," p. 93.
[9] Ibid., p. 95.

another form of consciousness alongside the one which answers to Kant's analysis.

When we proceed, however, to compare the "I-Thou" relation with the consciousness of the primitive man, we find little, if any, agreement indeed. To be sure, the principle of contradiction is disregarded, physical causality is unknown, absolute space and time are not even conceived and all phenomena are inextricably mixed with "mystic" entities. But, we have learned from Buber that the essential element of the relational attitude is the feeling of facing and conversing with another person. Does this feeling form part of the mental content of the primitive man? This question, we feel, can only be answered in the negative. The occult "powers" which the primitive man "perceives" all about him are so many additional inhabitants of his "ordered world." There is no evidence at all that they are to him more than so many "its," which he may use, compel or persuade, as the case may be, to do his bidding. Neither does he address his social group as a "Thou," as a being standing over against him; rather, in accordance with the "law of participation," he feels himself to be at one and the same time his own self, the totem animal and the social group. Again, as stated above, the primitive mind is rigidly deterministic and, hence, coldly inhospitable to the feelings of freedom and destiny which occupy so prominent a place in Buber's description of the "Thou" relation.

From all the above, it seems fair to conclude that Buber's claim that the "Thou" relation is habitual to primitive man, and hence, that it is native to the human mind, is unsubstantiated by the present knowledge of savage societies and is, therefore, quite improbable.

The assertion of the priority of the Thou relation to the ordered world of "It" is of the essence of Buber's philosophy and, by no means, an after-thought. Since the "I-It" world is a mediated and discursive world, construed as a falling away from a "Thou" that is dimly felt on the horizon of consciousness and the "I-Thou" relation is conceived as a direct apprehension, the "I-Thou" relation can occur before the "I-It" experience, but not the reverse. Having described the opposite of the Thou relation as the functioning of the discursive intellect. Buber is constrained to claim that "pre-logical" people, children and primitives, find their lives dominated by the "Thou" relation. The absence of corroborative evidence for this claim is therefore a serious difficulty for Buber's philosophy.

Though there may be many degrees of clarity in which it is manifested, the relational attitude is by no means a very rare phenomenon. Buber desires to regenerate society by its means; hence, at least weak instances of it must be within the reach of all. Accordingly we have to examine the "Thou" relation not as a subjective experience of Buber, but as an objective description of a form of consciousness, which now and then displaces the normal or common-sense consciousness of men. If true, Buber's description will agree, at least in broad outlines, with the recorded descriptions of similar experiences by other students of the psychic life. Certainly, if no parallel could be found in world literature to it, we should have to regard the "Thou" relation as the peculiar experience of Buber, of little or no value to the study of religion.

Actually, we find many works of mystical literature which, with varying emphasis, can be said to offer so many descriptions of the relational attitude.

The "Thou" relation can be classed as a mystical experience if we adopt the broad definition of mysticism given by William James in "Varieties of Religious Experiences." [10]

1. It possesses the quality of ineffability, since the message derived from the meeting with the "Thou" can find expres-

---

[10] See note 2 at end of book.

sion in actions only, not in words. When the attempt is made to crystallize the message in language, a self-contradictory statement is necessarily the result.

2. In Buber's description, the "Thou" relation possesses a noetic quality. Though one knows only one's own path to the meeting point and the "Thou," in its essential being is forever unknown, it still remains true that directions and guidance for life are found in this experience.

3. The element of transiency is, of course, characteristic of the "Thou" relation. It comes in the form of ephemeral glimpses into reality which are fated to endure but briefly, giving way to the "It" consciousness.

4. The "Thou" relation is also characterized by the quality of passivity. At the meeting point, the attitude of the "I" is described as a "waiting," an open receptivity.

For the purpose of classifying the various descriptions of the stages of mysticism, we shall here employ the scheme of Evelyn Underhill, in which the Mystic Way is discussed under the following five headings: 1. Awakening of the Self; 2. Purification and Mortification; 3. State of Illumination; 4. The Dark Night of the Soul; 5. The Unitive Life.[11]

Many descriptions of phenomena which fall under the first heading contain the essence of the "Thou" relation. The individual is suddenly made aware of a higher reality. His consciousness, which was up to that moment centered about his own instincts, is suddenly felt to be only a part of an infinitely wider consciousness. When this transition is both violent and sudden, it is called "conversion." Thus Starbuck says:—"This is the first aspect of conversion; the person emerges from a smaller limited world of existence into a larger world of being. His life becomes swallowed up in a larger whole."[12] The careers of nearly all mystics began with some such experience. While some employ the terms

---

[11] See note 3 at end of book.
[12] "The Psychology of Religion," Chap. XII.

"a great love," "a great light," [13] "a great beauty," others speak of a voice that comes to them.

The following elements enter into the experience of conversion according to James:

1. The conviction that an outside power is effecting the change.
2. A feeling of assurance concerning one's state and one's mission in life—theologically speaking, grace has been won.
3. A sense of the perception of new truths.
4. A sense of clean and beautiful newness, within and without.
5. The occasional appearance of "photims" or voices. These qualities can all be found in Buber's description of the "Thou" relation, though they are not always stated explicitly.

William James writes that some people experience the sensation of a person being at a definite point in space. It is really an hallucination that does not employ the visual or auditory organs. The interpretation of this experience is, of course, conditioned by the subject's beliefs. Religious people naturally interpret it theistically.[14] Religious literature abounds with records of people who felt the majesty of the unseen as profoundly real. "The darkness held a presence that was all the more felt because it was not seen. I could not any more have doubted that He was there than that I was. Indeed, I felt myself to be, if possible, the less real of the two." [15]

This sense of an invisible presence James rightly compares to the lover's sense of the continued presence of his beloved, even when the latter's features are not consciously repre-

---

[13] See E. Underhill's "Mysticism," 10th edition, pp. 224, 225.

[14] See "Varieties," p. 65, for the record of one who felt he was in personal relation to it.

[15] Ibid., p. 67. Innumerable Biblical references will come to mind.

sented. This observation accords with Buber's calling the apprehended invisible being a "Thou"; i.e.: a person turned toward the "I" and to whom the "I" has turned. The emotions which this state evokes are described by James as solemnity, joy mixed with fear, the sense of assurance following a sense of danger. This mixture of contradictory emotions is also found in the Thou relation. While meeting the "Thou" is supposed to result in a sense of assurance, we are told that the sense of security belongs only to those who live exclusively in the ordered world of "It."

According to Buber, "Thou" can be spoken to objects of nature. God's word is echoed by all things. Buber translates Plato's image of the world from visual into auditory terms. He seeks and finds God in nature. For the general feeling of God as immanent in the world and as radiating thru the veil of phenomena, innumerable testimonies are cited by the students of mysticism.[16] Evelyn Underhill calls the mystic stage where this phenomenon is likely to occur the State of Illumination. The person does not feel one with God, but as "dancing" about Him. The Psalms are dominated by this sense of God as immanent in nature. All artists possess to some extent the power to see glory in all things. Most of the instances cited by James and Underhill employ visual imagery to express the feeling of God's presence. In Buber's description, the visual element is not altogether ignored. Witness the description of saying "Thou" to a tree.[17] But the process of entering into relation with the Thou is to Buber, in greater part, auditory. The nearest parallels to this phenomenon are, therefore, the reported apprehensions of voices during certain stages of the Mystic Way. The mystics distinguish three different kinds of voices: 1. The "immediate" voice which speaks wordlessly to the mind; 2. The distinct interior voice; 3. The exterior voice. Of these

---

[16] See "Varieties," p. 253.
[17] "I and Thou," p. 7.

three, the first form is regarded as most genuine, though, to non-mystics, a wordless significant voice must seem a contradiction in terms. "The word which God speaks without intermediary is no other than His Word in the soul; a substantial word, silent and inarticulate, a vivifying and energizing word; as has been said, dixit et facta sunt." [18] In "Zwiesprache," Buber gives an account of the call which came to him from the night which, appearing at first in the form of a clear voice, was later heard as a silent voice. The transition from the second to the first form of hallucination was thus effected.

While we note the resemblance of the mystic auditory hallucination to the apprehension of the Thou, we must not fail to observe the vital difference between the two phenomena. With Buber, the Thou does not convey a definite message, whereas the medieval mystics and the Jewish Chasidim often guided their lives by means of these "voices." To be sure, Richard Rolle speaks of a "state of song" and Suso heard how angels sang certain sacred sweet songs within him. Yet these experiences are not identical with the call from the "Thou" which Buber describes. That call, described in "Zwiesprache" as rhythmical, is nothing more than the feeling of being in conversation with some one, plus the assurance that this event is of supreme importance.

There is no parallel in the "Thou" relation to the sad and depressing stages of the Mystic Way. The mystic life, like any organic phenomenon, follows a rhythmic law. There are the expanding joyous stages, the awakening of the soul or conversion, the state of illumination, and the unitive state. But the mystics also tell of the need of self-mortification and purification by ascetic means and they relate of the terrible hang-over of the "Dark Night." With Buber, mortification is altogether dispensed with, except insofar as we are urged

---

[18] E. Underhill, quoting Madam Guyon, "Mysticism," p. 328.

to give up the attitude of "me" and "mine." Nor does Buber know of the misery succeeding the "Thou" relation. There is no uncertainty and no qualms of conscience to the one who met his "Thou."

That union with God can possibly be achieved, Buber takes special pains to deny. All theories of absorption sin against the Thou relation, he asserts. The universe is fundamentally dual. The mystics who claimed to have attained the state of absolute union with God mistook the intensity of the relation for the fact of union. The experience of absorption he declares to be a phenomenon "of the brink to which reality extends and at which it grows dim." The experience of ecstasy and rapture, which represents to the mystics the consummation of the tortuous and toilsome path to God, is regarded by Buber as a degenerate form of the genuine religious experience. His argument is based primarily on his own metaphysical intuition that reality is in its ultimate nature pluralistic. However, he also contends, on strictly pragmatic grounds, that the experience of ecstasy and, in general, the assiduous cultivation of mysticism, bears no relation to the practical life.[19]

He regards the feeling of union with or of absorption into the Absolute as being a form of dreamless sleep which leads not to "lived reality," but to annihilation.[20]

We are thus justified in concluding that Buber is preaching a mild form of mysticism. He urges us to arrive at the state of Illumination, but to proceed no farther on the thorny path of mysticism. What Suso called "the entrance into the upper school," Buber asks us to reject just as emphatically as we are to discard the "me" and "mine" attitude. The milder forms of mysticism which James lists under the following headings look like so many variations of emphasis on the different aspects of the "Thou" relation, in an incipient

[19] See "I and Thou," p. 88.
[20] See note 4 at end of book.

form: 1. the state when certain words or scenes seem to strike us with peculiar emphasis; 2. the state of false recognition, when things appear as familiar though they were never seen before; [21] 3. the state when all things seem charged with meaning; 4. the state induced by certain drugs, in particular by the inhalation of nitrous oxide which leaves a sense of profound meaning, of a reconciliation having been finally achieved between all opposites, but which leaves no definite content; 5. the feeling of unity with God or with nature that is induced by the sight of certain striking natural phenomena and which has been described by Bucke and called "Cosmic Consciousness."

The reports of these phenomena, though differing in emphasis and in the choice of phraseology, seem really to refer to one basic experience, which different persons would naturally express differently in accordance with their special predilections. Broadly speaking, mystical experiences are described in either transcendental and metaphysical, or in immanent and personal terminology. Mystics of the latter group can be further classified according to whether their experience is predominantly visual or auditory. Buber belongs in this last category.

The main distinction of Buber's philosophy of mysticism is to be found in its practical implications. In simple terms, we are told to cultivate an attitude of openness to external suggestion and a floating sense of devotion. No Yoga can be given, which will assuredly lead to the "Thou" relation, Buber tells us, but we can consciously reject the self-centered attitude and we can summon all our energies in readiness to devote them toward the attainment of a goal, which the "Thou" relation when it should come will reveal to us. All things can speak to us and devotion to all things is devotion to God. We are to regard whatever situation we

---

[21] Compare third dialogue of "Daniel" p. 75, where the star seems to say, "all the time I was turned toward you."

are placed in as the starting point of an endeavor. The situation will itself reveal to us what our task is. Knowing our task, our acts constitute the reply of our selves to the call of God. By these acts, we become real, and help God to create the world. "God wills to be realized . . . and no realization can take place except thru man, who actualizes himself and all being." [22]

Evil exists, to be sure, but only as a problem and as a task. The perception of evil is a challenge to us—a challenge which we are to meet with our deeds. The reward of those who heed the call is the knowledge of being real, of being in harmony with the will of God which comes to them thru his Creation. Those who live for themselves alone are to be pitied since, like the opium-eater, they live in an unreal world of their own. He alone truly lives who knows his own self to be but the one pole of his being and who feels the ties of devotion, which, like the magnetic lines of force, stream from him to men and nature and thence to the other pole, God. To be religious is to be actual, is to live in perpetual conversation with God— a conversation which coming from God to us is expressed in the needs of the situation as it is understood by man in flashes of mystical insight and which, returning from us to God, is concretized in the form of deeds performed to meet those needs. Such, in brief, is the religion of Buber.

(*e*) PRACTICAL SIGNIFICANCE OF BUBER'S MYSTICISM

TO BUBER, THE "THOU" RELATION IS THE MOST IMPORTANT fact of existence. He feels that this experience is the one fact which modern man must learn and accept in the very depths of his being, if Western civilization is to be saved from disintegration. The "Thou" relation is more than a way of finding God; thru it alone man finds himself and

---

[22] Daniel, p. 77.

thereby obtains the necessary fulcrum by which the human world may be raised from the morass of sin and chaos into which it is now so rapidly sinking.

The acid test of any idea is the extent to which it retains the capacity to appeal to our sense of reality in the face of disaster. The advent of the Nazis to power provided this crucial test for Buber's view of religion. The genuineness of his conviction is shown in the lectures he addressed to Jewish audiences.[1] (1933–35) The onset of destruction did not daunt his spirit or cause him to despair in men. In "Die Frage an den Einzelnen," published in 1936, he reaffirms his unshakeable faith that the salvation of the world depends on men learning the arts of personal relationship and of communion with God.

The evil of the present day world, Buber argues, lies in the oppressive rule of the masses (Menge) and in the prevalence of the wrong ideal of individuality. This analysis is not self-contradictory, for it is only because the true meaning of individuality was lost that the mass arose as a vast, impersonal force, destructive of personality. Already in 1919 Buber addressed himself to the intellectuals with the prophetic rebuke, "Wer hat sie gross gemacht, die Menge? Der sie hasste und der sie verachtete, den es vor ihr schauderte und den es vor ihr ekelte, ja jeder, der sagte: Menge! —sie alle haben sie gross gemacht, dass sie nun aufbranden will zu eurem Geistburgen und heimlichen Bünden." How truly prophetic these words of Buber turned out to be! The ivory towers of the intelligentsia proved to be no protection against the upsurge of the mob.

Two ideals of individuality came down to the present generation, as opposed to each other as the two poles and yet converging at one point. Max Stirner propounded the theory of absolute egoism, a new version of Protagoras'

---

[1] "Die Stunde und die Erkenntnis," by Martin Buber.

formula, "Man is the measure of all things." "Truth . . . exists only in your head," "Truth is a creature," "For me there is no truth, for above me nothing can go," Truth is "my property," "What you call responsibility is a lie," [2]—these quotations amply illustrate the position of Stirner. His importance lies in the fact that he gave powerful expression to the tendency of "total selfishness," a tendency which grew apace in our century.

Buber agrees to Stirner's attack against the objective standards of truth and morality. The more we draw into ourselves, the more do we feel free from all outside constraints. And yet, Buber cannot accept the anti-social, anarchical view of Stirner. How shall we tread the path to our own individuality and yet avoid the pitfall of Stirnerism?

The only and effective reply to Stirner, Buber finds, was given by the great Protestant thinker, Sören Kierkegaard. The Danish philosopher also propounded the absoluteness of the individual. Yet the difference between the two conceptions is striking. To Kierkegaard, the individual is a task. One must become an individual. The category of the individual cannot indeed be taught; it is a capacity, an art, the deepest art of life. Only one requisite can be stated: one must "listen." One must put the whole of one's being in relation to God.

Stirner had shown the emptiness of purely noetic truth. Kierkegaard does not dispute that contention, but he points to the possibility of discovering a truth, which is not purely noetic, which one must "realize existentially"—that is, a truth which is obtained by the turning of the whole thing toward reality. "Der Einzelne ist die Wahrheit," Kierkegaard states. For truth is but another name for God, and man "expresses" God only when in total isolation from the world, he faces His Creator. Man becomes an "I" only in relation to God as his Thou.

---

[2] "Die Frage an den Einzelnen," pp. 20, 21.

Also, in regard to the question of responsibility, Stirner argued that it could have no meaning since no one can rise above his own self. But what Stirner is really assailing, Buber insists, is only the appearance-responsibility of a Reason, an Idea, a Nature, an institution. The living sense of response to a voice which addresses us with trust and appeals to our loyalty, a voice "as real as the voice of a friend,"— this responsibility Stirner and his like have never felt. Hence, their criticism is meaningless to those who have heard the "call." This is Kierkegaard's meaning when he insists that responsibility is always of the individual.

Thus far, but no further, Buber consents to follow the lead of Kierkegaard. When the Danish thinker proceeds to demand that allegiance to God be in no way hampered by attachments to men, Buber, in line with Jewish thought from Moses down, refuses to agree. To Kierkegaard the crowd was the great untruth. In a sense, Buber too accepts this idea for the saying of Thou to God can take place only in solitude. But, the Jewish mystic insists, the realization of the message thus received can only occur in the sphere of human relationships.

Kierkegaard is quoted as cautioning those who would become individuals. "Jeder soll nur mit Vorsicht sich mit den andern einlassen und wesentlich nur mit Gott und mit sich selbst reden." [3] This formula which couples talk with oneself and with God is irksome to Buber who regards talk with the "other" as being not essentially different from talk with God. Again, the admonition to preserve one's inner soul from too close contact with men is in direct opposition to the thought of Buber who teaches that God is only found by those who enter into the closest contact with men. For "God and man are not rivals." [4]

Kierkegaard's renunciation of marriage was prompted by

---

[3] Ibid., p. 31.

[4] Ibid., p. 34.

the thought that the love of God is incompatible with an "essential" love of woman. "In defiance of the whole nineteenth century, I cannot get married," the great Christian theologian exclaimed. Marriage diverts the love of the Creator to the created and drags man into the life of the community. No greater contrast to the teaching of Buber could be found. "God desires that we come to Him through the Reginas [5] that he has created and not by cutting loose from them." It is only a false image of God that is found by those who spurn the society of men and seek Him by the short-cut of solitary meditation. God is truly to be found only by those who take "the longest way," the way of active service to all men. Thus, marriage is the institution through which God is really found. For in it, the "Thou" relationship between two human beings is established in its purity. I love the "Other" and through it—only through it, God. The relation obtaining in marriage is exemplary of the relation one ought to adopt toward the community. "Die Menge zu entmengen!" We ought to break through the iron ring of classifications into which we tend to divide the people that we meet. The true individual is the one for whom the crowd does not exist as a crowd, but as so many concrete persons, so many candidates for the living "Thou" relation.

Accordingly, one must be conscious of his responsibility not only for himself, but for all the "others" which the God of history had thrown in his path. Of this responsibility, we may not absolve ourselves by making one grand decision, which is thereafter to guide our life for all the future. The party, the leader, the minister cannot answer the call which God sends to our own hearts. Neither can a definite set of rules be given, by which conduct may be regulated. Each hour must bring its own decision. "What God demands of me for this hour I experience, insofar as I do experience it,

---

[5] Regina was the name of Kierkegaard's bride, whom he loved. However, he broke the engagement for "religious" reasons.

at this same hour, not before it." [6] What the decision is to be, no one can foretell, as it comes from God and is not arrived at, on the basis of any calculations of success. Of course, the knowledge of all relevant facts is important; but this knowledge cannot serve as the substitute for the decision. "One thing alone is essential; that I open my ear to the situation as it presents itself to me, waiting for the appearance of the Word, until hearing flows into Being and I perceive what there is to perceive, and reply to that which was perceived." [7]

Is this advice to be identified with the common notion of conscience? Not with the superficial meaning of this term; the conscience of which Buber speaks must be rediscovered again and again—and that, "existentially," by a total concentration of one's entire being.

This position of Buber's is in direct opposition to the whole modern tendency to worship the collective ideal, the group rather than the person. Thus, Oswald Spengler [8] says that human groups are like "beasts of prey," and it is sheer folly to close our eyes to this fact. Carl Schmitt takes as the criterion for politics the contrast between friend and foe. [9] He and Friedrich Gogarten, a Catholic writer, agree in the assumption that man is basically evil. The latter makes all ethics dependent on politics. For man, being sinful, cannot know what is good; hence he must receive his ethical direction from the state. Individual liberty can only breed evil, chaos and confusion, since individualism is the source of sin. Thus, fascism, or the police-state, manages to put on a religious garb. Against this worship of collectivism, Buber points to the need for individual decision—a decision, made by man alone with God and his conscience. Man is not

---

[6] Ibid., p. 67.
[7] Ibid., p. 69.
[8] Ibid., p. 77.
[9] Carl Schmitt, "Der Begriff des Politischen."

radically evil or good he insists. Man is "fallen" only in relation to God, not to other men, or to any human institution. The basic religious and political attitude must be that of reverence and love for the human person, such as he is in all his otherness. No political institution is to be permitted to assume the role of sole intercessor between God and men.

"But I maintain that the human person occupies the irreplaceable central place in the battle between the movement of the world away from God and its movement toward God." [10]

Thus Buber's view of the nature of the religious experience leads him to formulate an ethics of creativity and to insist that the state has no right to interfere with the creative functioning of the human conscience. He seems to accept Fichte's contention [11] that man, knowing himself to be free, cannot do wrong.

In view of the ravages which the human personality has suffered in recent decades from the excessive emphasis placed upon the methods of the sociologist and of the psycho-analyst, the position of Buber must be welcomed heartily as a healthy reaction. The inevitable result of the methods which deal with human society in terms of mass processes is to reduce the conception of man to that of a figure in a chart. Once man is regarded as solely the object of a scientific inquiry, the basis of human freedom has been undermined. For science necessarily proceeds on the assumption that there is no freedom in the object of its study. Also, science assumes that the expert's opinion is alone correct, thus paving the way for tyranny by self-styled experts and cocksure doctrinnaires. Buber insists that man can rise above the conventions of society and by an "existential" mode of thought, derive counsel from God. Thru its possible relation to God,

---

[10] Ibid., p. 70.
[11] "Science of Ethics," p. 183.

the human personality derives an importance and an authority, which the dictates of the state may not ignore.

Though valuable as a protest against the tendencies to degrade the human personality, Buber's philosophy is not without dangers of its own. Those, who, like Buber, have felt the inner voice of God commanding them what to do and what not to do are, of course, beyond the reach of argument. True, their knowledge is not of the same order of certainty as mathematical truth. Yet, they are convinced that their orders are from God, and God will do no wrong. Those of us, however, who are constrained to judge the value of these "inner calls" by external standards, may well feel uneasy at the total absence of the rational element in the decision advocated by Buber. If only we were certain that the call came from God! But, what if Satan should intervene instead! How are we to tell the voice of the "Eternal Thou" from that of the "demonic Thou?" (Is not Hitler, too, a mystic?)

If God be not defined by any rational attribute, then is devotion to Him a snare, more than a beacon of light. How are men to know what God wills them to do? They are to turn with a heart full of devotion, we are told, to the things about them, and the answer of God will come. If it does! But, if God does not speak, the formal conditions of the experiment are likely to induce a sense of assurance of the ultimate value of the thing contemplated. In that event, the things to which we turn, whatsoever they be, will elicit our response. Loyalty to all things is likely to prove as pernicious a doctrine as loyalty to none.

That devotion uncontrolled by reason is a greater danger to society than selfishness, history proves abundantly. We find this truth scrawled all over the story of mankind, in letters of fire and blood. It may be that wars were once waged for economic ends, which the ruling group sought, but the masses of the embroiled nations could not have been induced to go to war if they were not lured thereto by devotion to the cause of nationalism. The glory of Greece, of Rome, of the Church, of the Prophet, of French culture, of the Germanic race—how many rivers of blood were poured to cool the wraths of the all too passionate devotions to these several ends! Buber assures us that devotion to all things is ultimately devotion to God. But opposite devotions clash and more violently so than opposing selfish interests.

Basically this criticism points to the inadequacy of the idea of God in Buber's thought. God never reveals Himself; he only reveals His Will. Living in response to His Will, we learn to know His Nature from the commands of His which we heed. We fill in our image of God by the lines of influence stemming from Him, which we embody in our lives through our actions. This really means that the idea of God cannot serve as a guide to our fund of devotion, since it is rather formed in our mind by the turns which our devotion happens to take. But without God as a directing influence, devotion to the things of the environment becomes pure idolatry, which is the original sin of mankind.[12]

The only guide for devotion which we find in the writings of Buber is the employment of the expression "Thou" to indicate the object of devotion. "Thou" is addressed to a person. The saying of "Thou" to an object is below the level of speech; in human relations it takes the form of speech; in relation to God, it soars above the level of speech. It follows that in our relations with men the saying of "Thou" is most clearly to be found. Universe loyalty is thus defined as being, in its higher manifestation and in preference, loyalty

---

[12] It is instructive to note the comparison of Buber's dialogue-living with Royce's "Philosophy of Loyalty." Royce, too, begins with loyalty as an ultimate value and is then compelled to evolve as a guiding principle for loyalty the maxim, "be loyal to loyalties." Buber, on the other hand, does not offer an explicit principle of guidance.

to men. I say loyalty to men, not to mankind, advisedly, for though Buber asks us to reject the loyalties to "my nation," "my race," "my religion," along with devotion to all other things that are "mine," the fact remains that we are asked to render devotion to the immediate social scene and to the men and women that actually evoke it. In practice, the view of Buber may well lead to intensified provincialism, nationalism, or of statism.

Unless the idea of God becomes a guide to the devotions of men, rather than the resultant therefrom, devotion to humanity will not prevail. For this purpose, the idea of God as love, or the source of all relations of personal love, is still insufficient. For love may be, and often is, capricious and clannish.

The idea of a God of love is capable of invigorating an ethical life, but not of replacing reason as a guide to the good life. In history, the worship of the God of love proved to be compatible with a variety of cruelties and brutalities which sane men have always deplored. If guidance is not derived from the idea of God, it will be derived from life itself, and the course of life is, from an ethical standpoint, perpetually downward.

The views of both Pratt and Leuba that the value of the mystic way consists in the interpretation of the experience, rather than in the nature of the experience itself, may not be entirely correct. Nevertheless, few students of mysticism will deny the decisive importance of the elements of interpretation in the development of the mystic's thoughts. What if the "converted one," heeding the call from the eternal Thou, performs an act which his rational self declares to be wrong? Shall he then declare the voice he had heard to have been demonic? Or shall he announce that God is beyond good and evil? The choice between these two alternative explanations is bound to affect the later life of the "convert."

It is evident from all the above that Buber's teaching can-

not be recommended as in itself sufficient to guide the destinies of men.[13]

---

[13] There are two ways of conceiving the guidance one may derive from
mystical insight. With the mystics of the Classical tradition we may regard
the "Unitive Life" as a "led life" in which every important decision is
directly conveyed to the mystic from God. George Fox and the Quakers
represent this belief at its best. The Baalshem, too, lives this philosophy
in Buber's tales. It is also possible to think of the mystic insight as being
an increase in creative spiritual power which results in ethical decisions only
indirectly. The decisions are likely to rise above the average standards of
the day, but they are neither absolute nor divine. Bergson and Hocking
concur in this view, albeit with significant differences in the nature of the
mystic's creativity.

Now, Buber seems to move between these two poles. From his language,
it is not always possible to tell which view he favors. It is doubtful whether
he would draw a strict line of demarcation between these views. In either
case, the fact that Buber has no theories concerning the nature of the Deity
renders his philosophy of life rudderless and adrift. Again, the fact that
God is not addressed in vacuo, but through the objects about us, necessarily
restricts the possible limits of God's message. If, now, we believe with
perfect faith that God has a definite message for us, it does not really
matter how we place ourselves in readiness to receive it.

If, however, the message is as catholic as the universe in which we live,
then it does greatly matter both in the life of the individual and of society,
what aspects of the environment we choose as the Thou of our self. Now,
Buber offers no principle of selection, whereby the Dialogue-life may be
directed. (See Hocking, "Meaning of God in Human Experience" Ch. 14,
Bergson "Two Sources of Morality and Religion" Chap. III, "Tales of
Baalchem," by Martin Buber.)

CHAPTER V

MORDECAI M. KAPLAN— RECONSTRUCTIONISM

(a) RELIGION AS A GROUP AFFAIR
(b) RELIGION AS A HEALTHY REACTION
    TO LIFE
(c) THE COSMIC SOURCE OF HUMAN IDEALS
(d) THE RECONSTRUCTION OF JUDAISM

IN AMERICA, THE LEADING MIND AMONG THE EXPONENTS OF modernistic Judaism is that of Mordecai M. Kaplan. As the most influential member of the faculty of the Jewish Theological Seminary, Kaplan impressed his thought on the minds of scores of young rabbis, who have become his faithful disciples. The publication of his major opus, "Judaism as a Civilization," served to crystallize the trend of religio-culturism, which later emerged upon the scene as Reconstructionism. It is still too early to evaluate the merits of this new movement, since its full implications have not yet been uncovered even in theory. A generation of American Judaism, at least, would have to elapse before the practical corollaries of the Reconstructionist doctrines will have affected the actual structure of Jewish life. Nevertheless, we feel that the movement has already assumed dimensions which entitle it to respectful attention. It is hoped that the critical analysis of the theoretical foundations of Reconstructionism, which is presented in this chapter, will prove helpful in molding the future shape of the movement. In the history of thought, the accidental association of ideas is known to have led frequently to the most unexpected consequences. It is the purpose of this chapter to expose the different threads of thought, which have been woven into the texture of Reconstructionism, in order that its real implications may be better understood. Since the literature of this movement is easily available, we shall not present a detailed exposition of it, expecting the reader to familiarize himself with Kaplan's works.

(a) Religion Is Essentially a Group Affair

THE BASIC THOUGHT OF KAPLAN IS THAT THE GROUP IS ALL important in the history of mankind. Kaplan is a sociologist, and he never for a moment permits himself to forget the all-pervading influence of society. In the beginning, was society. No phase of human life can be understood apart from it. No human experience is so intimate as to be wholly individual. Certainly religion is not exempt from this influence. In fact, Kaplan comes near to saying, religion is nothing but the consciousness of group values.

We shall not be able to comprehend the true meaning of his thought until we have become acquainted with the sources of his ideas. There is a school of sociologists, associated with the names of Levy-Brühl and Durkheim, which attempts to understand all the phenomena of present-day culture from a study of the civilizations of primitive peoples. The categories of thought which these sociologists claim to have found among the Hottentots and the aborigines of Australia they seek to apply to our own societies. Primitive peoples, it will be recalled, lack a clear consciousness of individual personality. Their "collective consciousness" is apparent in all spheres of primitive life, or, to put it more simply, the individual savage has no mind of his own. He "thinks" and "reasons" only as a member of his particular group. This "reasoning" does not follow the laws of strict logic. It may be called a special type of social or organic thinking. Religion, as is well known, pervades every expression of group activity among savages. They possess no social life which is not also an integral part of their religious life. They have no secular culture apart from religion, nor any group interests whatsoever that have not been sanctified by their faith. The aspirations of the tribe are inextricably woven into its body of religious practices and so-called doctrines.

Now, these sociologists conclude, religion is nothing but the manner in which the group consciousness of the tribe is expressed. What is important to the tribe is "sacred" to it. The significant experiences of the tribe are transmuted into a mythical biography of its god. In brief, there is nothing in the religion of the savage which is not a sublimation or a projection of the wants of his tribe. The savage feels the "collective consciousness" of his group as an irresistible pressure from the outside. He "projects" this group-voice first in the figure of a totem animal or plant, later in the other figures and myths which constitute primitive ritual. All such "projections" are embodiments of collective emotion, desire and hope. Thus group emotion is the essence of religion.

It is important to realize that this view departs radically from the theories concerning the origin of religion which have been in vogue since the very beginning of philosophical thinking. The origin of religion was thought to be fear of the Unknown, or a sense of awe in relation to the great universe, or a sudden realization of human weakness and "dependence," or a certain "creaturely" feeling which is characteristically human, or a special human endowment provided by nature to offset the weakening effects of the human intellect. According to all these theories, it is the human individual that is the subject of religious experience. According to the Durkheim theory, however, it is not man versus the universe that gives rise to religion, but man as part of society, versus nature as seen by society, that is the be-all and end-all of religion.

The theory of Durkheim appears to be a major cornerstone in the thought of Kaplan. Thus he writes [1] "but on the higher level of spiritual thought and conduct as on the lower level, the feeling of togetherness is indispensable to the realization of God, for without it we cannot experience God at all." All religion is based on the consciousness of

---

[1] "Meaning of God," p. 251.

society, "for it is only as a member of society that man comes to know God at all." The awareness of God comes only to those who possess a strong group consciousness.[2] The term sacred or holy is but another name for that of supreme importance to the group. Thus he writes,[3] "If we consider all the various objects, institutions and persons that have been declared holy, not only by the Jewish religion, but by any of the other religions, both those of antiquity and of modern times, we find that they are the objects, institutions and persons that particular groups felt to be of supreme importance to them." [4]

If it be true that the experience of religion is essentially the heightened consciousness of group interests and values, then it necessarily follows that religion has little or no reality apart from the vital problems of the nation or race in which it evolved. Religion is not a "world-view," or a set of metaphysical notions, or a definite manner of reacting to the Infinite. It is simply and solely a name given to certain aspects of group life. "Religion abstracted from the other human interests that express themselves in a civilization becomes irrelevant and pointless, a way of speaking rather than a way of living." [5]

Pursuing this line of thought further, it is apparent that in order to obtain a proper perspective in which to view the present problems of religion, it is necessary to see exactly what function a religion performs in the structure of the society, to which it is indigenous. If religion is primarily a social phenomenon, then it must be approached from the standpoint of a sociologist, who is not concerned with the "truth" of any social belief, nor with the "reasons" for those beliefs, but with the actual operation of the religious motive

---

[2] Ibid., p. 263.
[3] Ibid., p. 82.
[4] See also J. 317, M. 190, M. 258, M. 260.
[5] Ibid., p. 17.

in different civilizations. From the study of the place of religion in a human society, inferences may then be drawn concerning the specific problems of any religion in modern Western society.

There is a subtle yet extremely significant difference between inquiring "what place does religion occupy in ancient and modern societies?" and "what *function* does religion perform in a society?" The former question is thoroughly objective, taking nothing for granted. The second involves the conscious assumption that a society is an "organic" entity, in which every part performs a definite function, even as the different limbs in a living body. Thus, it is at least possible that religion is the result of individual reactions to the strange mystery of existence. These individual insights and beliefs become the property of the whole tribe through the normal processes of the dissemination of ideas, through the influence of a leading personality, or through mass conversions. The different religious ideas, then, interact with the other social forces, stifling some and stimulating others. Greek religion, for instance, encouraged the development of the arts, while it hampered the growth of ethical convictions —a fact already noted by Plato in the Republic. On the other hand, the Jewish religion stimulated the development of moral insight and devotional literature, while damming the creative impulses of the Jewish people in the fields of sculpture and painting. Religious ideas are social forces, at once constructive and destructive, operating in a social milieu along with other ideas and motives deriving from different sources. In posing to himself the question of the "function" of religion in a society, Kaplan assumes that every society is an "organic" entity in which the existence of every phase can be explained in terms of its utility to the total structure of society.

Reasoning further from this standpoint, Kaplan points out the functions of the God-idea in a human society. The need

of commanding respect for the laws of a tribe is one such
function; the need of impressing upon the members of the
tribe the importance of certain books, national heroes, and
some historical events is another such function. Through
the God-idea these things are endowed with the quality of
"holiness" and rendered inviolable. Thus, the social result
of religion, the element which Kaplan construes as its origin
and essence, is to preserve the sancta of the group. It is the
function of God and the servants of God to hallow the national will, "for the pragmatic significance of the God-idea is
the recognition of certain elements in life as supremely important." [6]

Armed with this knowledge, we are in a position to understand what forms a modern religion must assume in order
to conform to the needs of modern society. The general
requisite is, of course, that religion should stamp with its
approval those forces and tendencies in modern societies
which men today regard as supremely important. The assumption involved at this point is the one previously noted,
that primitive society and, hence, that primitive religion is
typical religion.

This assumption is important to the understanding of
Kaplan's system for it determines the essential phases of his
thought. Primitive societies are presumably stable societies.
Since we have no means of learning their histories, it may be
conveniently assumed that they have no histories and undergo very little, if any, transformation. Their societies are
in a state of equilibrium and may therefore be used as
standards by which to measure our own societies, that are at
present in the transition period. It need hardly be pointed
out that this assumption is no more than an assumption,
resting more on the meagreness of our knowledge concerning
primitive mentality and history than on any proved scientific
data.

---

[6] Ibid., p. 18.

The determining characteristic of a primitive culture is the absence in it of exact knowledge and the paucity of critical reasoning. The growth of reason and self-consciousness have steadily modified human societies. Assuming a continuous expansion and popularization of critical knowledge, it may be expected that modern societies will move ever farther away from the primitive type. As the clan and the tribe were slowly outgrown and rendered obsolete, so too will all national and racial sancta be discarded in the future, as too constrictive and divisive. To regard primitive society as typical is to eliminate the element of rationality as a potent factor from the study of human societies. Room is thus provided for all sorts of non-intellectual and anti-intellectual doctrines.

Despite these evident objections, Kaplan erects an imposing edifice of reasoning on this estimate of primitive society. Since religion among primitives is a group of practices and doctrines which perform the function of preserving all that is dear and important to the tribe, religion in the future must similarly be integrated with group traditions, hopes and aspirations. More specifically, religions in the future will be indistinguishable from the national civilizations of the different peoples in Europe and America. Each nation of the future will develop its own religion, even as each tribe in ancient times observed its own creed. Christianity will be broken up in a host of national churches, each hallowing the national treasures of its own past. The universalistic aspirations of Judaism, Christianity and Islam were erroneous and illusory. If not universal ideas, but the particularistic interests of groups are the essence of religion, it follows that national faiths are the only kind that have any chance of survival. Christianity aspired to embrace all mankind. This aim was in reality an extension of the ambitions of Roman imperialism. "The doctrine that no one could attain salvation except through the church was tantamount to the demand that the *reorganized Roman empire* constitute one's entire world." [7]   In the future, the "religious imperialism" of the Church will be overcome and national creeds, corresponding to and idealizing the different national patriotisms will sprout forth.   No longer will Jewish history and heroes form the foci of sanctity to the nations of Europe.   The growing self-consciousness of the different nations will gradually flower into folk religions, for "the way in which religion functioned in the past conformed with the social needs of human nature." [8]

From this viewpoint, Judaism may well look forward to the future with confidence, since it still retains its intimate connection with the Jewish people.   Judaism is even now the "folk religion" of Israel.   "The Jewish people has demonstrated the validity of the principle, which has been repeatedly verified by the experience of mankind, that a folk religion retains its relevance and vitality so long as it confines itself to those who have evolved it." [9]   Having thus brushed aside with the magic wand of contempt nineteen centuries of Christian experience, Kaplan proceeds to the deduction that the vitalization of the Jewish religion demands the intensification of Jewish national consciousness.   Judaism should be interpreted as a civilization, no longer merely as a religion.   All aspects of national experience and hope should be thoroughly integrated with the Jewish religion, so that its character as folk religion may be clearly exhibited. It is in the interest of religion to stress what rationalists may call the secular phases of group life.   "Paradoxical as it may sound, the spiritual regeneration of the Jewish people demands that religion cease to be its sole preoccupation." [10] Jewish worship will regain its once electrifying power for the

---

[7] "Judaism as a Civilization," p. 340.
[8] Ibid., p. 341.
[9] Ibid., p. 343.
[10] Ibid., p. 345.

Jew when his national communal life will have been re-established. "It is significant that in past ages, when Jews led an autonomous communal life, this particular complaint that the individual could not experience God in the worship of the synagogue was unheard of." [11]

Kaplan is not unmindful of the danger of national religions turning into consecrated chauvinisms—a tendency which has been in progress in Germany for many years, and which gave rise to many forms of neo-paganism, a la Alfred Rosenberg, since the advent of the Nazis to power. He feels, however, that this danger can be held in check by the force of "personal religion," which is the religion of the great minds that dare place the authority of their conscience above that of the creed of the group. At this point, the inner contradiction of Kaplan's thinking comes to the surface. He notes that "personal religion" is universalistic,[12] whereas folk religion is in effect the self-worship of a group. He realizes, too, the great need of "personal religion," which he describes as attainable only by a small percentage of humanity. Nevertheless, he does not inquire whether the two can logically coexist. In the struggle for existence of nations and individuals, folk religion and personal religion naturally lead to two different courses of action. Which is the *right* path to follow? What is the *true* view of man's rights and duties? The terms "right" and "true" are jealous gods, that brook no partners. If personal religion be true, then is folk-religion idolatry. In actual practice, ideas are always at war. But, how can one who belongs to the elect and possesses "personal religion" teach a form of religion which is untrue?

It may be observed at this juncture that the doctrine which teaches that religious experience is essentially awareness of group values can be applied to modern religion in a totally different manner than in the one chosen by Kaplan. We may

[11] M. 246.
[12] J. 348.

take due account of the growth of ethical feeling, which knows neither political nor racial boundaries. When we are at our best, we think in terms of all mankind, as the all-inclusive society of the future. This is not individualistic, "personal" religion. The modern "folk" is humanity itself. Once the atavistic wave of Nazism had sunk back into the oblivion of barbarism and the world had resumed its forward march, the emergence of this united humanity could not be far off. To say that self-identification with the evolving humanity of the future is of the essence of religion, would indeed be to express the spirit of modern religion—in truth, of all prophetic religion. The replacement of the group-element by the ethical element is the mark of all higher religions.

But, Kaplan could legitimately stump us with the question, have human beings already reached the stage where they are conscious of all humanity as being their group? At this sad hour in world history, when moral feeling has ebbed to an unprecedented low level, we must hesitate to answer in the affirmative. In the long run, we are certain of the triumph of humanity, but in the next century or so we cannot dogmatically assert what the pattern of men's loyalties will be. Thus, it may well be that Kaplan's predictions concerning the course of religion will prove true for a generation or so, before the pendulum swings again toward a religion of humanity.

To summarize the discussion in this section, Kaplan takes his categories of religion from the study of primitive society. Among primitives, religion performs the function of preserving the elements of tribal life that are important to the life of the group. In modern times, the intimate connection between religion and national life has been lost. This is especially true of the Christian faiths—hence, their weakness. Judaism retained its vitality only because it remained the national civilization of the Jew. Reform Judaism which sought to sever all ties with the national heritage of Israel is doomed to degeneration and failure. In the future, national faiths will be the rule rather than the exception. Accordingly, it behooves the Jewish people even now to strengthen its national culture and to reinterpret its heritage, so that Judaism may be reconstructed as a "folk-religion."

(b) Religion Is a Healthy Reaction to Life

We come now to an analysis of the specific content of religion according to Kaplan. On the one hand, he realizes that, while consciousness of group values is the form which religion assumes, it does not constitute its entire content. No amount of patriotism can, as such, become synonymous with religion. Kaplan, indeed, says of patriotism that, "it is in a large measure the modern form of folk religion."[1] Nevertheless, he concedes that national loyalty is not quite the same emotional and ideational complex as religion, though in function they may be alike. Religion possesses a content of its own, by virtue of which it is enabled to exercise its several "functions." This elementary observation is not disputed by Kaplan. On the other hand, it is not possible for him to recognize as the content of religion, that collection of explanations and "reasons" by which every creed justifies its rites and ceremonies. To do so, would amount to disavowing his central thesis that it is group emotion which is the basis of religion. There must be something, outside of group emotion, which is none-the-less common to all forms of religion. To an analysis of Kaplan's ideas on this subject, we must now turn.

Kaplan sees religion as growing out of all the forces of life. Thus, he recognizes in religion an emotional, a volitional and an intellectual element. Various forms of religion may emphasize one or another of these elements; yet, all three are to be found normally in all creeds. The emotional

[1] J. 337.

element presumably is that of self-identification with the group. Upon this emotional base, the conative and intellectual elements erect the structure of religion.

The conative element in religion is, to Kaplan, a direct development of the will to live. Impelled by this will to live, man ascribes value to all thoughts and things which aid him in the struggle of existence. Looking for salvation, man identifies as Divine all the things that aid him in his quest. The term "salvation," as used by Kaplan, means simply "happiness," except that this word possesses for him a flavor of sanctity. Thus, he writes, "When our mind functions in such a way that we feel that all our powers are actively employed in the achievement of desirable ends, we have achieved personal salvation." [2] This description of salvation differs in no essential respects from the definition of the term happiness, except for the ambiguous words, "desirable ends," which may be interpreted in both an ethical and a personal sense— i.e., the "ends" may be those desired by the individual person, by the moral nature of man, by society as a whole, or by God. In the writings of Kaplan, these several meanings appear to be meant at different times. [3]

[2] M. 53.

[3] Thus, he recognizes, in man's ethical impulses, motives essentially different from the ordinary feelings of mankind. Of humanism, he writes, "But this interpretation is inadequate, because it fails to express and to foster the feeling that man's ethical aspirations are part of a *cosmic urge,* by obeying which man makes himself at home in the universe." (italics mine) M. 244. In the same connection, he identifies as the "dynamic of ethical action" the spirit of worship. Again on page 115 of the same book, he writes of "something in the human being that craves giving itself to others" without pronouncing any metaphysical judgment concerning this "something." Kaplan speaks indeed in many passages of the realization of human aims as being assured by the structure of reality. Yet, this belief in itself does not make every ethical impulse as such, divine and authoritative. In places, Kaplan insists that the "ethical strivings of man" are not outside nature. On the contrary, he declares, "all that religion calls upon us to believe is that the element of helpfulness, kindness, and fair play is not limited to man alone, but is diffused thruout the natural order." M. 75. This passage is an echo of the famous thesis of Kropotkin that cooperation is a general character-

His dominant position seems to be that the goal of personal happiness involves the happiness of society as a whole. "Selfish salvation is an impossibility, because no human being is psychologically self-sufficient." [4] To be individually happy, our friends must be similarly blessed and their friends, too, by similar reasoning, must be free from sorrow. Thus the quest for individual happiness involves the ideal of an order, in which all men will be enabled to realize their wishes and to attain the goal of happiness. The forces and things which help in the realization of this ideal are Divine.

The first part of this argument, which seeks to base altruism on selfishness is, of course, an age-old and respectable philosophical doctrine, though, to non-philosophers, it was never more than a pious quibble. Really selfish people have never yet been fooled by it. For, the argument leaves out of consideration the degrees of interest which the individual, on a purely selfish basis, possesses in the well-being of his fellow-men. While that concern is present in theory to the intelligently and resolutely selfish, it is but a tiny fraction of their concern with themselves and, hence, of negligible value in practice. Certainly, their concern with the well-being of society is too flimsy to serve as the foundation of social idealism.

In any case, Kaplan asserts that the search for happiness is the impulse which confers the title of "sacred" on things. Whatever contributes to the happiness of the person, the group, or mankind is holy. This valuation requires no intellectual assumptions; it derives directly from the individual's will to live. The normal person who loves life and is

---

istic of living creatures. In general, it may be said that despite occasional expressions, Kaplan does not think of the moral law as being intrinsically different from other human impulses—a theory which Kant had made famous. He follows the relativistic and pragmatistic school of ethics, the greatest exponent of which is the American philosopher, John Dewey.

[4] M. 53.

endowed with a healthy constitution, will naturally classify
things as either evil or good, depending upon the degree of
help he can obtain from them in his quest for self-fulfillment.
The adjective "holy" he will bestow on things that are of the
highest value to him. "The distinction between the holy and
the profane, the sacred and the secular, is essentially the same
as the distinction between the valuable and the worthless, the
important and the trivial, the significant and the meaningless." [5]

To this extent, then, religion does not involve the acceptance of any belief in historical or metaphysical propositions. It is simply an affirmative attitude to life in general.
Thus, he writes, "The God-idea is not an idea but the reaction of the entire organism to life, the reaction by which
man's will to live overcomes the fears and the miseries that
only a being of his mental capacity can know." [6] In another
place, he writes of an *"organic acceptance"* [7] of certain elements of life and of "the 'yea' of our entire personality," [8]
as being the basic attitude of religion. The opposite of religion, in this sense, therefore, is not disbelief, but pessimism,
cynicism, defeatism and perhaps, intellectual detachment.
The question at issue is whether life be worth living and the
answer to this question can only be the famous adage, quoted
by William James in his discussion of this question, "it depends on the liver." The religious attitude is simply the
reaction of a healthy and energetic person to life.

This view of religion appears to exlude from the circle of
the blessed a number of very pious people, who looked upon
this world as a vale of tears, doomed to disappear in a final
blaze of destruction. The gloomy judgment, in which the
schools of both Hillel and Shamai concurred that "it were

[5] M. 82.
[6] J. 330.
[7] J. 397.
[8] M. 27.

better for man if he had not been born" was, on this view, not conceived in the spirit of religion. The entire world-view of the Puritan, or of the Catholic, who regards this world as evil, steeped in the morass of "original sin" and the bliss of the other world as reserved only for the small minority of mankind, is essentially unreligious. From an objective, psychological standpoint, the "varieties of religious experience" can not be restricted to the class of the healthy-minded only.[9]

This hypothesis that religion is a healthy reaction to group life and to life in general, avoids the biggest obstacle to religious faith in modern times—the fact, namely, that it is a faith, requiring intellectual assent to a set of propositions. If the ideational element of religion is minimized or eliminated completely, there is no longer any possibility of conflict between science and religion. Science is simply systematized human intelligence and knowledge. It can have no quarrel with "an attitude to reality," save as that attitude gives birth to concepts of God and judgments concerning His work in the world. In a modern religion, those concepts and judgments will be derived from experience, even as it is interpreted for us by the progress of science itself.[10]

Still, there is a hitch to this comfortable reasoning. For, Kaplan knows that religion cannot quite get along without the idea of God as an actually existing Being, concerned with the destiny of men. A "God-idea" that is only a sanctimonious echo of human will and emotion will simply not do. We must believe that God really is, not only that we want Him to be. Reduce this intellectual element as we may, we cannot ignore the fact that modern man is a rational being and that group emotion and exuberant vitality in any conceivable combination or permutation, do not spell religion. With all

---

[9] See "The Varieties of Religious Experience" by William James, who classifies religious experience in the two categories of "healthy-minded" and "sick-minded."

[10] J. 307.

his efforts to tone down the intellectual element in religion, he knows that there can be no religion without it. Group-emotion finds expression in national patriotism, social ideal-ism gives rise to humanism; mix them as you will, patriotism and humanism—exasperatingly enough, do not quite add up to religion. An element of belief is indispensable. Thus, we come to the third basic thought in Kaplan's philosophy of Judaism.

(c) THE UNIVERSE IS SO CONSTITUTED THAT HUMAN IDEALS ARE CERTAIN TO BE ULTIMATELY REALIZED

THE RESIDUAL ELEMENT OF BELIEF, WHICH RELIGION CAN-not but insist upon, is that the universe is so constructed as to make sure that the ideals of humanity will ultimately be realized.

These ideals are not to be conceived in a static sense, as blueprints for the world of the future. The ideals of man-kind are always projections, embodying the desire to escape from an existing, unpleasant situation. Hence, the realiza-tion of some ideals brings with it the creation of new prob-lems and the genesis of new ideals. Life can be depended upon to provide fresh problems for every generation. Thus, the one and only belief of Kaplan's theology may be re-phrased as follows: There is in the universe a Power, sym-pathetic to the cause of humanity. Accordingly, we are justi-fied in believing that the universe as a whole and human so-ciety in particular will approach ever closer the highest ideals of mankind. In Kaplan's own words, "when we believe in God, we believe that reality—the world of inner and outer being, the world of society and of nature—is so constituted as to enable man to achieve salvation." [1]

Upon this belief, Kaplan knows that he must insist if he is not to give up the attempt of finding a philosophy of re-

---

[1] M. 26.

ligion and be content instead with mere humanism. The step from humanism to religion is taken when *hope* for continuous improvement of human society is transformed into belief in the necessary fulfillment of the hope. This step, small as it may appear, involves a leap into metaphysics, however unwilling the author himself may be to launch upon such an adventure. For if the attainment of human salvation is to be "guaranteed," there must be a force within nature even now, strong enough to effect this result.

This Power in nature, Kaplan identifies as God. Thus, he writes, "God may therefore be defined as the Power that endorses what we believe ought to be true, and that guarantees that it will be true." [2] The God-idea, according to Kaplan, must be able to do two things for the modern man—it must accord authority to man's ethical strivings and it must assure him of the ultimate realizeability of these aspirations. Without these two assurances, religion is impossible and idealism is sheer heroic futility. "There is so much of defeat and frustration, lingering disease, death of friends in the prime of life, so much unnecessary suffering and heartless wrongdoing, that if we are not fortified by faith in a Power that endorses what in our most illumined moments we believe to be right, and that makes for its realization, we cannot regard the ought as more than idle fancy, and the hope of a better world as anything more than mirage." [3]

Having arrived at these two propositions as descriptive of what the idea of God should do, we must next seek a more exact definition of what it is that God actually does—i.e., we must learn what activities in the present world Kaplan identifies as being those of God. The questions we must seek to answer are first, whether God is identified with the whole of nature or whether He is conceived only as a Power within nature or again whether He is a Power, standing out-

---

[2] M. 324.
[3] M. 326.

side nature and effecting His will through certain forces that
derive ultimately from Him.

In the writings of Kaplan, these questions are not clearly
envisaged, leaving his concept of God extremely vague and
ambiguous. In his "Judaism as a Civilization," Kaplan as-
sails the dichotomy between the natural and the supernatural
as an outworn superstition, that is the source of much intellectual confusion and spiritual perplexity. The world of the
spirit and the world of nature, the physical order and the
moral order, God and the universe are one. "The so-called
laws of nature represent the manner of God's immanent functioning. The element of creativity, which is not accounted
for by the so-called laws of nature and which points to the
organic character of the universe or its life as a whole, gives
us a clue to God's transcendent functioning. God is not an
indefineable being who stands outside the universe. God is
the life of the universe, immanent insofar as each part acts
upon every other and transcendent insofar as the whole acts
upon each part."[4] According to this quotation, Kaplan accepts the first alternative, identifying God with nature, taken
as a whole. True, he speaks of the "life" of the universe and
not of the universe itself as being God. If the laws of nature
however, are descriptive of the functioning of this "life," it
is nothing but a name for the totality of forces that keep the
universe in motion. In this sense, God is the natura natu-
rans of Spinoza,[5] the underlying unceasing energy of the
universe.

---

[4] J. 316.

[5] The expression, "insofar as the whole acts upon each part," introduces
an order of causality, which is not scientific, and which is related to ordinary
scientific causality in much the same manner as the supernatural, miraculous
order was related to the natural one, in the scheme of the Jewish Medieval
thinkers. It is impossible to learn from the expression itself to what phenomena, in the physical or in the human world, our author is referring.
The phraseology is reminiscent of Hocking's "Meaning of God in Human
Experience." Obviously, it would take us too far from our subject to discuss
all the implications of Hocking's thought, which, after all, may not quite

Naturally, if this be the meaning of God, there is no need for any element of belief. But, there are in this definition two expressions that point to certain philosophic interpretations of nature. When Kaplan speaks of the element of creativity, as being the result of God's transcendent functioning, we realize that the term "creativity" simply has no meaning apart from the philosophic tradition, of which the most brilliant exponent was Henri Bergson. This deduction is strengthened by the fact that the phrase descriptive of "creativity," "not accounted for by the so-called laws of nature," cannot be taken in a literal and old fashioned sense, since Kaplan, it need hardly be said, does not believe in miracles. It was Bergson who in his book "Time and Free Will" taught the world the significance of a third concept, standing midway between the two traditional alternatives of determinism and free will. When an act is done through the effort of the whole person, not merely through one of his impulses, that act is a new "creation." In his later book "Creative Evolution," Bergson pointed out that certain facts of animal life could not be explained by the Darwinian principles of selection. Those phenomena he described as caused by acts of "creation," by the power of the underlying "life" of the universe, the élan vital.

Now, it is certainly possible to base a philosophy of religion upon Bergson's view of the universe. Many thinkers have done so, and Bergson himself had declared his views in his wonderfully suggestive work "Two Sources of Morality and Religion." But, then, one must be consistent in his views. If it is indeed Bergson's philosophy that Kaplan had in mind when writing the sentences quoted above, he should have stated that fact in his book, inasmuch as certain in-

coincide with our author's philosophical ideas. The point to remember is that the expression does not refer to any easily cognizable events such as the untutored eye may glimpse. The expression is borrowed from a system of thought, the author's or someone else's, and is simply meaningless without that background.

ferences must necessarily be drawn from the philosophy of
Bergson, which are of direct concern in the practice of religion and morality, and which in many cases are quite the
contrary of Kaplan's own deductions. Thus, Kaplan describes the theological doctrine which views God as actually
loving man, not only as the source of love in man, as not
"modern" and false. To Bergson, on the other hand, God is
essentially love. Also, to Bergson, "personal religion" is the
source of true religion, whereas "group religion" is merely
an irrational device, provided by life, to counterbalance
the destructive effects of the intellect, and meant therefore
only for the initial stages of man's intellectual development.

The point to bear in mind is that nature as it is seen and
observed, apart from any philosophical traditions, does not
show any instances of "creativity," of "life," of phenomena,
not accounted for by "so-called laws of nature." It is idle
therefore to urge men to believe in God, that is defined in
those terms, without revealing the world-view from which
they have resulted. God as creator, in the Biblical sense,
was a definite Idea. His nature might have remained
shrouded in mystery, but His work was there for all to see.
God as the source of "creativity" in Kaplan's sense, is simply
nothing at all, until and unless a philosophy of the universe,
containing a theory of "creative causality," is presented.
Since Kaplan is concerned with discovering a view of God
that would guarantee ethical progress, he cannot be content
only with the discovery of a biological force, a will to live,
or a will to power. He must seek to find a force that is at
once creative and ethical. This result, certainly a big order,
cannot be attained by the simple device of borrowing terms
out of their contexts.

Kaplan seems to think that the "organic" view of the universe is all that modern religion needs, on which to base its
postulate of the ultimate triumph of the moral order. On
the basis of this view, expounded most clearly in the writings

of Whitehead,[6] every part of the universe is affected by every other part, and the character of the whole universe determines the "ingression" of new elements and their interdependence. The world is like an organism in which every part is determined by the whole. When, now, the religious attitude superimposes upon this world-view the belief that the whole universe is good or "worth-while," we have all that is necessary for an intellectual basis of religion. Thus, he writes of God as "the apotheosis of the interrelated unity of all reality."[7]

This solution is not the dominant one in Kaplan's thought. He realizes that to ascribe goodness to the whole of existence is a vain subterfuge, issuing in no real consolation. To say that the moral ideals, entertained by man, are part of the "organic" character of Being, which is a continuous and never-ending process, and then to assert that in time these ideals will be realized, is to straddle an extremely wide territory. The first assumption tends to blunt the edge of the ideals in mankind, affirming them to be of like essence with all the other morally indifferent aspects of the universe—the colors of sky and forest, the soothing sound of the rustling rivulet and the sudden shock of the thunderbolt. The second assumption asserts, on the contrary, that there is a vast difference between the various data of the universe, that while the humanly disagreeable events are marked for disappearance and death, the moral and esthetic values are destined for unlimited growth and final triumph. The artificiality of this solution, if not its inherent self-contradiction, is thus clearly apparent.

To say that the world is an organic unity is of significance from a moral standpoint only when it is shown on what basis this unity is established. Terms, such as "harmony," "in-

---

[6] See also, Hocking "Meaning of God in Human Experience" who mingles this view with a theory of mysticism.

[7] M. 226.

tegration," "organism," "interrelated unity," mean precious
little apart from the knowledge or the belief concerning the
manner in which the different values are "integrated" or "harmonized" or "united." If the moral values are supreme in
the mind of God, to whom the entire physical universe is but
the environment needed for the working out of an ethical
purpose, then indeed we have, in effect, the Jewish view of
God. But, such a view posits an unbridgeable chasm between the moral ideals and the physical data of the universe,
between the "work of God" and the "will of God." The
realm of ethics cannot be placed above the realm of physical
events, unless God, the cosmic source of morality, is conceived as standing outside and above the sway of physical
nature. We must think of God as the Creator of the universe
and the Author of the moral law. This is quite different from
the simple recognition of physicists that the universe is an
"organic" unity. It is certainly not without significance
that pantheists could not recognize ethics as an independent
science of right and wrong. Spinoza, who expounds in a
most logical manner an "organic" view of the universe,
preaches an essentially amoral doctrine of human conduct.
For, certainly, the physical universe knows neither ends nor
values and is not cut out to suit the fancies of a Candide.

The unwillingness of our author to recognize the logical
implications of his postulates is illustrated in his estimate
of the importance of the ancient question of creatio ex
nihilo. "To the modern way of thinking," he writes, "its
connection with spiritual life is remote, if not altogether irrelevant." [8] That question, it appears upon reflection, is still
of essential significance to the religious mind. God, as the
author of morality, is supreme over physical nature. If this
supremacy is not to be interpreted in a Zoroastrian sense, as
ultimate victory in a struggle of nearly equal forces, then
God must be regarded as the only real force. In other words,

---

[8] M. 62.

there exists no force apart from God. This is the basic assertion of Judaism, as of all higher religions. Now, the alternative to creatio ex nihilo is the assumption that there is another cosmic force, outside of God—matter, chaos, or what you will.

The essential difference of the Jewish religion from the pagan creed is expressed in the non-mythological character of its creation story. While all mythologies portrayed creation as being the result of the transformation of some primal matter or of a struggle between two sets of demonic powers, the Jewish religion saw the Will of God as the one and only force. The assumption of an underlying eternal matter mirrored the pagan belief that the forces of nature are vaster and more inclusive than the gods. The implacable sword of fate, moira, hangs above the heads of all beings, mortal and immortal. The underlying chaos of the universe will in the end assert itself, civilization will go up in flames, and a "twilight of the gods" will ensue. The Jewish intuition of the supreme power of God was bound to express itself in creatio ex nihilo as soon as the question presented itself to them.[9] The issue of creatio ex nihilo is thus seen to be of pivotal significance, to the problem of religion.

Kaplan's failure to recognize this fact is illustrative of his general pragmatic tendency, to undervalue the importance of the intellectual element in human life.

In his book, "Meaning of God in Modern Jewish Religion," Kaplan tacitly abandons his former attitude of identifying God with the underlying "force" or "energy" of the universe. Thus, in referring to the prevailing tendency of thinking of

---

[9] See J. Kaufman—"Toldoth Hoemunah Hayisrealith" pp. 251–252, where the spiritual implications of this controversy are fully discussed. See also D. Neumark, "Toldoth Haphilosophio b'Yisroel," where the doctrine of creatio ex nihilo is placed in the center of Jewish thought. Halevi's view of the unimportance of this dogma and Gersonides' acceptance of the doctrine of primal matter, do not invalidate the conclusions to be drawn from the mainstream of Jewish thought.

ultimate reality in these terms, Kaplan remarks, "To apotheosize force or energy is contrary to that intuition of the Jewish spirit which, from the time that Jewish religion may be said to have come into existence, always identified God as that power in the universe which sponsored the ideals that gave meaning to life." In this sentence, it appears that Kaplan rejects the doctrine that God should be identified with the "force of life," the totality of existence, or the "organic" unity of the universe.

The view of God which appears to be most dominant in Kaplan's thought accepts the second of the three alternatives mentioned above. God is conceived as a "force" or a "power" or a "process" working within the physical universe. The world, we are now asked to think, is not all of one piece. It contains parts that have been conquered by the power of God. Those are all the data which appear to us, humans, as being of value—all the things which are good or true or beautiful. The evil in the universe or, generally, those phases and aspects of nature that are not favorable or that are indifferent to human ends, are simply the spheres of the universe, which God has not yet taken over. In this sense, God is a cosmic force for the good. There are other forces in the universe that are indifferent—Kaplan would not say hostile —to human weal or woe. But, there is also a force that labors unceasingly for mankind—for righteousness, for cooperation, for freedom, for the regeneration of human nature, in general, for all that men call salvation. God is "the totality of all those forces in life that render human life worthwhile." [10]

It must be noted that Kaplan does not simply identify God with that power within man that labors to make the world a better place to live in. If that were his intentions, he would still be a humanist, not a religionist. His God would then be man himself. This Feuerbachian substitution,

---

[10] M. 133.

Kaplan does not accept. That force for the good, then, is "not ourselves"; it is a power outside man, a "cosmic urge." Thus, Kaplan writes, "Life seeks to make of every organism, whether individual or social, a perfect pattern in which every part contributes to perpetuate and enhance the whole, and in which the whole energizes every part. This effort of life to achieve and express unity, harmony and integrity is what makes life holy; this is the evidence of the divine; whatever thwarts this tendency is sin." [11]

We, thus, have the conception of a God that is not all nature, but that labors within nature for certain ends. So far, so good, but the conception is really a would-be conception, since it is not carried far enough to convey definite meaning. The definition starts out with the phrase "life seeks." If our author is really speaking of a definite force, then his meaning can only be that the "force of life" is God. This conception would involve only the principle of vitalism, the theory that there is such an element as a "force of life," a vital principle that is absent from all lifeless objects. This assumption is entirely possible and it accords with many of the ideas of our author. But, he hesitates to identify God with the "force of life," since that "force" is presumably non-ethical. This "force" is after all common to man and beast. Hence, deductions based upon the actual observation of the way the "force of life" operates in nature are bound to be below the standards of humanity. Nietsche's "transvaluation of all values" is derived from the contemplation of the "struggle for survival" and the "survival of the fittest," principles which describe the manner in which the "force of life" is observed to operate. Peter Kropotkin found the desire for cooperation diffused throughout nature, and Bergson evolved a religion of mysticism from his theory of a "force of life." But, Kropotkin's data are rare oddities and Bergson's theories are by no means simple observations. They depend on a

---

[11] M. 245.

long string of arguments which our author may or may not accept.

For this reason, Kaplan in other places does not identify God with the "force of life." It is not all the power of life that is God, but a power in life. He is "the totality of all those forces *in* life that render human life worthwhile." We may presume, then, that only those forces which make for freedom, for righteousness, and for human happiness are God. This conception comes close to the traditional Jewish doctrine of God, insofar as the latter taught that God's main *concern* was the righteousness and well-being of mankind.

But, there is a significant difference between the traditional view of God and that of Kaplan—a difference which exposes the inadequacy of Kaplan's conception. The God of Israel was transcendent to the universe, standing outside of it and molding it by degrees, as "the potter moldeth his clay." Certain acts could then be attributed to God, without involving the assumption that the physical causes of those phenomena were in themselves divine. The splitting of the Red Sea before the children of Israel was an act of God. But, the wind which God employed as His instrumentality was not a part of God. Relationships could be identified as divine, as evidences of the presence of She'chinah, while the forces which brought about those relationships were not necessarily identified as permanent agencies of the Deity— let alone, as God Himself. Kaplan, on the contrary, insists throughout on the immanence of God, on the theory that God is an actual force or group of forces within the structure of existence. If, then, any event is seen to further the course of humanity, the effective cause of that event, the force which brought it into being, must be regarded as divine. Conversely, if certain events or facts obstruct the progress of humanity, their effective causes must be regarded as not yet divine, or, to be really consistent, as diabolic. In this manner, we are led into a morass of confusion that is surely not divine. Consider this anomaly—the "force of life" which causes plants to grow and flowers to bloom is not divine in itself, but when human beings are around, that "force," of a sudden, becomes a part of God. There is no force of chemistry or of physics that is not productive of human evil as well as of human good, depending upon the peculiar conjunction of circumstances at any particular time and place. Hence, to identify any "force" of existence with God, as an immanent Being, is simply a play of words.

The only way for Kaplan to escape from this infinite confusion is to identify those motives in man that aim at the good, the true and the beautiful as being God. Since those motives never lead to anything but good, it is not illogical to identify them with the Deity. The acceptance of this alternative, however, would require of Kaplan that he ascribe goodness to motives, not to actions, even as Kant had done. Like Kant, too, he would have to draw a sharp line of division between the different ideals of man. If religion is to be based upon ethics, then the science of the Ought must be shown to be intrinsically different from the science of nature, belonging, in fact, to a different order of Being. Kaplan is not conscious of this necessity. He is a Deweyan and all interests of life appear to him to be intrinsically alike. He operates with the conceptions of happiness or salvation, not with those of right and wrong, which alone can lead to an ethical philosophy of life and religion.

Thus, he does write in places as if God were effective in existence, solely through the efforts of man. "On the other hand, from the point of view of the sovereignty of God as immanent in human society, the responsibility for ushering in the kingdom of God on earth rests squarely with mankind." [12] If God is indeed a "creative" force, as Kaplan declares in some passages, then it may be expected that He will cause the hearts of men to be more responsive to the

---

[12] M. 119.

demands of ideals, that He will give men a "new heart," as the prophet Ezekiel had predicted. Bergson, it may be remembered, does teach us to look forward to that consummation, on the ground of the "creativeness" of God. In ruling out this possibility in principle, Kaplan limits the name of God to the actually observed strivings of men. As noted above, he makes no effort to determine which strivings are from God. It cannot be reiterated too often, that terms like "integration," "unity," "harmony," etc., which Kaplan sometimes employs as determinative of what is divine, mean absolutely nothing from an ethical standpoint. It is the basis on which unity or harmony or integration is achieved that matters. The League of Nations represented the ideal of unity; so does Hitler and his "New Order." The first was ethical; the second is not. The ethical nature of the one and the unmoral character of the other are determined by standards other than unity.

Moreover, it may be asked, if God is but the strivings of man, how is He at the same time a "cosmic urge"? How can we feel assured of the eventual fulfillment of the hope in the attainment of human salvation? These questions bring us back to the conception of God, discussed before— the "organic unity" of the universe, the "creative urge," the "life of the universe." Thus is revealed the full extent of the ambiguity of the conception of God in Kaplan's works. He attempts to write as a theist and as a humanist at the same time, to insist on belief in God and then to reduce His dimensions to the vanishing point. The result is, to judge by the writings of Kaplan to date, a sorely incomplete philosophy of religion.

In this critical analysis of his conception of God, we have endeavored to carry out a task which Kaplan himself regards as unnecessary and irrelevant to religion. We have attempted to know exactly the meaning of the words which he has used to enunciate his conception. We have employed the instrument of reason to whittle down a conception that does not issue from the field of reason. The belief that the moral impulses of mankind are "rooted in reality" is derived from an emotional intuition, and is therefore supra-rational. The state of mind of the religious person may be expressed as follows—"I believe that God is on my side. What He is, how or when he works I cannot surmise. But, this I know, that, behind the veil of seemingly indifferent phenomena, there functions a Power of goodness and love, impelling the world ever higher on the road toward the goal of a God-like humanity. I feel this truth with all my being. It rises with force and clarity to my consciousness whenever I am at my spiritually best, whenever I rise to the highest levels of spiritual thought and action that I am capable of. Such an ever-present, universally diffused and keenly felt intuition cannot be wrong. This intuition is all that I require for my religious life. Religion cannot go beyond this step. It lies within the province of metaphysics and not religion to ask all the embarrassing questions that you have put forward in the preceding paragraphs. Metaphysics is irrelevant."

This argument is very popular among American preachers of religion. It derives no doubt from the general practical tendency of the American mind. It is not theories or doctrines or abstract conceptions that matter, but the facts of actual experience. Life is wiser than mere wisdom, and it stultifies with the greatest of ease the most "irrefutable arguments" of the ivory-tower intellectual. This tendency received academic approval in the pragmatist movement which appeared to substitute the question, "does it work?" for the question, "is it true?" James, it will be recalled, had declared that "truth is that which works." Any proposition which brings desired results is insofar forth true. If then, the belief in God "works" in the sense of bringing peace of mind and strength of will to believers, it is validated by experience and, therefore, "true."

This attitude is based upon a variety of misunderstandings and half-truths. We cannot here enter upon a complete criticism of the pragmatist position. It is sufficient for us to realize that the phrase "truth is that which works" is clearly ambiguous. When, being in a practical mood, we are concerned with the implications for actual life of a certain proposition, then the test of "working" is necessarily conceived in practical terms. When, however, being in a reflective mood, we are concerned with the exact meaning of a proposition and its "consistency" with other valid ideas, that are stored in our mind, then the test of "working" is conceived in intellectual terms and is carried out entirely on an intellectual plane.[13]

The question at issue, then, is whether or not religion can get along without intellectual reflection. To this question, there can now be given only a negative answer. To be sure, a religious person need not be a metaphysician and know all the answers on his fingertips. But then, he must be satisfied that he knows what he is talking about whenever he indulges in critical reflection, if his religion is to be enduring and inspiring.

There is one test which no real religion can afford to fail, and that is the requirement that its conception of God should be sufficiently precise to refer to a definite entity. It is this requirement which Kaplan's religion has thus far failed to meet. From the standpoint of the philosophy of religion, then, "Reconstructionism" is still incomplete. This observation does not, to be sure, deprive it of the right to exist as a modern version of the Jewish religion. Every living religion, that is really rooted in human experience, precedes, as a faith, its intellectual justification. But, it must strive to attain that consummation, turning its original insight into a clear and consistent world-view. Otherwise, that insight is

---

[13] Of pragmatists' views on test of "consistency" see R. B. Perry—"Trends in Modern Philosophy."

bound to fade in the sober light of day, giving way to un-mitigated blindness and sheer futility.

Some writers point to the Hebrew prophets and Hebrew religion generally to prove the claim that religion does not require the doubtful aid of philosophy. It is quite true that the Jewish rabbis were not philosophers, but, perhaps for that very reason, their idea of God was as far from nothing-ness as any conception could be. If anything, it was, in philosophic strictness, too rich in meaning. How fantastic to compare the living God of Israel with "the name given to those processes and relationships that make for human wel-fare." The God of the prophets was all that, to be sure, but He was vastly more than that. He was a Person, possessed of a Will, a Mind, a Memory. All the apparent inconsisten-cies of the rabbinic view of God, were due to the power and the grandeur of the conception, not to its tenuousness. Ra-tional criticism could only reduce the dimensions of the God of Israel, sloughing off meanings and shades of meanings from the original resplendent "cloud of glory." In the case of the Reconstructionists, on the other hand, philosophical analysis is necessary to bring real meaning to the shadow of mere words.

Moreover, the prophets did not claim to have discovered a new conception of God. They spoke in the name of the God of their fathers, not being aware that they were teaching anything new. The absence of critical reflection in ancient times permitted the adoption of traditional beliefs. Kaplan, on the other hand, attempts to construct a new faith on the basis of his own experience and reflection. This is obviously quite another matter. A new belief must fight for adoption with the already established ideas; it must prove itself.

Assuming for a moment that Kaplan's view of God is a valid conception, we must now inquire what reasons he cites for the belief that God really exists—that there is, indeed, a Power, not ourselves, working for righteousness and that the cause of humanity will ultimately triumph. At times, Kaplan writes in a fideistic vein, arguing that God cannot be proved and that belief in Him is "an assumption that is not susceptible of proof." [14]   This assumption is necessary for moral living. Hence, those desirous of dedicating themselves to high ideals are compelled to assume that their ideals will be realized. Thus, all righteous persons will accept the hypothesis of the existence of God, since "belief in Him is a necessary concomitant of all idealistic endeavor." [15]

The fideistic position was set forth by James in his brilliant essay "The Will to Believe" or as it was called in the original manuscript "The Right to Believe." James points out that in life, belief must go far ahead of reasoned conviction. The weakness of the human mind and the brevity of human life compel us to choose between two equally rational alternatives. Where the testimony of reason is not decisive it is proper to accept the hypothesis which will help us to live a good life. Since the arguments for both theism and atheism are inconclusive, the decisive consideration should be the moral motive.

Another argument for the existence of God that Kaplan sometimes offers is the one of intuition. This intuition is at times described as "emotional," or as "the yea of our entire personality." At other times, this intuition is portrayed as a real source of knowledge. The intuition of the worth of high ideals, proves that those ideals are "rooted in reality," are valid from a cosmic viewpoint. "For human personality, with its reference to goals of human behavior beyond our capacity, yet demanding our fullest devotion, points to a power that makes for righteousness—not ourselves." [16]

As will be seen in the last chapter, our own opinion is that the last argument is indeed the most fruitful one. Kaplan,

---

[14] M. 29.
[15] M. 325.
[16] M. 309.

however, does not pursue this line of reasoning very far.

From all the above, it is clear that Reconstructionism did not yet develop a philosophy of religion sufficient for its needs. While it has broken with the traditional view of God, the movement has not so far succeeded in developing its own conception of God to the point where it could again serve as the basis of a life of religion.

(d) THE TRADITIONAL PRINCIPLES OF JUDAISM MUST BE CONSCIOUSLY REINTERPRETED

THE NEED FOR CONSTANT REINTERPRETATION OF TRADITION is easily apparent. Every student of the history of civilization is aware of the gradual changes in thought and custom that every society undergoes. Society is in a perpetual flux, even when the changes are too subtle to be noticed by the contemporary observer. Religion, as an organized social institution is naturally affected by these changes. Since historical religions are based on the authority of ancient books, it is natural to expect that every age would interpret those books in the light of its own ideas and prejudices.

Judaism was not an exception to this general rule. The Holy Books of Israel brought different messages to the teachers of the different epochs in Jewish history. The naive expressions of one age could not be accepted literally by the proponents of a more subtle and reflective age. Since they could not believe that the revered authorities of old have indeed erred, they usually maintained that the old expressions were to be interpreted in a symbolic manner. There was no deception involved in this process, in the past, since the new interpreters did not realize that their views and standards differed in the slightest from those of their ancestors. Thus, David is portrayed in the Bible as a warrior, a man of flesh and blood. In the Talmud, he and all his cohorts are presented as learned rabbis, whose main preoccupation was the discussion of the minutiae of the Law. To the Rabbis of the Talmud, the ideal man was the student and teacher of the Law. Thus, they could not think of the great King David in any other light. Since he was the ideal Jewish personality, the father of Jewish kings and the progenitor of the Messiah, he could not have been aught else except an ardent expounder of the Law. Lacking a sense of historical criticism, it was possible for the Rabbis to remake King David in their own image without feeling that they were departing from tradition.

This method of unconscious reinterpretation was aided by the homiletical attitude, which sought to derive pertinent teachings from the passages of the Law. In this process, the moral lesson and the degree of ingenuity manifested in the apt application of a verse to a vital problem were more important than the historical accuracy of the interpretation. The comments of the Haggadists were not to be examined on the score of truth so much as on that of morality and spiritual utility. In this manner, every generation of Jews was able to add of its experience to the continuous stream of Jewish tradition.

In modern times, history has become a science. It is no longer possible for modern Jews to accept any interpretation of an ancient passage as true which is not in accord with the principles of historical criticism. When we ask ourselves what the meaning of a passage is, we are dealing with a question for which objective standards have been developed. Hence, it is impossible for us to adopt the traditional line of thought—"my thoughts are true, therefore, they must have been intended by our ancient teachers." The modern sense of historical accuracy forbids this easy method of reconciling the old with the new.

Again, there is too wide a gulf between Kaplan's religion and that of traditional Judaism to be thus lightly bridged over. In the past, the changes which Jewish thought underwent were slight and unimportant, in comparison with the radical modification which, in the opinion of Kaplan, the modern temper requires. For, now, the foundation of Judaism, its belief in a personal God who watches over the affairs of men, has been removed. The God of Kaplan, it is repeatedly asserted, is not a "personal God." Also, the Torah is no longer to be regarded as the word of God in the old sense. All things "sacred" to the Jewish faith are now to be understood as merely "supremely important" to the Jewish people. Such wide divergence from traditional Judaism cannot, in honesty, be reconciled with historical Judaism.

How, then, is the bond of continuity between modern religion and traditional Judaism to be maintained? Kaplan faces this problem squarely and he offers the following solution. We must seek to discover, he declares, what values the old principles and practices were meant to embody. Next, we must endeavor to envisage clearly what our own views concerning these values are. Having attained this knowledge, we shall be in a position to pour the new wine into the old vessels, vitalizing the traditional words and acts with the set of values and meanings that are dear to us. Thus, the Sabbath was meant to impress upon the Jew the ideal of salvation. In traditional Judaism, the term "salvation" referred to the other world, "olam shekulo Shabbos," the world which is all Sabbath. This world of hustle and bustle, this ceaseless march of indifferent phenomena, of blessings and catastrophes which seem to have no relation to the virtues of the good and the sins of the wicked, this "world of deeds" is but one side of existence, the side completed in the first six days of creation. But, there is also another order of existence, a realm of the spirit, where the moral laws of God are completely vindicated. In that world, the good and the faithful will find their reward and their happiness, the perfect consummation of their life, their salvation.

In modern times, Kaplan continues, we can no longer believe in an other-worldly existence. Salvation for us can only mean the attainment of happiness in this world. The assurance that the blessings of salvation are ours, if we but strive for them can today mean only this—that happiness is indeed within human grasp, that life is worth living. Human life can be continuously improved to the end when "all our powers are harmoniously employed in the achievement of worthwhile aims." This must be the meaning of the Sabbath to the modern Jew.

Another reason for the observance of the Sabbath was the commemoration of the covenant that Israel made with God. "And the children of Israel shall keep the Sabbath, to observe the Sabbath for their generation, an eternal covenant." The idea that God really concluded an agreement with any nation cannot today be accepted in a literal sense. The covenant idea must be reinterpreted to signify the consciousness, on the part of the Jewish people, of their duty to bring their contributions to the altar of the common progress of humanity.

In a similar manner, Kaplan proceeds to reinterpret all the Jewish holidays and many of the rituals connected with them. While one may dispute his interpretation of any specific Jewish custom, one cannot argue against his general method of interpretation once his views of God and religion have been accepted. Since group life is the matrix of religion, the historical continuity of Jewish life must not be interrupted. For this reason, the solution of Reform Judaism, which breaks completely with traditional Judaism, cannot be accepted. On the other hand, the method of unconscious reinterpretation is no longer effective.

The only possible objection to "functional reinterpretation"—open to those who accept the other main theses of Kaplan—is the fear that its casuistic artificiality may be repellent to many Jews. This fear, we feel, is not justified. The notion of progress is now all-pervading, and people are becoming accustomed to the thought that, even in religion, the beliefs and customs of earlier generations are less authoritative than those of our contemporary philosophers and religious leaders.

In addition to reinterpreting specific customs and beliefs, Kaplan's reconstruction of Judaism involves a shifting of the center of gravity from religion to nationalism. As remarked above, religion and nationalism have always been blended together in Judaism. But, the two motives of allegiance have long ago arrived at a definite modus vivendi. In the forefront of the consciousness of the Jew was his duty to God. His loyalty to his people was largely an unconscious motive, though admittedly powerful. When the Jew asked himself the why and wherefore of his existence, his answer was always culled from the sphere of religion. God had revealed His true Will and His real Nature to Israel. Every Jew is therefore fortunate in falling heir to this Divine truth which is alone the source of salvation. What matter if during our brief sojourn on this blood-drenched earth our lot as Jews is less pleasant than that of other nations? "More beautiful is one hour in the world to come than the entire life of this world." [1] The dominant and conscious motive of Jewish life was, therefore, a religious one.

Kaplan's reconstruction proposes to make loyalty to the Jewish nation the dominant motive of Jewish survival. As Jews, we wish to continue our national existence. The expression of our national existence in the Diaspora is Jewish community life, in all its aspects. Undertakings for charity, Palestine work, Jewish culture and education—all are elements of Jewish national life. Of Jewish cultural values, the Jewish religion is supreme in importance, firstly, because the final fruit of every national civilization is a national religion; secondly, because religion has in the past been the main element of Jewish culture. Thus, while the synagogue

---

[1] Abboth, 4, 17.

retains its central importance in Jewish culture, it is only one of many Jewish institutions. The community is the unit of Jewish life, not the synagogue. It is the immediate task of Jews to organize Jewish life on a community basis, so that concrete expression could be given to the doctrine that Judaism is more than a religion, that it is, in fact, a civilization.

This demand is, of course, intended principally for the Jews of America, since, in the countries of Europe, organization of Jewish life on a community basis was the rule rather than the exception. However, even in the European countries, the Kaplanian conception of Judaism as a civilization could not fail to introduce a radical rechanneling of Jewish energies. For this conception calls upon all Jews to help, not only in the preservation of Judaism, but in its enhancement and further development. We must not rest content with tabulating the results of Jewish "contributions" to this or that aspect of civilization. We must endeavor to continue the progress of Jewish culture in all fields of endeavor. Instead of confining our reverence for Torah to the study of the Talmud and its commentaries, we should apply the same ardor and the same self-abnegating pursuit of knowledge to work out methods and standards for the solution of present-day problems in the light of morality and religion. The ideal of "avodah," or worship, should not be limited to the continuous performance of ancient rites and the dry repetition of standardized prayers. We should seek to produce new prayers and new ways of arousing within men the consciousness of the Divine. The development of Jewish music and Jewish liturgy should be encouraged by the Jewish community. Similarly, in regard to the third pillar of Judaism, ge'milus hassadim, the same progressive, forward-looking attitude should be adopted. The "performance of deeds of loving-kindness" takes in the whole vast field of the community's responsibilities to its destitute and in general the duties of man to man. In the past, it was the spirit of Judaism which led to the creation of all manner of social agencies for the alleviation of the misery of the unfortunate. Our consciousness of pride in the achievements of our people should lead us to strive, as Jews, to excel in the fields of human kindness and social responsibility.

The leading motive in all these activities may be summed up in the word "creativity." Jewish life even now is full of potentialities in divine directions. It can be made beautiful and inspiring, thereby demonstrating to the world that nationalism can become the social force, which is needed to arouse all the impulses for goodness, truth and beauty, that are normally dormant in the human breast. In fact, Kaplan urges, we should regard it as our God-given duty to prove to the world the ways in which the wild and dangerous force of nationalism can be brought into the service of mankind. By channeling the energy of nationalism into the fields of culture and religion, we solve the famous riddle of Samson, bringing the sweet out of the strong. The contribution of different nations to humanity's symphony of cultures is essential to the growth of human culture as a whole, for growth is always achieved through diversification. When nations will learn to compete with each other in the task of making life beautiful, the curse of nationalism will have been turned into a blessing. To the attainment of this "mission" the Jews should consciously dedicate themselves, for it is in line with their historical tradition. Already, in the days of Moses, the Jewish people turned itself into the "servant of God," thus grafting a universalistic religion unto their racial stem. The Jewish people is the only one today that has achieved a truly national religion, which is, at the same time, a religion of love and good-will to all men. This consummation is devoutly desired by the author for all nations, and the "little child" of Israel must lead in the task.

It is idle to discuss here the wisdom of shifting emphasis

from the motive of religion to that of nationalism, since this shift of emphasis is the direct corollary of the thesis discussed in the previous sections of this chapter. Without doubt, the motive of nationalism has been shown to be liable to the most vicious type of abuse, in the movements of fascism and nazism. On the other hand, one could make out a similar case against religion on account of all the misery and bloodshed which have been caused in its name. Certain it is, that the motive of nationalism is an evil force when not balanced by a deep conviction in the reality of the universal values of ethics. In Kaplan's version of Judaism, the force of Jewish nationalism is blended with the firm faith in universal religion—a faith which is strong and earnest though its intellectual formulation is still inadequate. Can this balance, so laboriously achieved by the solitary thinker, be permanently maintained by whole nations? Who can, at this time of confusion and impending chaos, presume to peer into the future? Who can predict whether mankind will spurn nationalism, as a reaction to the catastrophic situation which this social force has engendered, or whether it will devote itself still more blindly and with even more ruthless fanaticism to the worship of this modern Moloch? This much is clear that, not doctrines, but the swift-moving current of economic and martial events will determine the future attitude of mankind to the ideal of nationalism.

"The hidden things are for the Lord, our God, and the revealed things are for us and our children forever"—to think, to pray and to hope.

CHAPTER VI

SUMMARY AND CONCLUSION

(a) THE COMMON CORE OF MODERN
JEWISH PHILOSOPHY
(b) THESES FOR A PHILOSOPHY OF RELI-
GION

(a) The Common Core of Modern Jewish Philosophy

IN THIS CHAPTER, WE SHALL ENDEAVOR TO FORM A connected picture, out of the seemingly independent discussions in this book. Having scrutinized in detail the philosophies of Cohen, Rosenzweig, Buber and Kaplan, we turn now to the task of obtaining the necessary perspective in which they may be viewed as a whole. In the preceding chapters, these philosophies are expounded and criticized in their own respective terms and realms of discourse. The impression was, therefore, conveyed that each thinker constructed his own system of Judaism, with little or no reference to his contemporary colleagues. To be sure, there is little direct influence that these four exponents of modern Jewish philosophy of religion exerted upon each other. Yet, there are certain basic ideas that are common to them all. These ideas are more important by far than the numerous points of difference between them.

Together, the four systems discussed in this book constitute the typical trends of modern Jewish philosophy of religion. Outside of the Orthodox and neo-Orthodox philosophies, there have not been produced other works on the Jewish religion that introduce any new element, or that contain a fundamentally new approach.[1]

---

[1] Leo Baeck's "Essence of Judaism" is an excellent and balanced work, but it is eclectical in nature. Schechter's "Aspects of Rabbinic Theology" is primarily a historical study. Montefiore's little book on his philosophy of religion is written in a superficial and practical vein. D. Neumark's philosophy expressed in his extended criticisms of Cohen in the "Hatoren" have not been presented in a systematic manner in any of his published works. Felix Adler's ethical philosophy of life does not belong in this book since Adler saw no value in Judaism. For the same reason we did not include in this book the views of those Jewish thinkers who wrote on philosophy and religion in general, without any direct reference to Judaism.

Our search for the points of contact between the philosophies of Cohen, Buber, Rosenzweig and Kaplan resolves itself, therefore, into an attempt to establish whether there are any basic convictions, apart from Jewish ritual and ceremony, that are common to all great Jewish thinkers. Naturally, we cannot expect sameness or even similarity in the detailed exposition of their systems, since there is no accepted philosophical tradition in the modern world. In the Medieval era, there were many acrimonious conflicts over philosophical propositions, but in the background of those disputes, there was a body of principles, methods, terms and dogmas employed by all who ventured to explore the infinite sea of thought. In our own era, this situation no longer obtains. There is no "logic" acceptable to all, no unquestioned universally revered philosophical tradition, not even one set of technical terminology. Consequently, it is to be expected that modern Jewish theology will be discussed in the light of diverse philosophical viewpoints and that it will be radically reinterpreted to suit the opinions of the different trends of modern thought. Yet, if Jewish philosophy of religion is to be Jewish as well as philosophy, it must contain certain fundamental convictions, that are really derived from Jewish tradition, not merely artificially interpreted into it.

On the surface, it may appear that there is little, if any, common ground to the four philosophies that are discussed in this book. Cohen was an extreme rationalist, carrying faith in reason to unprecedented limits. He refused to take for granted any data, other than those of reason. At the base of his system, he placed the astounding assertion that reason is capable of producing its own ideas and developing its own concepts, without the aid of data derived from experience. To be sure, Cohen regarded reason as incapable of obtaining metaphysical knowledge. He insisted on a severe distinction between objective knowledge and metaphysics. But, at the same time, he thought of reason as a timeless world-process, entirely self-sufficient as an instrument of knowledge, containing the seeds of its own infinite development. He scornfully repudiated any form of intuition as a source of true knowledge and he had no patience with materialists and empiricists. The conclusions of "pure reason" alone are true knowledge. Everything else is sheer opinion, or as he put it, a task for knowledge.

Buber, on the other hand, is a neo-Mystic. While he differs from the "grand mystics" in maintaining that no union with or absorption into the Divine Being is possible, he is a mystic in the sense that he seeks a direct contact with God. The speculations of reason, "pure" or not, are mere bubbles on the surging waves of reality. Disinterested thinking can only lead to an unreal artificial world of laws, principles and material elements—a world that is largely the product of our own mentality. The only way to approach reality is through the Thou relation. It is "blind" love, not the cold eye of reason that is capable of penetrating to the core of things.

Rosenzweig called himself an empiricist. He was a believer in experience, in the sense that his philosophy was founded upon an experience—the experience of revelation. This experienced intuition was employed by Rosenzweig to reverse the entire course of philosophy. His refutation of that vast system of thought, which was unfolded by degrees from Thales to Hegel, was based upon our alleged dissatisfaction as individuals with the consolation of philosophy. The individual's fear of death, Rosenzweig asserted, is not allayed by the admonition of the philosophers to contemplate the Absolute. Evidently, he argued, there is something in the nature of man that escapes the net of philosophy—a something, which reason can only regard as a Naught. Yet, it is a fruitful naught, the matrix of the true human self. Rosenzweig insisted, in substance, that the whole of man must be taken as the test of a philosophy, not his reason

alone. Otherwise, he claimed, philosophy is but a half-truth.
As contrasted with the German idealistic school, Rosenzweig
may therefore be called an empiricist. It is hardly necessary
to point out that there is no connection whatever between
him and the English empirical school.

Kaplan is a pragmatist. His main interest throughout his
writings is practical. Sharing the disdain of the American
pragmatical school for the speculations of the metaphysicians, Kaplan is concerned only with establishing those beliefs that have a direct, practical bearing on life. The one
belief of religion that really matters is the assertion that
there is a Power—not ourselves, that makes for righteousness. This belief helps man to live a noble life; therefore, it
is both good and true. A healthy man will accept it and
build his life upon it. Apart from this belief, Kaplan regards
all phases of human experience as equal in value. There is
no Absolute Moral Law, nor any set scheme for approaching
the Divine. Human happiness, or salvation is the ultimate
test of any belief or course of action. The bewildering flow
of variegated human experience is the final reference and
test of all truth.

Notwithstanding these basic differences, there is a core of
belief that is common to all these philosophers and—what
is more important, common as well to the long line of Jewish
sages and prophets, from Moses down. This core of belief,
it will appear upon analysis, is the main theme and the real
starting-point of all these thinkers, forming the one cornerstone of their respective systems of thought.

We shall approach most conveniently this all-important
common ground of Jewish philosophers through an examination of the following question "what is the source of ethical
value?"

As human beings we are prone to pass judgment on all
things. We either approve or we disapprove of the millions
of phenomena that enter within the range of our experience.

In most cases, the reasons for our value-judgments are the very evident ones of self-interest. Adjectives such as pleasant, painful, enjoyable, boring, promising, ominous, reassuring, menacing, etc. are obviously conferred on things because of our concern with our own welfare.

Now, the question arises whether the judgments, good and bad, right and wrong, ethical and unethical, are similarly based on subjective considerations, or whether they are derived from our apprehension of the existence of some objective standards. Why do we uncompromisingly approve of charitable deeds and disapprove of acts of robbery, disloyalty and duplicity? Our own personal interest is, in many cases, unaffected by the deeds that we so warmly applaud or by those that we so heartily condemn. Since self-interest is not the source of these judgments and since, furthermore, they are characterized by the quality of objectivity, are we justified in assuming the awareness, on the part of men, of an impersonal moral law in accordance with which the judgments of right and wrong are made?

This question as to the source of ethical valuation is, of course, a very ancient one. It would take us far beyond the limits of our subject, if we attempted even a bare outline of its history. Suffice it to say that a large and respectable group of thinkers, headed by Aristotle, have maintained that all human judgments could be understood as variations of self-interest. Various ingenious explanations have been offered for the apparent objectivity and earnestness of "the voice of conscience." Generally speaking, these theories may be classified as either materialistic or humanistic. In the former category belong all the explanations which "explain" morality away in the process of trying to understand it. The best known modern representative of this group is Friedrich Nietsche, whose apology for unbridled brutalitarianism was based upon his purported discovery of the origin of traditional morality in the thwarted will to power of the slave-peoples, primarily, the Jewish nation.[2] In the latter category belong those doctrines which maintain that the ethical insight of human beings is somehow valid, though that insight is really a development of the instinct for self-preservation. The humanists take the civilized conscience of man as their standard of reference. All human interests are good and the ethical strivings of man are of essentially the same value or authority as other human desires and aspirations.

Cohen, Buber, Rosenzweig and Kaplan—all agree in rejecting both materialism and humanism. They concur in maintaining that there is something about our experience of the moral law, which cannot be reduced to self-interest. You cannot analyze the voice of conscience in terms of selfish or indifferent impulses, without proving false to it. The moral law appears in consciousness as an absolute command, spurning all selfish and unworthy motives. It can only be understood on its own face value, as an objective law of action, deriving from the structure of reality. An essential part of ethical experience is the feeling that there is an outside source to our judgments of right and wrong, that the stamp of validity attaches to our apprehensions of the rightness and wrongness of things.

This conviction is not only common to the philosophers discussed in this book; it constitutes the main vantage point of their respective philosophies. While they express this fluid intuition in radically different ways, they agree in founding their systems of thought upon it.

Cohen begins his system with the "basic law of truth" (Grundgesetz der Wahrheit). Truth, he then goes on to say, is the recognition that the two directions of spirit, logic and ethics, must be "pure." The requirement concerning the "purity" of ethics in turn implies the assertion that the judgments of ethics are intrinsically valid and authoritative.

---

[2] F. Nietsche, "Genealogy of Morals," p. 24.

We must not attempt to find the origin of morality in the consciousness of social pressure or in the sublimation and rationalization of some unworthy motive; the "basic law of truth" directs us to treat ethics as an independently authoritative and valid science.

If we should now inquire for the reasons that lead Cohen to accept his so-called "law of truth," we shall be confronted with the answer that truth is its own final authority. In other words, Cohen's philosophy of life is based upon an original insight into the objective validity of ethical judgments. To be sure, Cohen insisted that philosophy must not start with anything "given" by experience or intuition. But, then, that insistence was an impossibility, to begin with. Cohen's initial axiom, the requirement that logic and ethics should be "pure," must itself be assumed. In the final analysis, then, Cohen's system is based upon the conviction that our ethical experience contains the seal of objective validity. The concept of God, which logically belongs at the beginning of Cohen's system, further supports this observation that the intuition of the authoritativeness of the moral law and of its ultimate vindication is the starting point of his thought.

Buber's "Thou-relation" may also be classified as an ethical experience. As we have seen before, this relation is the concentration of the individual in the feeling of love. Whenever this relation appears, communion with the Deity, to a limited extent, is established. "The extended lines of relations meet in the eternal Thou; by means of every particular thou, the primary word addresses the eternal Thou." It is through love, then, that man reaches out toward the Deity. Without doubt the impulse of non-sexual love should be regarded as ethical in character. Many thinkers viewed the feeling of love as the highest culmination of ethical experience. Buber's claim that reality can only be attained through the Thou-relation, involves, therefore, the conviction that the road of ethics alone leads to God. Ethical thought and life are the response of man to the call of God. "Dialogue-living" is real, valid and authoritative.

The sense of the omnipresence of God, breaking through the "It-world" with overwhelming suddenness and power, is, to Buber, a valid intuition of reality. Yet, this mystical apprehension of God's presence is attained only through the long sustained practice of concentrating and directing our entire fund of devotion upon the needs of our fellow-men. The Thou-relation is at once and essentially, both ethical and religious. It is religious not only in the superficial sense of being commanded by God, but in the deeper and more intimate sense of a direct communion with God.

The philosophies of Cohen and Buber appear to be so contrasting in character that it is difficult to realize that they derive from similar intuitions concerning the objective validity of ethical experience. The assurance of objective reality in the feeling of rightness may be expressed in two ways. It may be construed as arising from our awareness of the reign of a cosmic law or a series of laws, according to which the right acts and attitudes in every conceivable situation are determined with inflexible definiteness. Or, the source of validity of ethics may be identified as the Will of God, and the answer in every situation is accordingly sought through a fresh orientation to the Being of God.

The systems of Buber and Cohen represent extreme developments of these two alternatives, respectively. Cohen began with the recognition of the "lawfulness" of ethical judgments. He noted the similarity in development of both logic and ethics and, in his "Grundgesetz der Wahrheit," he set forth the requirement of "purity" for both these directions of spirit. "Purity" is, clearly, a technical designation for absolutely perfect and self-sufficient lawfulness. While in his "Ethics," Cohen stressed this aspect of the ethical will, in his later writings, he came to recognize more and more the importance of the reference to God, which is vaguely implied in the apprehension of ethical values. Buber, on the other hand, chooses to ignore the element of rational lawfulness in ethical experience altogether. The validity of ethical insight is not due to any agreement with a cosmic law, but to the call of the Divine Voice. The reference to God, implied in the Thou-relation, is the one essential element of the ethical, or, as he would say, of the real life.

Cohen's interest is essentially that of cognition. Hence, in dealing with the meaning of the ethical values, he expressed the intuition of their validity, from the viewpoint of knowing, as "truth." In his later writings, Cohen conceived of this basic certainty as the guarantee of God. It cannot be emphasized too often that the concept of God is the most central idea in Cohen's philosophy. Though God is an "idea" and a "methodological concept," He is nevertheless a real Being, unique and transcendent. We must not be deceived by the language of Cohen. Writing from the standpoint of epistemology, he naturally wrote only of ideas and concepts. Still, in his view, God partakes of the processes of both will and thought and is the ultimate Reality. Thus, the apprehension of the validity of ethics contains, with Cohen, a direct reference to God, as the Source of ethics.

Buber's interest is practical. Scanning the wide field of ethical experience, he concludes that the life of ethics cannot be expressed either in cold principles, or in bare maxims. Ethics is neither thought, nor will, nor feeling, but life, the fulness of life, which is all-inclusive. Wherever self-less love is expressed, there Buber finds the perception of ultimate reality and a reference to God, as the final focus of all earthly Thous—the eternal Thou.

The common elements in the basic insights of both Cohen and Buber are, first, the state of mind in which both the good and the true are sought as one. They start with the feeling that these two goals are somehow one, that there is a common core, accessible to the heart of man, which is at once valid and right. In the "Thou" relation, the will to serve God and the will to know God are merged. Similarly, the "law of truth" stands at the borderlines and unites the processes of thought and will. Secondly, there is a sense of the "reality" of the ethical life—that is, the feeling that the good life is in accord with the eternal structure of things. To Buber, the "dialogue" life is the only "real" life and the reward of morality is the knowledge of being real. Cohen, too, sees no sanction to ethics. The good man has the satisfaction of knowing that his life is steered in the direction of the three "pure" processes of Being. Thirdly, both believe that the ultimate validity of ethical motivation is due to the Will of God. Buber's thought is expressed in the belief that all love is love of God; every Thou-relation is an address to the eternal Thou. Cohen's belief takes the form of the principle that the validity of the direction of pure will and its eternity are guaranteed by the God of truth.[3]

Rosenzweig's basic intuition is similar to those of Cohen and Buber. It will be remembered that Rosenzweig's philosophy is based upon the experience of revelation. The love of God streams into the heart of man, who is, thereupon, constrained to reply with love to his fellow-man. Rosenzweig believes that human love is derived from the love of God and that the love of man to his fellow-man is an integral link in the eternal triangle of creation, revelation and redemption. Clearly, then, there is no essential difference between Buber's and Rosenzweig's versions of the nature of the ethical-religious experience.

Kaplan's one belief is, as we have seen, the affirmation that ethical rightness and wrongness are rooted in the ultimate structure of reality. God is the Being, Who assures the final

---

[3] Franz Rosenzweig in his "Einleitung" finds the common ground of both Buber and Cohen in the concept of correlation. We noted that point in our discussion of Cohen's concept of God, but, in our view, the similarity is more verbal than actual.

triumph of the ideals of mankind. Kaplan does not describe the line of demarcation between the consciousness of ethical and non-ethical ideals, nor does he indicate how God functions in the world. Obviously, if ethical values are to be accorded supreme ontological status in the scheme of existence, they must be conceived as endowed with distinguishing characteristics, which mark them off decisively from the stream of ordinary phenomena. Nevertheless, in spite of his failure to draw such a line of demarcation, Kaplan, in his own way, bases his religion upon the assertion that our awareness of ethical values includes a perception of their objective validity and a reference to God as their Guarantor.

Thus, we see that the four greatest and most typical exponents of recent Jewish thought agree in basing religion upon the perception of ethical values. Though they represent widely differing philosophical movements, these thinkers agree that, at bottom, religion and ethics are one and that the voice of conscience is somehow also the voice of God. In this belief, modern Jewish philosophers continue to cultivate the original insight of their ancestral faith.

Jewish monotheism was derived from the impulses and longings of ethics, not from reasoned speculations concerning the cosmos. For this reason, there was always an impassable gulf between the monotheism of the Greeks, especially of Aristotle, which was based upon the recognition of the metaphysical unity of the world, and the monotheism of the Hebrew prophets, which was so powerfully epitomized in Abraham's query, "Can it be that the Judge of the whole world will not do justice?" God as the "Righteous Ruler of the Universe" and God as the Source of "Order" in the world are the two conceptions, stemming from Judaism and from Greek philosophy respectively, which theologians, since Philo, have sought to harmonize.[4] Modern Jewish philoso-

---

[4] See Josiah Royce's article on "Monotheism" in the Encyclopedia of Ethics and Religion, Vol. VIII, p. 819.

phy continues, in the main, to be derived from a heightened sense of ethical values. In all its diverse ramifications, modern exponents of Judaism remain true to the deep insight of Elijah that God is not to be found through the contemplation of the fire and wind of the physical universe, but that the "still, small voice" of conscience is indeed the voice of God.[5]

(b) Theses for a Philosophy of Religion

In the preceding pages, i have endeavored to present a strictly objective account of modern Jewish philosophy. However, I am conscious of the fact that a completely impartial history of philosophy cannot possibly be written. The essence of philosophy is the description and explanation of things from certain viewpoints and you cannot chart the map of viewpoints without revealing the coordinates of your own thought. For this reason, many philosophers began the exposition of their own systems of philosophy with histories of philosophy, believing that their views of the development of thought were clear illustrations of their own basic ideas.

In order to enable the reader to judge this work for himself, it is necessary that I set forth here the basic principles of my own thought, insofar as they are relevant to the construction of a philosophy of religion.

1. From a logical standpoint, complete skepticism is possible. We may sit down in an easy chair, pass all the data of our mind in review and demand incontrovertible proof from them that they are not all part of one grand illusion. To an aggressively skeptical state of mind, all "proofs" must be further substantiated through "proofs of proofs" and so on, ad infinitum. In the pale light of skepticism, all facts and values assume of necessity the ghostly aspect of unreality. Thought itself is powerless to arrest this process of total dissolution, through militant disbelief, whereby the world and

---

[5] See supplementary note to this chapter.

its contents is turned into an ephemeral nightmare. But no such power is required by thought, since the pressure of life itself soon puts an end to the unearthly speculations of the skeptic. Away from the easy chair and within the seething cauldron of life's actual problems, no one but the insane will question the reality of the existence of the world or of man. Our "animal faith," to employ a celebrated phrase of Santayanna, brushes aside with supreme unconcern and ease the vast array of logic so tortuously assembled by the philosophical skeptic.

When we pose to ourselves the question of the ultimate foundation and purpose of existence, we are similarly able in strict logic to adopt an agnostic attitude. Perhaps, there is no eternal Reality behind the flux of phenomena, we may say, or if there be such a Reality, it is to us totally incomprehensible. The best we can do, it may be argued, is to designate that Reality as the Unknowable. This attitude, too, is refuted, not by any rational means, but by the fact that *human* life and *human* ideals continue to demand that we orient our lives to some valid goals. As skepticism in regard to the existence of the physical universe is overcome by the pressure of animal impulses, so is agnosticism in regard to the ultimate nature of reality surmounted by the spirit of man which impels us never to give up the search for God, for truth and goodness. Complacent agnosticism is itself a sin against the human spirit. In spite of past failures, it is our spiritual duty to employ our best lights in the attempt, at once human and divine, to know the Unknowable. From this sacred endeavor, we may not fall back in weak despair without losing our title to the crown of human dignity. "For the righteous man falleth seven times and riseth up again." [1]

If, then, we spurn the deathly refuge of the skeptic, we can only answer the basic question of philosophy, "what is

---

[1] Proverbs 24, 16.

the essence of all things?" by postulating frankly a reasonable assumption or by referring to an intuition of reality. This fact becomes evident through an examination of the nature of logical thought. Deductive logic proceeds from the general proposition to the particular instance. Possessing the major premise, we are enabled, through deductive logic, to note the appropriate minor premises and to draw the correct conclusions. But, the final major premise, how can it be obtained? Here is where thought ends and intuition begins. Inductive logic proceeds from the particular to the universal. Major premises are built up through the consideration of a number of relevant individual cases. Strictly speaking, inductive logic requires the verification of all the instances that are comprised within the major premise. Otherwise, the major premise must still be regarded as unproved. In the case of the question before us, inductive logic is obviously inapplicable. Clearly, then, our views on the essence of things will be based on an intuition. There is room for reason in the criticism of alternative answers, of course. Thus, I agree with the idealistic criticism of the materialistic position on the ground that the concepts of matter, force, energy etc. are not valid metaphysical concepts. I further believe that the progress of science has rendered materialism totally untenable. But, when we come to the presentation of a positive answer concerning the essence of things, we are compelled to fall back upon our own deepest convictions.

There is no way of evading this choice of an intuition. Cohen dared to reject all "given" elements in the construction of his system. So long as he was occupied with the problems of logic, he managed to retain this position. But, we have seen, that when he came to construct a philosophy of life, he found it necessary to begin with the "law of truth." A similar examination of all great philosophers will show, I believe, that no one can build the palace of metaphysics who does not himself provide the cornerstone.

2. The principle which we have to lay down at the base of metaphysics cannot be an arbitrary assumption. The recognition of the dependence of a rational philosophy upon a basic intuition does not grant a general license for all manner of irrational and unproved beliefs. In the history of thought, disappointment in the power of reason led all too often to the silly excesses of romantic subjectivism, which, in its turn, sooner or later, culminated in a neo-obscurantism. No intuition deserves to be taken account of which is not shared by the generality of mankind.

The difference between an intuitional truth and a rational axiom is that an axiom retains the quality of certainty at all times, so that we are never able to doubt its validity. The metaphysical intuitions, on the contrary, appear to us as overwhelmingly and incontestably true only at certain moments. Thus, Bergson's intuition of the élan vital, Schopenhauer's intuition of the cosmic Will, Jacobi's intuition of freedom—all these insights, we are told, come only at rare moments of intense concentration.[2] In other words, the claim of the intuitionists is that knowledge concerning the ultimate structure of the universe can be reached by us, only when we *are* in certain states of mind. We must assume a certain "existential" attitude, as the German thinkers put it, before we can glimpse reality. At the base of reason, it is what you —the whole of you, are that counts.

3. In seeking to solve the riddle of existence, we face the choice of beginning either with the lowest or with the highest concepts. In the first case, we assume simple elements— Democritean atoms, or electrons, or some general form of

---

[2] Already Maimonides in his introduction to the "Guide" speaks of the elusiveness of truth, which flashes lightning-like upon the mind of man, only to give way to total darkness with equal suddenness.

matter in motion, or a series of "neutral" essences. From these elements, we then proceed to explain the emergence of the more complex organisms, through the operation of some simple mechanical rules. In the second case, we begin with an all-inclusive concept, the Absolute, Self, or Reason, or the Infinite, or Personality, and then attempt to reason down to earthly things.

It obviously makes a big difference in the final result, as to whether we begin with the simplest or the most complex concepts. If everything is, at bottom, particles of matter in motion, then the distinguishing traits of mankind appear to be accidental phenomena, mere temporary freaks of existence. We are higher than the universe and rightfully look down upon it. If, on the contrary, we begin with the highest concept, then man's spirit is more akin to reality than his body. Man looks up to the universe and is the more at home in it the higher he rises to the loftiest spiritual levels of which he is capable. From a strictly logical viewpoint, both assumptions are equally admissible. The final decision must come from an extra-logical source, from the depths of our own being.

4. At this point, the intuition of the objective validity of ethical values must be taken into consideration. In moments of intense moral fervor, we feel that rightness and wrongness are eternally fixed in the scheme of things; that it is not our own personal dictates and impulses that are the source of ethical feeling; that the sense of authority attaching to our ethical judgment is not derived either from the opinions of other men or from the unconscious influence of society; that the things we call "good" and "bad" are similarly designated by the Eternal One, Who stands outside of us and yet dwells within us, speaking through our mouths in moments of great, ethical exaltation.

This intuition is the basis of my philosophy and religion. I believe it, not only because on many occasions it has come to me with dazzling clarity, but, far more because this insight has been shared by the great thinkers of humanity, in particular, by the religious geniuses of Israel. To be sure, an intuition is a fluid state of mind, which cannot as a whole be imprisoned in some hard formula. Every statement in which this intuition has traditionally been phrased necessarily reflected the philosophical background and particular bias of those who have experienced it. We have seen before how beneath the apparently opposed philosophies of Judaism of our generation, there is hidden one group of insights, pointing to the divine origin of ethical values. By seizing upon different aspects of this intuition, philosophers may evolve widely varying world-views, the common source of which it is difficult to discern.

We are concerned with discovering whether there is indeed vouchsafed to man, albeit admittedly at rare moments only, an intuition of the eternal validity and of the extra-human source of ethical values. In advocating an affirmative answer to this query, I point to that long line of Hebrew prophets, who taught that God, the Creator of the world, to Whom alone true Being can be imputed, is also the Source of morality. It is the opinion of nearly all scholars that the Jewish teachers have arrived at their monotheistic faith through their intense moral enthusiasm. Their religion arose and developed out of their intuition of the absolute authority of the moral law. Among the Greeks, it was Plato who gave to the world the classic formulation of this belief, in the thought that the Good, the True and the Beautiful are One. Kant, in modern times, attempted to formulate in rigid terminology the dictates of the "practical reason," which he conceived to be a divine and eternal law, akin to the timeless principles of logic.

There are many scholars who maintain that the objectivity of ethical values is due to the unconscious pressure of society. Thus, Durkheim wrote, "If religion has given birth to all that is essential in society, it is because the idea of society is the soul of religion." [3]   I do not believe that consciousness of society is the source of the highest ethical experiences.   The greatest advances in ethical feeling were consummated in the hearts of those few who dared to oppose the mass-mind.   The mob is always stolid and blind, motivated most powerfully by the least common denominator of moral feeling.   Durkheim's "idea of society" does not, therefore, refer to any consciousness of the opinions or wishes of the actual human society in which we live, but to some vague abstraction.   Furthermore, the conviction, that ethical validity derives from sociological forces, if actually believed in, is likely to dispel belief in ethical validity altogether.   For it is of the essence of the highest ethical experience to feel that the source of its authority stands outside and above the shifting sands of popular approval.

We do not always apprehend in consciousness the objective validity of ethical values.   It is possible for us to view moral action from an indifferent, non-moral standpoint.   In that event, we see nothing peculiar in the life of morality, nothing, that is, which cannot be explained on the basis of ordinary, human impulses and drives.   But there are moments in life, when, no longer skeptical and indifferent, we feel the values of morality to be supremely real, more real even than our own lives.   At such moments we cannot but regard the materialistic explanations of morality as utterly false and irrelevant.   Most of us, in the ordinary run of things, take moral values for granted and are not much concerned over them.   When, however, we are suddenly confronted with an outrageous crime, we realize, through the violence of our indignation, that the springs of morality are very deep indeed, streaming forth from some mysterious, divine source.

5. The intuition of objective ethical validity leads directly

---

[3] "Elementary Forms of Religious Experience" p. 419.

to the conclusion that there is a Divine Will, operating behind the veil of phenomena. Ethical values are obligatory for us, because they are willed by a Supreme Will. They could not appear to us as objective, if they did not exist apart from human minds. But values can have no existence apart from a Mind which envisages them and a Will, which, in willing them, confers upon them the status of values.

This conclusion may be drawn, no matter in what form the intuition of the validity of ethical values is conceived. In a general way, we may say that intuitional ethics may be divided into two classifications, under the headings, "justice" and "love." In the former category, ethics is conceived as a system of eternal laws, to which men on earth ought to conform. In the second category, the moralist stresses a feeling of attraction toward an elusive goal. The two different ways of construing the meaning of the ethical experience are illustrated in this book, in the philosophies of Buber and Cohen. In either case, the idea of God is found to be implied, in one way or another, in the basic insight of the moral life.

6. On the basis of this argument, I believe that metaphysics should start with the highest concept available to man, that of Personality. We are unable to give a full account of what is meant by God as Personality, any more than we can tell all about our own persons. The term personality is the most inclusive in our vocabulary. It includes the elements of matter, spirit, will, caprice, character, emotion, mind and the mysterious unity in which they are all fused together. By thinking of God as Personality, we indicate that from His Nature, all the multiple and diverse phenomena of existence are somehow to be explained.

For a long time, it was believed that philosophers could only believe in a "negative theology." God had to be defined in negative terms only and every adjective referring to His real positive action could only be taken in a symbolic sense.

I believe with Rosenzweig that God is to be conceived as a Living Person, containing within His Being the contradictions of necessity and freedom, eternity and timeliness, matter and spirit, lawfulness and creativity, "midas hadin" and "midas horaḥmin." Is not the human self a similar unity of diverse elements? I do not believe that we can possibly hope to improve over the conceptions of the God of Israel in Talmudic literature, where He is pictured as at once "Our Father," "Our King," "Lord of the Universe" and "God of Israel," "The Place" and "the Merciful." "Wherever you find the greatness of God, there too you find His humility," we read in the prayer-book. God as the metaphysical principle of unity and God as the source of ethical values are one or, as the Rabbi Levi Isaac of Berdichev was wont to phrase this truth, "God as the Far and God as the Near is One." [4]

A conception of God, reached through the process of progressive abstraction, can only be of the most general sort. Hence, it cannot possibly permit such warm attributes of His Nature as the language of true piety and genuine prayer requires. But a monotheism which derives from an intuition of ethical validity leads naturally to that view of God, which does justice to His relations with man and the world. There are in the ethical experience elements of both generality and particularity—the apprehension of a universal law of justice as well as a call to love. There is no reason, then, to decree that God cannot think of or love the individual. I see Rosenzweig's great contribution to the philosophy of religion in his contention that God does indeed love the individual.

Against the concept of God as Self or Personality, the argument is often advanced that we have no knowledge of any self. The term "self" or "person" is based upon the absence of analysis, it is pointed out. Thus, Hume and more recently Bradley have shown that we have no perception of

---

[4] K'dushath Levi, "Mishpatim." See also Leo Baeck in "The Essence of Judaism," who enunciates this principle at great length.

self. They searched their minds and found nothing which endured through time, apart from the changing flux of mental representations. It was this criticism of Hume, which, more than anything else, led to the abandonment of the concept of a "personal" God, since there appeared to be no real meaning vested in that term. Yet, the argument of Hume is nothing but a quibble; I cannot imagine how, with his procedure of eliminating particular mental data, any other result was possible. McTaggart has shown that we do possess an awareness of self.[5] I feel that, little as we may know concerning the inner unity of personality, the term itself is one of the least equivocal in human parlance.

In any event, it is only as Personality that God can be worshipped. In recent years, the tendency has arisen to think of God as a Process, or a Force, or a Principle. John Stuart Mill suggested that God be worshipped as a power within reality, working steadily for the good, omnipresent, but not all-powerful. This God-force manifests itself especially in the endeavors of mankind to subdue nature and to improve the structure of society. Mill's reversion to neo-animism was motivated by the apparent insolubility of the problem of evil on the basis of traditional theology. A similar attitude prevails among some of the "Reconstructionists." Thus, Eugene Kohn writes, "a God who is the source of evil no less than of good and who is conceived as having the power to save mankind but not using it, cannot command the reverence due to a God." [6] In this disdainful manner, he brushes aside three millenia of monotheistic piety, offering us instead the view of a God who is only an "aspect of reality." It is not my purpose to examine in detail views, which have not yet been fully developed. Here, I wish only

---

[5] David Hume—"Treatise of Human Nature." Bradley—"Appearance and Reality." McTaggart—article on "Personality" in Encyclopedia of Religion and Ethics.

[6] Reconstructionist, Vol. 7, No. 2, March 7, 1941.

to indicate that the conception of God as "personality" is alone capable of affording a rational solution of theological problems, while retaining the capacity of evoking the spirit of worship. It is of the essence of personality to unify and to integrate, to make room for the ideal, while yet the real continues to exist.

All so-called contradictions in the traditional concept of God revolve round the apparent conflict between the Will of God and His work. Yet, if we are not to be guided by the law of the jungle, this distinction must never be lost sight of. On the other hand, any doctrine which implies a complete severance between these two phases of the activity of God must end eventually in the reduction of the stature of God to that of man.

The solution of the problem of evil, which Cohen proposes, in which suffering is interpreted as "yissurim shel a'havah," "afflictions of love," appeals to me most. The point to remember is that the concept of God as the ideal personality presents many aspects, contradictions if you will, sublimed into a higher unity in the Consciousness of God. We may remonstrate with Him even as Jeremiah, complain and protest even as Job, praise and extol even as David. But it is to Him, to Him Who is mysteriously one in all His many-sidedness, that, in our moments of humble piety, we always return.

Conceptions of God as a "power" or as a "process" are altogether worthless for religion. The concept of "power" is derived from the science of physics, where it is employed to designate a potential force. Clearly, then, this term cannot be applied to God, since He must be an actual Being. If God is an actual "force" for the good interacting with the ethically neutral forces, then we should identify the effective causes of everything that is good with God—an obvious absurdity. The term "process" is one of relation, possessing no inherent meaning of its own. It becomes significant only when it is indicated what kind of process is meant.

God, as the Supreme Personality, remains an inscrutable Being. This means for religion, that we approach Him in humble supplication, conscious of our human limitations. In philosophy, this concept of God presents innumerable problems, which it is our task as thinkers to resolve. At the base of human thought, lies the feeling of humble reverence. We cannot, as living beings, see the Face of the Lord. Moses, through his humility, came closest to God. There can be no cocksureness in matters of religion, then. Often the restless agnostic comes nearer to genuine piety than the professional religionist. For piety is, at bottom, a seeking and a quest.

7. We have seen before that the awareness of the validity of ethical values comes to us in rare moments, but it is upon the insights gained in those moments that the entire moral structure of mankind is perilously reared. Every generation inherits a certain fund of moral idealism from the accumulated experience of its predecessors. But, the genuinely moral sentiments in our heritage are bound to wane, unless they are periodically strengthened through renewed devotion to the Source of ethical motivation. If worship is neglected and disdained, then, in the course of time, morality loses its distinguishing fervor. It is inevitable that it should then be classed along with other human impulses as merely a form of subtle selfishness, required by "common sense."

The highest ethical experience is a reply to a Thou as well as an awareness of the eternal "rightness" of ethical life. It is this double nature of the ethical experience, which accounts for the ancient controversy, as to the relative merits of the concepts of "justice" and "love" in expressing the essence of the moral life—a controversy, which Achad Ha'Am and many others thought was the main issue between Judaism and Christianity. Really, the religious element which enters into the highest forms of ethical awareness can only be described as love, whereas the ethical motives in ordinary life are better subsumed under the term of justice. Without this saving grace of devotion to a Person, the element of lawfulness in ethics steadily loses its appeal, wilting away like an uprooted tree. During the first stage of irreligion, the Kantian stage, the moral law appears to be suspended in mid-air. Then, it gradually falls to earth, either as materialism or as humanism—no longer distinctly itself.

Worship is the exercise whereby the attempt is made to keep moral fervor at a high level. In reminding ourselves of our relation to the Supreme Being, we strengthen the ties of ethics which are common to man and to God. Through worship we endeavor to reach that high state of spiritual exaltation, when the reality of the good is experienced most poignantly. To be sure, worship does not always accomplish this result, but, if it achieves this purpose once in a lifetime, it is more than justified as a regular practice.

The intimate relationship between religion and ethics serves to explain why public worship is often so much more inspiring than private prayer. We must unlimber our bonds of oneness with each other, before we can feel the ties that bind us to our Father in heaven. Here, too, we find a major reason for loyalty to the inherited forms of particular religious groups, for people of a like education and background acquire more easily the feeling of unity and brotherhood. Thus, public worship is an ethical duty, for it is our obligation to strive always to be better than we are.

But worship is more than a spiritual exercise for the ends of ethics. It is one of the follies of our time, that support for religion is sought in the fields of sociology and political science with the claim that "social justice" and "democracy" are secure only on the basis of a strong religious faith. Whatever truth is to be found in those claims may be sufficient to justify public support for religion; it cannot serve as a good incentive for religion itself. However, the truly religious require no extraneous motivation. Witness the joy of the Psalmists in their communion with God. Those who have once experienced the pure earnestness and the deep sense of devotion which floods the whole of one's being, submerging, if only for the moment, all that is petty and unworthy, will not require special reasons for religious worship. They will feel it both a duty and a privilege to pray, even as they feel it a duty and a privilege to do good and to shun evil, for the root of religion and ethics is one.

Is worship a form of communion with the Deity or is it primarily a dedication of oneself to the Will of God? Students of the history of religions know that in the lower forms of religion, worship is an element of secondary importance in the sacrificial ritual. The value of worship is thought to lie in its efficacy as a means of bringing down the Grace of God, in one form or another, to the suppliant. The fact that religious worship has so often been the prelude to bigoted hatreds of all sorts is doubtless due to the circumstance that the element of dedication to a life of ethics, as the Will of God, has been ignored and worship was thought of in non-ethical, ritualistic terms. When religion is not guided to its goal through the voice of conscience, it is liable to sink to the level of black magic and become a vehicle for mass-fanaticism and blindness. On the other hand, the voice of conscience should be recognized as hailing from beyond ourselves, being indeed a faint echo of the mighty call of God to man. Worship, then, is primarily self-dedication and secondarily, communion with the Will of God.

8. The above outline of the philosophy of religion agrees, I feel, with the innermost essence of Judaism. It remains to point out the obvious truth that there are values to the entire body of Jewish life, over and beyond the truths contained in this exposition. Judaism is a revealed religion.

The meaning of this term can only be understood against the background of the long and glorious role which the Jewish religion played in world history. If we believe that the course of human events is directed by the Providence of God, we must look upon our role in the cosmic drama as a Divine command. Rosenzweig's theory of revelation, expounded at length before, will be found to accord with an enlightened view of tradition and with the ways of thinking of the earnestly critical modern mind.

In recent years, the question has been hotly debated, is Judaism primarily a religion or a civilization? This question is generally so phrased as to preclude a definite answer in favor of either alternative. Judaism is, of course, more than a national civilization. On the other hand, religion is not just a philosophy of life; it is that plus a regimen of conduct intended to saturate all phases of life with the spirit of faith. Thus Judaism is the central, all-pervasive and all-absorbing element of the civilization of the Jewish people.

Judaism may be described as a civilization in the sense of being the treasure of a definite historical group. It is the duty of every group to keep alive for humanity the ideals of its peculiar heritage. Group effort is needed to maintain group-values, especially the values of religion, which are inaccessible to the naked eye—much less, to the naked heart. Not one of the finer treasures of the culture of a group— neither its better music nor its noblest literature, nor its greatest works of art, nor the basic faith underlying its form of government—could be transmitted from one generation to the succeeding one without some form of social organization and common endeavor. For the flesh is weak and the upward climbing of the human spirit requires constant prodding.

To ask whether Judaism be a religion or a civilization is not so much a question of definition and historical study, as it is one of motivation. Its real meaning is, which motive for the maintenance of Jewish life shall we stress, the nationalistic or the religious one? In other words, what is involved is a change of valuation and emphasis. I am opposed to this change for many reasons, principally because I believe that the motive of nationalism is productive of good only when it is kept in the background, as subordinate to the universal ideals of ethics and religion.[7]

To close with a word of exhortation, I feel that it is impossible to over-estimate the role which a genuine renaissance of the Jewish religion could play in protecting the Achilles heel of Western civilization, its gradual loss of a religiomoral bases. Our people in this country and in many other lands are favored with a high degree of culture, and we are very much in the public eye. If we could win our people back to real piety, not merely to passive observance of certain rituals or to weak panderings to popular taste, we shall have unleashed intellectual forces which cannot fail to influence powerfully the entire trend of current events. In the past, our people performed this function for the world. Somehow, the lines of history follow ancient grooves. This, then, is still our task and this our destiny—to labor for the revival of genuine piety among our people, so that we may bring nearer the promised day, when "the knowledge of God will cover the earth as the waters cover the sea."

---

[7] See my article, "Judaism as a Civilization—A Critique," in the "Opinion," June, 1934.

BIBLIOGRAPHY

WORKS BY MARTIN BUBER

1. *Reden über das Judentum,* Rütten & Loening, Frankfurt am Main, 1923. This edition includes the essays which are also published separately and are referred to in this book. (2 & 3)
2. *Der Heilige Weg,* Rütten & Loening, Frankfurt am Main, 1919.
3. *Cheruth,* R. Lowitt Verlag, Wien, 1919.
4. *Mein Weg zum Chassidismus,* Rütten & Loening, Frankfurt am Main, 1918.
5. *Daniel,* Gespräche von der Verwirklichung, Insel Verlag, Leipzig, 1920.
6. *Die Rede, die Lehre und das Lied,* Drei Beispiele, Insel Verlag, Leipzig, 1920.
7. *Ich und Du,* Insel Verlag, Leipzig, 1923. In this book references are to the English translation published by T. & T. Clark, Edinburgh, England, 1937.
8. *Worte an die Zeit,* Zwei Hefte, Dreiländer Verlag, München, 1919.
9. *Zwiesprache,* Schocken Verlag, Berlin, 1932.
10. *Die Stunde und die Erkenntnis,* Schocken Verlag, Berlin, 1936.
11. *Die Frage an den Einzelnen,* Schocken Verlag, Berlin, 1936.
12. *Kampf um Israel,* Schocken Verlag, Berlin, 1933.
13. *Jewish Mysticism, and the legends of Baalshem,* being a part of the work, "Die Chassidischen Bucher," translated by Lucy Cohen, London and Toronto, J. M. Dent & Sons, Ltd., 1931.
14. *Die Jüdische Bewegung,* Jüdischer Verlag, Berlin, 1920.
15. *Das Königtum Gottes.* 1938.

WORKS ON MARTIN BUBER

1. *Martin Buber, Sein Werk und Seine Zeit* by Hans Kohn. Verlag von Jakob Hegner in Hellerau, 1930. In this book, a com-

plete bibliography of all the minor articles and works not directly relevant to our subject by Martn Buber and on him, down to the year 1930, is given.

2. *Derech HaKodesh* by M. Glickson in Hebrew monthly. "Maavaroth" Jaffa, 1928, Vol. 1, p. 339.
3. *Martin Buber, Sein Gang in die Wirklichkeit*, by Wilhelm Michel. Verlag Rütten & Loening, Frankfurt am Main, 1926.
4. *Martin Buber and Neo-Mysticism* by John J. Tepfer, Central Conference of American Rabbis, Yearbook, 1934.
5. *Martin Buber und die Wiedergeburt des Judentums aus dem Geiste der Mystik*. Verlag Herrmann Meister, Heidelberg, 1924.
6. *Religion as a Psychic Necessity*, in "Psyche," London, April 1927.

WORKS BY HERRMANN COHEN

1. *Kants begründung der Etik*, Berlin, F. Dummler (Horrwitz und Grossman), 1877.
2. *Logik der Reinen Erkenntniss*, Berlin, B. Cassirer, 1902. Referred to here as Logic.
3. *Religion und Sittlichkeit*, Berlin, M. Poppelauer, 1907. Referred to here by abbreviation R. u. S.
4. *Schriften zur Philosophie und Zeitgeschichte*, Berlin, Akademie-Verlag, 1928.
5. *System der Philosophie*, 2nd Vol. "Etik des Reinen Willens," 1904, Berlin, B. Cassiser. Referred to here as Ethics.
6. *Jüdische Schriften*, 3 vol. Ed. Bruno Straus, Berlin 1924.
7. *Der Begriff der Religion im System der Philosophie*, Verlag Von Alfred Topelmann (Vormals J. Ricker) Giessen 1915. Referred to here by abbreviation B. d. R.
8. *Die Religion der Vernunft* aus den Quellen des Judentums, Gustav Fock G. m. b. H. Leipzig 1919. Referred to here by abbreviation R. d. V.

WORKS ON HERRMANN COHEN

1. *Herman Cohen*, Walter Kinkel, Verlag von Strecker und

Schroder, Stuttgart, 1924, where, too, an exhaustive bibliography of Cohen's works is given.

2. *Der Gottesbegriff in der Philosophie Hermann Cohens,* by Siegfried Ucko, Inaugural-Dissertation, 1927.

3. *Die Begründung der Etik bei Hermann Cohen,* by Johannes Weise, Inaugural-Dissertation, 1911.

4. *Hermann Cohens Religion der Vernunft,* in "Monatschrift für Geschichte und Wissenschaft des Judentums," 1921, by Albert Lewkowitz.

5. *Die Religions Philosophie des Neukantianismus,* in "Zeitschrift für Philosophie und Philosophische Kritik," Bd. 144, 1911, by Albert Lewkowitz.

6. *Einleitung* by Franz Rosenzweig, in "Judische Schriften" 1st Vol.

7. *Hermann Cohen, schitoso bemusor umishnoso bayaaduth,* by Jacob Klatzkin, in Hebrew, Berlin, 1923.

8. *Die Religionsphilosophie des Neukantianismus,* by J. Hessen, Freiburg, 1924.

9. *Kritik der Neukantischen Philosophie der Gegenwart,* by K. Kesseler, Leipzig, 1920.

10. *Hermann Cohen's Etik* by W. Herrmann, in "Christliche Welt," 1907.

11. *Die Religion der Vernunft,* by K. Bornhausen, Kantstudien, 1924.

12. *Hermann Cohens Philosophische Leistung unter dem Gesichtspunkte des Systems,* by P. Natorp, Berlin, 1918.

13. *Das Reine Denken und die Seinskonstituierung bei Hermann Cohen* by Josef Solowiejczyk, Inaugural-Dissertation, Berlin, 1932.

14. *Die Unterscheidung von Mythos und Religion bei Hermann Cohen und Ernst Cassirer in ihrer Bedeutung für die Jüdische Religionsphilosophie,* by Alfred Jospe, Inaugural-Dissertation, Breslau, 1932.

15. *Shito Yehudith Bephilosophio Habikoreth,* by David Neumark in Hebrew Magazine, "Hatoren," April 1924, May 1924, Nov. 1924, July 1925, December 1925.

16. *Religion of Reason,* by Dr. Trude Weiss Rosmarin.

WORKS ON PHILOSOPHY AND RELIGION BY FRANZ ROSENZWEIG

1. *Das Stern der Erlösung,* 1st edition, Frankfurt am Main, 1921. 2nd Edition, Schocken Verlag, 3 volumes, 1929. Referred to here as S. d. E.
2. *Kleine Schriften,* Schocken Verlag, containing "Das Neue Denken," a lengthy essay. 1935.
3. *Briefe,* Schocken Verlag, Berlin, 1937.

WORKS BY MORDECAI M. KAPLAN

1. *Judaism as a Civilization,* Macmillan Co., New York, 1934 referred to here as "J."
2. *The Meaning of God in Modern Jewish Religion,* Behrman's New York, 1937. Referred to here as "M."
3. *The Reconstructionist* magazine.

Das Judentum und die Strömungen des neunzehnten Jahrhundert, Albert Lewkowitz.
Philosophie des Judentums, J. Guttman.

SUPPLEMENTARY NOTES

It must be observed that, on the basis of Cohen's own hypothesis, the idea of God cannot be regarded as simply a deduction from the law of truth. Since truth signifies agreement in the methods of ethics and logic only, conclusions regarding the respective actualities of the two sciences cannot be inferred from it. We must remember that in the physical world, Being would remain even if the actual world were destroyed. Else Cohen would not have found it possible to equate being with thought. True, the idea is hypothesis, but once tested, it remains true and real, even if the physical world is destroyed. Again, mathematical thought would not be affected by the destruction of the physical world. Why then should ethics be considered as invalid and illusory if its corresponding actuality never comes to pass? As a matter of fact, the ethical ideal is not conceived by Cohen as capable of attaining the same kind of actualization that physical reality possesses. If Cohen had argued that pure will and pure thought are alone capable of constructing their corresponding actualities, he would have been justified in concluding that the law of truth leads directly to the idea of God. But in the case of mathematical logic, it is doubtful whether Cohen makes any such claim. Between the categories of logic and the phenomena perceived by our senses, he postulates the Category of Consciousness. This Category makes possible the perception of the merely possible and existent, forming the bridge between Being and Existence. Hence there is no necessary connection between being or thought and the actual world. It is difficult to see how the actual world could be identified with thought so long as the former is still perceived as under the dominion of time. True, the physical world is the task for thought, but whether all existence will eventually be conceived as being, is not clear in Cohen.[1]

---

[1] See the discussion of the relation between thought and "Wirkichkeit" in "Die Begründung des Seins und Seinsprinzip bei Herrmann Cohen," by Joseph Soloveitchik.

CHAPTER II, SECTION (*e*)

Note 1. It will be recalled that this too is the view of Kant. See his book on "Religion innerhalb der Grenzen der blossen Vernunft." Kant interprets in that book the symbols of the Christian faith in a manner which makes ethics their sole content and value. His Christianity is a mere useless attire of ethics.

Note 2. See B. d. R. p. 15 & p. 119, where he concludes: "So ist die Eigenart der Religion eine Grundbedingung der Systematischen Einheit des modernen Kulturbewusstseins."

Note 3. Cohen would object most violently to any conception of religion which separates it from cognition and regards it as a realm of unique value. In his system both ethics and esthetics share in Vernunft. Hence he cannot allow a total severance of fact from value. The intimate relationship of these elements of experience is in fact assured in the idea of truth and in that of God. Yet the fact remains that by the method of correlation only the value of the respective terms for each other can be deduced. It is in this special sense that we refer to the belief in the "uniqueness" of God as a value judgment. (See note 4)

Note 4. The view here presented is in contrast with the interpretation of Paul Natorp (Vorträge der Kantgesellschaft Nr. 21, 1918, p. 35) in which the evolution of Cohen's view of the uniqueness of God is made to depend on the latter's development of the concept of man's individuality. The development of both the uniqueness of God and the individuality of man were, in our opinion, the result of Cohen's growing realization that religion is a "Standpunkt zur Welt," a deliberate change of emphasis. Siegfried Ucko in his thorough study of Cohen's view of "uniqueness" feels that Cohen wrestled long with the formulation of this concept, as it seems to lead into the sphere of the irrational. Nothing could be further from Cohen's way of thinking. An examination of the passages in which the term "uniqueness" is applied to God, shows that reference is made either to the transcendence of the concept of God, as explained in "Ethics," or to the changed emphasis which distinguishes the religious consciousness, as expressed in the above reference (from B. d. R. p. 25). The absence of any conscious recognition by Cohen of the newness of this concept, a fact which Ucko notes, is in itself evidence enough that no more significance is to be attached to this term than is here given. Cohen's use of this term is sufficiently explained by its prominence in Medieval Jewish philosophy and by the echoes of it in the Bible, which he claims to find. (See Siegfried Ucko—"Der Gottesbegriff in der Philosophie Herrmann Cohen's," pp. 30, 41. Also R. d. V. pp. 41–58). Note especially the statement in B. d. R. p. 32, that in monotheism it is not God as such, but God in relation to man that is in the center. The point here made is stated almost explicitly in R. d. V. p. 58. "Wäre Gott nur ein Gegenstand der Erkenntniss, dann Konnte er nicht der einzige Gott sein; denn die Erkenntniss hat noch ganz andere Objekte und probleme. Der einzige Gott muss daher ein anderes Verhalten des menschlichen Geistes zu ihn bedingen. So wird die Liebe ein Erfordernis dieses Verhalten zum Einzigen." Moreover, it may be pointed out that Cohen spoke of the "unique" God as the foundation of culture in a lecture delivered in 1907, or long before his exposition of the correlation of man and God. (See Jüd. Schriften, p. 4, vol. 1, also p. 20) Paul Natorp in the essay mentioned above suggests the view of God as the principle of limitation, the idea which requires that all processes of spirit be lawful. For this reason, to think of Him is also to will and direct one's feeling to Him.

Note 5. Franz Rosenzweig views the discovery of the concept of correlation as a landmark in the history of thought. He regards this concept as affording an alternative method in the construction of a philosophical system, unrelated to the method of "Source" and "Production," concepts followed by Cohen in the construction of the rest of his system. In Rosenzweig's view, this method represents a break with the idealistic school which Cohen up to that point followed. Thus the assertion in the fifth chapter of the "Religion of Reason" that Vernunft is itself the creation of God, appears to Rosenzweig as a break with German idealism, which, since Hegel, tended to identify Vernunft, in one form or another, with the Absolute.

This view, however it may accord with the oral lectures of

Cohen, which Rosenzweig attended, is not the one which a perusal of the writings of Cohen justifies. The conception of correlation is not used as a "Grundbegriff"—that is, as one affording certain knowledge concerning the basic structure of reason. The employment of this concept in religion is fully explained on the basis of its methodological character as explained in the "Logic." Cohen himself refers to that description of the concept of correlation when he applies it to religion.[1]

It should be remembered that the corrrelation is established between two terms, the meaning of which has been deduced by the "production" method of ethics. Religion does not simply assume the idea of God as present in the human mind; it relies on ethics, systematically speaking, for the evolution of this idea. Similarly, the other end of the correlation, man, is not just the empirical person. It is the empirical individual taken along with his tendency to become the ethical self.[2]

The view that reason is the creation of God is fully explicable on the basis of the character of God as deduced in the "Ethics." God assures the reality of the ethical ideal and as the idea of truth, He underlies and conditions both ethics and logic. Since the three directions of spirit are conditioned by God, we may, if we choose, express this relation in terms of creation. In so doing we do not attribute any temporal beginning to reason and hence do no violence to truth. Our positive gain is the expression in religious terms of the recondite concept of the transcendence of God. This procedure is but a part of Cohen's general scheme to interpret relevant facts in terms of the correlation of man and God and of his attempt to "idealize" historical religions—that is, to give philosophic content to ancient dogmas.[3]

Note 6. As will be seen in the latter part of this essay the correlation of man and God takes place in the sphere of feeling as well as of logic and ethics. God is not merely known and willed; He is also longed for. To avoid confusion, we here select for prior analysis the logical and ethical aspects of religion. It will be our task subsequently to inquire whether the clouds of emotion, which, in

---

[1] B. d. R., p. 47.

[2] R. d. V., p. 132.

[3] Franz Rosenzweig's Einleitung in Jüd. Schriften, vol. 1, pp. XLV–LXV.

Cohen's view, envelop his religious terminology, are not due to what Cohen would call mythological associations.

It is difficult to see how God can be at once idea and ideal. As an ideal of conduct, God can only be conceived if He be clothed in human attributes. The whole meaning of the ethical life lies in the struggle against the resistance of the flesh. Cohen claims that a society of beings living ethically by instinct would not be an ethical society. Yet there is no possible analogue to that element of resistance in the nature of God. Again, God cannot be conceived as an ideal, in the sense of a goal toward which human actions are to tend, for there is nothing ethical in the nature of God. He is neither action nor movement, but a fact of reality or of cognition, depending upon the two standpoints from which His nature can be viewed.

Nevertheless, in his works on religion, Cohen repeatedly refers to God as an ideal, thereby confusing the concept of God with that of the ideal society. Thus when he interprets the attributes of God as the norms of man's conduct, it is impossible to reconcile his meaning with the idea of God, expounded in his systematic philosophy.[4] God is Holy, whereas man is to become holy.[5] "Und diese Bestimmung des Seins begrifft bei Gott nicht seine metaphysiche Kausalität, sondern sein zweckhaftes Handeln, welches das Musterbild bedeutet fur die zweckhafte handlung des Menschen."[6] If the meaning of this sentence were taken seriously by Cohen, he would have proceeded to deduce the duties of man from the conduct of nature. As God maintains nature for the sake of the ethical ideal, so too is man to maintain his own nature for the same goal. Yet it is obviously bad advice for men to take the conduct of nature as their model. This principle would have led, in the last analysis, to a pantheistic ethics, which, to Cohen, is a veritable abomination. Ethics would have been deduced from God as the ideal personality. The only ethical principle which Cohen does, in passing, deduce from this view of God as the ideal is that man must set it as his task to rise above sensibility, "even as God is removed from the

---

[4] R. d. V., Ch. VI.
[5] R. d. V., p. 111.
[6] R. d. V., p. 112.

sensible realm." [7] Yet the meaning of this rising above the sensible can after all be determined only on the basis of an independent analysis of man's epistemological and psychological problems.

In the following sentence, Cohen admits in his own peculiar left-handed fashion that the view of God as an ideal is basically meaningless. "Wenn man die Paradoxie nicht scheute, konnte man denken, die Heiligkeit bestände gar nicht sowohl für Gott als vielmehr für den Menschen."

As I see it, Cohen sometimes uses the term God loosely, as identical either with the ideal society or with the ideal person. The difficulty is that an ethical ideal can only refer to action. God, on the other hand, is an idea which implies action in the realm of Becoming, but is not itself action. Hence God can only be viewed as an ideal if He is taken along with some associated ideas. Thus when God is set up as the Urbild, whose attributes are the norms of man's conduct, He is viewed as an individual of ethical perfection. Again, Cohen sometimes speaks of longing for or love of God as being love for the ethical ideal. [8] These loose usages of the term God are perhaps justified by the fact that the religious attitude is not a strictly cognitive one.

Note 7.   See R. d. V., p. 76. The "Uniqueness" in this connection can only mean transcendence, though it would seem that transcendence alone is incapable of performing this function. For God assures the existence (Dasein) of nature, whereas the idea of truth can refer only to Being. We thus come back to the difficulty indicated before in the idea of God.

Note 8.   It is worth nothing that in contra-distinction to Buber, Cohen opposed the Zionist movement. He saw in the Zionist movement an attempt to escape the lot which God had assigned to the Jewish people. "They want to be the equals of other nations," was his common taunt to the zionist leaders. "Sie wollen ja glückselig sein," epitomized his condemnation of the movement. It is not the fate of Israel as a group to be happy. As the bearers of the monotheistic faith, the Jews must lack those political accoutrements, in which the nations of the world find their pride. They

---

[7] R. d. V., p. 112.
[8] R. d. V., p. 188.

must represent in the concert of nations the type of the hero of monotheism "the suffering servant." Is the Jewish people then to be regarded as a nation? Yes and no. In his reply to Buber, he makes the distinction between "nationality" and "nation," asserting that only the first term can legitimately be applied to the Jewish people. His point is that these social forms of organization—the clan, the tribe, the nation, the race, are *in se* of no ethical value. However, they may be "idealized"—that is, ethical structures of society may be founded upon them. Thus the actual state is based upon the existent fact of nationhood. But the fact of nationality can be idealized in yet another way. A group, possessing common ancestry, language, tradition, and background, may become the basis of a religion, not only of a political state. This indeed is the story of Judaism. The example of the Jewish people, proving as it does that nationality and statehood need not go together, is sorely needed in the modern world, which in the last two centuries has known no surcease from the tempests of nationalistic ambitions for self-government, produced by the erroneous belief that the "natural" end of a national group is to exercise dominion over itself. Cohen regarded zionism as a base surrender of the messianic ideal to this modern superstition—a surrender, altogether unworthy of the historical function of Israel. Strictly speaking, Cohen's position could be harmonized with that of "cultural zionism," though not in the form which that movement assumed in the writings of Achad Ha'Am and Martin Buber, since Cohen did not believe in the interpretation which the latter thinkers gave to the concept of "national soul." The term "Nationalgeist" is often employed by Cohen. The mystery of the monotheistic consciousness is ultimately to be sought in the peculiar genius of the Jewish "Nationalgeist," since monotheism is the product of the whole people. Yet it appears that he means by "the national spirit," the totality of a historical tradition, not a characteristic set of psychic potentialities and propensities. He would not have objected therefore to cultural zionism if it were conceived in religious terms, as the attempt to provide a more suitable environment for the cultivation of a monotheistic culture.

See R. d. V., pp. 28, 30, 42, 183. See the exchange of open letters between Martin Buber and Herrmann Cohen, printed in the

"Jüdische Schriften" of the latter and "Die Jüdische Bewegung" of the former. See Franz Rosenzweig's "Einleitung"; note passage in "Religion und Sittlichkeit," p. 74, where he expressly repudiates the theory that history is in any spiritual sense molded by the forces of race and blood. See Achad Ha'Am's essay, "Torah Sheblev." Of contemporary thinkers, Mordecai M. Kaplan presents a view which is in many ways similar to that of Herrmann Cohen, as can be seen in our discussion of his views.

Note 9. English moralists have held that pure egoism is also an ethical impulse. The views of Bentham and Clarke on this question are well known. Butler believed that morality consists of two movements of the will, egoism and benevolence, both of which were intrinsically right. H. Sidgwick too regards it as self-evident that it is right for a person to seek his own welfare, so long as that endeavor does not conflict with the clear dictates of conscience. Even Kant concurs in this position. Thus the third example which that philosopher gives of the way in which maxims of conduct are to be deduced from the Categorical Imperative deals with the manifest duty to develop one's own talents to the full. Kant does not justify this ethical command by any reference to the general good of society. He simply affirms that "as a rational being, he necessarily wills that his faculties be developed since they serve him and have been given him for all sorts of purposes." It would seem, however, that this maxim is not really derived from the Categorical Imperative, but from Kant's belief in the benevolence and perfection of nature which bulks so large in his pre-critical writings and is clearly evident in the first example which he adduces to show the applicability of the Categorical Imperative.

To Cohen, only the one movement of the will toward totality can be ethical. To be sure, Cohen postulates two forms of will, stemming from Respect and Love, respectively, of which the latter is conceived as applying to an individual or to a group of individuals. Thus love and the virtues deriving from it establish closer bonds of union between man and wife, members of the clan, the tribe, the nation, etc. Love contains an element of selfishness and is therefore to be subordinated to the virtues founded upon the feeling of respect for human rights in the abstract. In this manner, Cohen admits admixtures of egoism into the movement of pure will. Yet it is evident that the extreme case of unadulterated egoism can in no way be regarded by him as a form of pure will. Hence Cohen can find no room in his ethics for the urge to develop one's own individuality, save in the form indicated above. (See Henry Sidgwick's "Methods of Ethics," Book II, Ch. 1; See H. Cohen's "Ethik des Reinen Willens"; See Kant's "Fundamentals of the Metaphysics of Morals," Abbot's translation, pp. 39, 40; See Lovejoy's "The Great Chain of Being" on Kant's views of nature).

Note 10. It is important to note the difference between the two conceptions of "guilt" (Schuld) and sin (Sunde) in Cohen's philosophy. Guilt is a mythological concept. In all mythologies, the fate of men is associated with their guilt. This guilt was conceived, paradoxically enough, in non-moral terms. It applies to acts without reference to motives. It is the violation of a law, rooted in the nature of things, for which punishment must needs follow. Guilt may be inherited or it may attach to a person by reason of his membership in a certain group. The individual as such does not figure in mythological thought. The dominant interest of mythology is fate and guilt is merely the correlate of fate. Guilt and punishment are the eternal twins of mythology.

Scientific thought, Cohen insists, must dispense with the notion of "guilt." The science of jurisprudence, which is the historical embodiment of ethical knowledge, still retains traces of its mythological origin insofar as it continues to make use of the principle that guilt must be punished. Jurisprudence must dispense with this primitive association of guilt and retribution. The penal code should be regarded as describing the present structure of society. The judge is not a moralist, but an engineer, a troubleshooter, charged with the duty of keeping the machine of society rolling along.

Sin is an altogether different notion. It refers to the individual in his own solitariness; it begins and ends in the recesses of his own soul. The person feels a contradiction in his own self. His is the ethical will and his, too, is the unethical act. The sense of individual responsibility is a necessary manifestation of pure will. Sin is the violation of one's own code, whereas guilt is the transgression of an external law. Guilt is conceived as a bodily impurity which can be expurgated by bodily punishment, by sacrifice, or by the various rites of mythology. Sin is purely an affair of the soul. The ethical consciousness compels one to be conscious of his own sin, though it does not itself provide the scheme whereby one may be liberated from this oppressive feeling. It is the language of religion which alone is capable of achieving this task. Cohen attributes the realization of this truth to the prophet Ezekiel.[9]

Note 11. The idea that the repentant sinner desires his own chastisement is, of course, not peculiar to Cohen. Kant had employed this doctrine in his attempt to interpret the person of Christ as the idea of humanity. All punishment is, to the good man, substitutional suffering, since the person who places his will entirely in the service of "practical reason" voluntarily accepts the punishment due to his former selfish acts. This doctrine is not to be confsued with Socrates' voluntary submission to the laws out of a sense of gratitude or fairness, as it assumes a necessary and universal relation to exist between sin and pain.

The question arises whether Cohen's acceptance of this view is not in direct contradiction with his assertion that only mythological reasoning sees a necessary relation between sin and suffering. In Cohen's view, the connection is between suffering and redemption. Pain is not the end of the drama of life; far more, its beginning, the perpetual effort needed for progress in eternity. Still we may inquire why ethical progress should of necessity require pain and sacrifice. Is it not possible that a remnant of what Cohen calls mythological reasoning is responsible for this association? Cohen does not explain why redemption necessarily requires penance. He seems to take it for granted that the progress of will can only go through the alternate stages of pain and redemption. His thought appears to be that it is of the very nature of the movement of will to overcome obstacles.

Will and the ethical life are unthinkable without resistance.[10] Therefore an ethical act that is directed inwardly can find the equivalent of resistance only in the feeling of pain.

This position does not imply favorable judgment on asceticism. For not all pain, by any means, contributes to the ethical goal. "Strictly ethical is only the punishment which the penitent recog-

---

[9] R. d. V., ch. 11.
[10] E. 388.

nizes and takes upon himself." [11] This pain is, at its most poignant
level, regret over the failures of mankind to live up to the demands
of the spirit, the anguish of the soul at the sight of stupidity,
cupidity and oppression.[12] (For Kant's view on substitutional suffering and the voluntary acceptance of pain, see his "Religion innerhalb die Grenzen der Blossen Vernunft." For a view which
claims that the criminal has the right to be punished, see Hegel's
"Philosophy of Right," part 1).

Note 12. It should be borne in mind that when Cohen discusses
the meaning of any principle of Judaism, he does not claim to present the historical meaning of that principle. His explicit purpose
is to "idealize" Judaism—that is, so to interpret the tenets and
customs of the Jewish religion as to make them serve the purpose
of culture, as he understands the term. He does not tell us what
Judaism does say, but what it ought to be interpreted as saying.
This process of idealization he regards as motivated and justified
by the virtues of piety and loyalty. Idealization is the normal
process of religious evolution. It is not a deliberate falsification,
for "idealization" merely brings to light some unexpressed tendencies and causes a veil of oblivion to fall on other ideas, thus
maintaining a thread of historical continuity, however tenuous.
(See R. d. V. pp. 94, 173, 428; also "Jüd. Schriften, vol. 1, pp. 18,
41. For a similar doctrine of interpretation, though with a radically different emphasis, see Mordecai M. Kaplan, "Judaism as a
Civilization," p. 389).

Note 13. "Der höchste Wert der Religion wird verdunkelt, wenn
man nicht den Messianismus als die reinste Frucht des Monotheismus erkennt." [13] To Cohen the doctrine of Messianism was more
than a pious belief in progress. In his view, the worship of progress by materialists was little more than self-delusion, since the
measure of progress was not the increase of human power, but the
growth of human nature. In his philosophy, the ultimate reality
of humanity is even now a fact of Being. It will be recalled that,
in his view, time cannot change the nature of Being, exercising, as

---

[11] R. d. V., p. 378.
[12] R. d. V., p. 265.
[13] R. d. V., p. 345.

it does, dominion only over the actual world.   Hence progress is not merely an accidental affair, like a snowball rolling down a hill; its beginning and its end are securely fastened here and now in the idea of God, at once the base and summit of Being.   To deny the Messianic doctrine is to deny the reality of mankind, is to think in terms of the empirical groupings of men and hence to expose ethical progress to the mercy of chance winds of passion.

Chapter iii, Section (c)

Note 1.   Since the system of Rosenzweig rests upon the experience of revelation, it may be called a mystical philosophy.   However, the term "mysticism" has been employed in so many connections, acquiring various and often diverse connotations, that it may be well to point out here the different ways in which Rosenzweig's experience of revelation compares with the various forms of mysticism.

1. Mysticism has been defined as a theory of existence based upon an immediate experience.   (Royce)   This definition is, of course, extremely broad.   Yet, it refers specifically to the philosophical mystics of the type of Plotinus and the German school (Tauler, Bohme).   These men claimed to have experienced a feeling of unity with the whole universe.   "All is one," they proclaimed pontifically.   By a long process of training, they asserted, they managed to attain a state of mind, when all lines of division between things had disappeared and the world was seen to be one "in reality," sweetly one with God.   Hence, the actual world was conceived as real only for those who had fallen away from God, and in direct proportion to such degeneration.   Rosenzweig quite emphatically does not belong to this group.   As we have seen above, he rejects the notion that man and God are really one.   For this reason he doubts the validity of the insights of the metaphysical mystics.

2. The term mysticism is sometimes employed as a synonym of the term pantheism, expressing the belief that God is present everywhere.   In this sense, Rosenzweig may be described as a mystic, but with important qualifications.   He does draw a distinction be-

tween the phenomenal world and God, who is the true and eternal Being behind the constant march of ephemeral phenomena. But, he insists that God is recognized as a personal being, though the meaning of the term "person" must remain obscure. In one of his letters, Rosenzweig points out that both Jeremiah and Spinoza speak of God as being everywhere. Yet, there is all the difference in the world between their conceptions of the Divinity. Whoever does not feel this difference can never be taught to comprehend it, he asserts. And Rosenzweig is a disciple of Jeremiah, not of Spinoza.

3. When a philosopher has once been described as a mystic, he assumes the status of an esoteric teacher in the eyes of many. It is argued that his doctrines cannot possibly be of any significance to the generality of mankind, based as they are upon an experience which, valid or not, is enjoyed only by an exceedingly small number of persons. This attitude is not at all justified in the case of Rosenzweig, since he views the experience of revelation as possible to all men. It is not necessary to be born a "spiritual genius" or to undergo a long period of training. All that is needed is to cultivate an "open mind," or rather an "open heart." Keep the windows of your soul open, he advises, and the love of God will stream in sooner or later. This, too, is the reason for the daily practice of religion. The value of religious ceremonies consists in the "purification of man" ("l'tsoref bohen eth habrioth") that is, in the training of men to be receptive and responsive to the Word of God, when it comes.

4. Does God or man take the first step? This question is of critical importance in the history and philosophy of religion. As is well-known, Protestant theology has generally insisted that God necessarily takes the first step. "Grace" is a free gift of God, which does not depend upon any act of man. In the experience of religion, it was asserted, man feels wholly powerless and passive, while the Divine influence courses thru him. In this sense, Protestant Christianity is mystical. On the other hand, in Judaism, the contrary doctrine prevailed. Man must pray with all his heart and soul. Only then is he heard by God. The deed of man must precede the grace of God. In the religious experience, then, the part of man is an active, not a passive one.

In his main work, Rosenzweig portrays the course of redemption as beginning with the initiative of God. It is the love of God, which comes first, arousing man to a knowledge of his destiny. However, in his comments on the poems of Jehuda Halevi (II edition p. 180), he answers this question by saying that both traditional answers tell only part of the truth. In reality, revelation is a dialogue relationship. In standing before God, man feels his powerlessness and, hence, asks for the aid of God, but at the same time he understands clearly that God demands that step from him. In a dialogue, Rosenzweig declares, it is not the beginning, but the end that matters. And the last word, of course, is said by God. In proof of his compromise view, Rosenzweig brings the many Midrashim where Israel appears in conversation with God.

5. The relation of the prophetic to the mystical experience has not yet been adequately studied. In the first decade of this century, when mysticism was regarded as the essence of religion, some students of the religious experience chose to draw a sharp distinction between the psychology of prophecy and that of mysticism. The Semitic people, it was said, knew only prophecy— that is, the psychic phenomenon in which the man feels that God has entered into him; whereas, the Aryan nations knew of mysticism, the state of mind in which man feels that he has entered into and united with the Deity. It is hardly necessary to point out that in Judaism, at least, the view that God enters into the prophet was never current. Rather, it was believed that God speaks to the prophet. There is the unity of dialogue between God and the prophet, but never the unity of persons or even of wills (as St. Bernard taught). Thus, it appears that Rosenzweig's view of revelation is in harmony with the general trend of Jewish religious thought. The prophet in Judaism is the ideal religious personality. It is in this light that he is portrayed by Maimonides in the "Moreh." In Rosenzweig's view, prophecy, in a strictly limited sense, is affirmed to be possible to all men.

6. At times, the term "mystic" is used to describe an anti-intellectualistic or irrational position. In popular parlance, any one who declaims against the "tyrannical sway of reason" is promptly labeled as a mystic. Thus it is imagined that all mystics are perpetually at war with common sense. In the case of Rosenzweig,

this presumption is completely erroneous, as he condemns in no uncertain terms the irrationalists in both philosophy and religion. To be sure, his system is based upon an intuition. But, then, he insists, this intuition is as much a part of the world of experience as any other objective event. Reason, Rosenzweig maintains, is a part of man, but a part only. That is to say, the way leading to Truth or Reality is wider than the path of reason alone. As is explained in the second section, our apprehension of truth is the one avenue of knowledge. Reason itself is based upon this inner apprehension, this basic trust, which, at its highest, is found in revelation. There can be no conflict between reason and faith, because faith is an inner perception, an experience, and all reason is based upon an element of faith. This is an important element of Rosenzweig's thought. With evident feeling, he rebukes those Christian theologians who represent religion as belonging to a "fully other" sphere of existence, and thereby erect an impassable wall between religion and science. There is only one truth, and the love of God is truth: belief in reason and in reason alone is but a weaker form of the love of truth.

This conviction is found in all the works of Rosenzweig, but a particular apt expression of it occurs in his comments on Halevi's poem, "The Far and the Near." (II edition of Halevi's poems p. 188) He asserts there that the basic insight of the Jewish religion is the proclamation, "that the Far God is not other than the near One, the Unknown no other than the Revealed, the Creator no other than the Redeemer." Thus, the one God, who in the glow of revelation is inexpressible, simply because He is so near, becomes with the cooling of the original experience and with the progress of reason more expressible and even provable in abstract terms and principles, as the Far God, as Substance, as the Last Cause, or as the Source of ethical values. And the God of reason is, in the last resort, the same as the God of experienced revelation.

7. In conclusion, it may be inquired how Rosenzweig classified himself. Nowhere in the "Stern" does he affirm connection with any of the philosophical schools, except when he professes to adopt the late-Schellingian world-view. In the last paragraph of "Das Neue Denken," he says that, if his thought must be labeled, he prefers the designation "absolute empiricism." This classifi-

cation is indeed an apt description of Rosenzweig's method. Thruout his writings, emphasis is placed on the actually observed data. In his proof of God he begins with the observed quality of the Divine. Rudolf Otto's "Idea of the Holy" presents a point of view that is similar to Rosenzweig's. The substitution of speech for thought as the proper instrument for the understanding of reality derives partly from this empirical approach. Every event or group of events, Rosenzweig declares, must be known by a method peculiar to itself. Hence, philosophy can be no more than narration —i.e. an actual retelling of the drama of creation.

Note 2. Language, Rosenzweig contends, is more expressive than art, the method which Schelling advocated as the proper organ of metaphysics. Developed in the form of stem and branches, it parallels the actual course of events. Language is "the original symbolization of actuality itself and it therefore appears in the closest feeling of identity with this actuality" (S. d. E. Vol. II p. 81). "We describe the course which we believe with the words that we trust . . . and it is easy to trust speech, for it is in us and about us, and no other (agency) comes to us from the outside and echoes back from our inner (self) to the outer world. The word is the same as it is heard and as it is spoken. The ways of God and man are different, but the word of God and the word of man are the same. What man in his heart comprehends as his own human speech, is the word which comes from the mouth of God."

The replacement of reason by speech as the proper philosophical organon is made more intelligible by the following considerations. Thought is not merely the making of mental images. As long as the knowledge of mathematics was confined to simple arithmetic, geometry and algebra, it was still possible to think of reason as being a "seeing of the mental eye." With the discovery of calculus and higher mathematics, this view of reason was no longer tenable, since derivatives and integrals cannot be visualized. Thus, it was that Hegel came to regard thought as a process which works by its own laws. This view of reason was accepted and modernized by Hermann Cohen, who claimed that the sum total of the processes of thought represented the whole of reality. Rosenzweig has this view of thought in mind throughout his works, and, it is for thought in the Hegelian and Cohenian senses that he substitutes dialogue-speech. In place of the famous Hegelian dictum, "The real is the rational," he announces that dialogue-speech is the real. The Hegelians place their faith in the workings of the thought-processes, whereas Rosenzweig prefers to trust "thinking for a Thou." In either case, the "real" is a mental process. Truth is not a matter of "seeing" but of trusting to a process, that, evolving by its own laws, drives inevitably from premise to conclusion. Thus, Hegel's dialectic reasoning and Cohen's "pure" thinking, "pure" willing and "pure" feeling find their counterpart in Rosenzweig's "speaking."

The one who first suggested speaking to a Thou as being the proper method for the apprehension of reality was Ludwig Feuerbach in his "Essence of Religion."

Note 3. The idea of deducing reality from the "naught," Rosenzweig borrows from Hermann Cohen, though the method is an adaptation of Hegel's thesis, antithesis and synthesis.

Rosenzweig's "yes," "no" and "and" are not identical with the respective categories of Hegel, the main point of difference being the fact that, to Rosenzweig, the "no" is as original a process as the "yes," not simply a negation of the latter.

Note 4. In "Das Neue Denken," (375) Rosenzweig explains the meaning of "yes," and "no" as corresponding to the definition of substance of Spinoza. The "yes" is Spinoza's conception of "in se esse," the "no" is the "per se percipi."

In the primary words, the predicate is the primary "yes," while "no" is expressed in the subject, though in an actual sentence, the reverse relation is true, as indicated above. "The predicate is indeed in the individual case always something particular, therefore, negative; according to its original concept, however, determination is positive—the pure so. That this So becomes a thus and not otherwise, occurs only when to the original one, the other is added. Only thru this transition to plurality is determination turned into negation" (S. d. E., Vol. I. p. 38).

Note 5. In accordance with the late Schellingian philosophy of nature, Rosenzweig regards the course of events in the world as being uniformly from the particular to the universal. Every event enters the actual world as a particular individual, and then tends to approach a Universal. The "forms," in the platonic sense, exert a pull on the multitudes of freshly born events, gradually impressing them within the world order. On the basis of this theory, the "no" of the world is prior in time to its "yes," the forms. The reverse, however, is true in the cases of both God and man, where, as we have seen before, the essence precedes the appearance. Rosenzweig noting this "difficulty" in his scheme, concludes that the world is not yet. Its "yes" is only an anticipation of the future. The world is not yet complete. It is in the process of attaining perfection.

CHAPTER IV, SECTION (a)

Note 1. Later, Buber was to find the same spirit in the Hebrew Bible. With the purpose of exhibiting this spirit to the modern reader, he set out to translate the Bible anew. This translation, undertaken in collaboration with Franz Rosenzweig, was intended to illustrate the meaning of religion at its purest. In the Bible, Israel, as a group, leads a dialogue-life with God, as the great Thou. The beauty of the translations published thus far won universal acclaim. In "Das Kommende," Buber examines the meaning which the Kingdom of God had for the Israelites of the Bible days.

Note 2. (In reference to his feeling of insecurity in "Daniel"). The feeling of fear seems to be an essential element of the religious consciousness. Thus Kierkegaard regarded "Angst" as the expression of man's spirituality. Rudolf Otto described the feeling of "mysterium tremendum" as being the most potent "moment" in the idea of the holy. Students of religion, like Ribot, Leuba and McDougal especially stress its significance.

Note 3. This experience of a fundamental duality within the soul can be paralleled by a number of instances which James brings in his chapter on "The Divided Self" in the "Varieties." Such a comparison would bring to light a seemingly vital difference. For,

(See Rudolf Otto "The Idea of the Holy," "Sören Kierkegaard," "The Idea of Dread." See J. B. Pratt "The Religious Consciousness" p. 71 for further references.)

whereas Buber's was the experience of a felt division, the cases cited by James are all descriptions of a divided will, capable of being covered by Paul's succinct exclamation, "What I would, I do not; what I do, I would not." This apparent contrast does not appear to me to be fundamental, as Buber's experience can be explained as a symbolical representation in consciousness of the conflict of wills occurring in the subconscious.

Buber's own explanation is, of course, that the feeling of duality is an apprehension of the real, for the universe which subsists behind the veil of phenomena throbs eternally in pulsations of activity directed from pole to pole. It is the destiny of man to help along in the work of creation by reconciling his felt duality through appropriate activity in the world. At the heart of man the currents of reality beat. He alone can complete the circuit of their course by his will and activity.

It is to this stage of his thought that Buber's views on the nature of the Jewish character are due. He simply labeled as Jewish the type of soul, which, in his view, was most sensitive to the messages of reality.

Note 4. Buber's language is here in evident agreement with Dewey's conception of God as the name given to the totality of the forces that make for the improvement of human life, a view taken over by Kaplan. Buber also agrees with Dewey in placing emphasis on the adjective "religious," rather than on the noun, "religion." To both thinkers, religion is an attitude, taken in respect to all things. But, whereas to Dewey, God remains just a name, to Buber, God is a person, felt as present in the concrete situation. Both Dewey and Buber recognize the manifestation of God in the same forces; the former refuses to move beyond this point, the latter postulates a Person, the answer to whose call is reflected in the ideal forces of the universe.

Note 5. See Jung's work on "Religion and Psychology" where the results of an investigation of religious dreams are reported. Jung is inclined to assume a religious motive as the cause of this kind of dream, especially when they occur in a series.

(See James' "Varieties," Chapter on "The Divided Self," also p. 24 in this chapter.)

CHAPTER IV, SECTION (b)

Note 1. From a strictly psychological viewpoint, it will be conceded that the awareness of the presence of a person in the immediate vicinity involves elements of consciousness which are not aroused by the awareness of an object. Thus, Prof. Leuba writes in "Belief in God and Immortality," [1] "The essential constituents of the experience of the presence of a person in a case of ordinary perception are neither sight nor sound, nor even touch; but the very complex sensory-motor activities which commonly follow upon these perceptions. When we see some one and feel his presence, our whole psychophysical attitude is modified; the facial and bodily expressions are altered, feelings and emotions are generated and, in addition, thought is given a new direction; it centers about our relations with the person of the presence of whom we are aware." It is a far cry from this description to Buber's account of the same phenomenon. Buber regards the common awareness of a person as being a weak instance of a fact of being, which, at rare times, is manifested in its full power and glory. Hence, he is concerned with the extreme cases only, though he purports to find the same relationship on the sub-human level, in an incipient form.

Note 2. In Buber's view, there is no special characteristic of the feeling of the divine apart from the apprehension of a Thou, which, on returning to the "it" world is felt as somehow transcendent, since that Thou managed to evade the common fate of the species, which is to turn into an "it." Not that some men don't treat God as an "It," but those who have once said "Thou" to Him, cannot afterward be content with any "It" attitude toward Him. It follows that according to Buber, there is no differentia of the sacred as such. This view comes, ironically enough, close to the view of Durkheim, who regarded society as the real source of the feeling of sacredness. The differences between the two views are obvious. But the similarity of their views is highly significant. Both regard the apprehension of the divine as being in essence the same kind of response that man makes to man.

---

[1] Pp. 48, 49.

(See E. Durkheim, "The Elementary Forms of the Religious Life")

CHAPTER IV, SECTION (c)

Note 1. Prof. Pratt describes the course of the mystic ecstasy as being a progressive diminution of the ideational element and an intensification, relative or absolute, of the emotional content. We should therefore expect an upsurge of the affective currents in any mystical experience and make the proper allowance for this fact.

Note 2. The feeling of belonging to a being, standing over against one, can further be analyzed into a sense of the presence of a Person and the sense of satisfaction of a Platonic love. The sense of presence is one of the unexplained, perhaps the one element of mysticism that is unexplained by the formal and physiological conditions of the mystic experience. (See J. B. Pratt, "The Religious Consciousness.") Leuba's explanation of the mystic trance as being a form of self-hypnosis, applies with peculiar force to Buber's experience of the "Thou." In this case, the image of the "Thou," emerging out of the subconscious, takes the place of the hypnotist for the conscious self. The feeling of belonging together would, on this view, be due to the general tone of agreeable relaxation, which accompanies the act of submitting to the will of the hypnotist, associated with the awareness of the presence of another person.

Note 3. No doubt it is possible to explain the experience of relation by the methods of modern psychology, as a complex manifestation of the workings of one or more of the lower instincts. Buber's case, however, cannot be refuted in this way since this procedure rests on the assumption that the parts in terms of which an experience is explained are more ultimate than the experience itself. This assumption Buber would deny most vigorously. The only justification for choosing any element or principle as metaphysically ultimate, apart from the success with which it can be shown to harmonize with the rest of experience, is the fact that it

---

(See J. B. Pratt, in "The Religious Consciousness," p. 397, also Pratt's citations from Prof. Coe on p. 450.)

(*Op. Cit.* pp. 428, 429.)

strikes us as being finally and irreducibly real. To Buber, the fact of relation appears infinitely more ultimate than the finely spun theories of psychology. On purely logical grounds, there is no way of deciding this issue.

Note 4. The distinction between "person" and "thing" can be made in philosophically exact language, so as to indicate an ultimate metaphysical dichotomy. (see William Stern, "Person and Sache," Leipzig 1906) In Grundgedanken der Personalistischen Philosophie," pp. 8, 9, the same author offers definitions of "person" and "thing," which are easily translatable into Buber's terminology of "Thou" and "It."

Note 5. This analysis of the metaphysical system implicit in the "I-Thou" relation bears obvious resemblance to the classical systems elaborated by mystics, of Catholic tradition. There is a realm of grace supervening above this terrestrial world, which the mystic in his ecstasy enters. In that realm of grace, the love of God enters into the soul of the mystic, or there occurs a union of wills, but no actual union with or absorption into God takes place.

It is instructive to note the manner in which Karl Heim has elaborated Buber's discovery of the "Thou" relation into a reflective and systematic philosophy of religion. The influence of Buber on the great German theologian is especially evident in the first two editions of the latter's "Glaube und Denken." The third edition of this volume is published in an English translation as "God Transcendent." In it Heim states, "It is one of the decisive discoveries of our time that the relation brought about when an "I" meets a "Thou" is quite different from the relation between an "I" and the "It" confronting it" (p. 153).

He explains this difference as being of a dimensional nature. He points out that a radical distinction can be drawn between two kinds of boundaries—boundaries of content and boundaries of dimension. The objects that are separated by a boundary of the former sort restrict each other. The boundary of the latter type occurs between two infinitely extending "Spaces," which interpenetrate without limiting each other. Heim lists five characteristics, by which the two types of boundaries may be distinguished, of which the most significant one is the observation that the perception of a dimension depends on a radical change in the being of the subject. "It is only by a special mode of existence that we can enter into a space and take station in it, subsequently observing and thinking from that particular standpoint" (p. 74). A new space cannot be apprehended "from the standpoint of a mere spectator, but only on the ground of my total existence" (p. 75). Events that appear paradoxical, as contradicting the law of excluded middle, from the standpoint of a certain number of dimensions, become self-evident when a new dimension is introduced.

Now, Heim argues, the ways in which an "It" is related to an "I" or the "It" world of one Ego to the "It" world of another Ego, or an "I" is related to a "Thou" are all describable as involving boundaries of dimension. The "I-Thou" relation is to be viewed as being in a separate dimension from that of the "I-It" attitude. The paradox involved in the attempt to treat a "Thou" as an "It" Heim expounds as follows: "I can either be the person I am; and then I cannot be the other man; or I am the other person, and then I cannot be the person I now am. . . . But this "either-or" is paradoxically broken through, when I regard you not as a "He" or an "It" but as a "Thou." For thereby I have indicated you as a being whose right I have acknowledged to say "I am." I have therefore given you authority to be the central point of the whole and to treat everything else, myself included, as a "not-I." The attempt never quite succeeds. Thus there arises a tension between two points, each of which must claim to be the centre of the whole and to regard everything else as "Not-I" (p. 159).

We have here quoted at some length Heim's version of the "Thou" relation, in order to bring out the radical modification which Buber's doctrine of the "Thou" relation had undergone at the hands of the Protestant theologian. Thus, with Buber, the "Thou" relation is essentially one of devotion and love. He who says "Thou" can only love and rejoice to serve. When an "I" truly meets a "Thou," there can be no question of opposition or of a conflict of wills. It is of the essence of the relation, that it can only be formed in love.

In the case of Heim's description of the "Thou" relation, it is evident that it is essentially a conflict of wills, which may or may not be reconciled. The characteristic tension of the relation is due, in his view, to the struggle for supremacy between the two wills and the two subjective worlds corresponding to the two persons. Instead of being the appearance of a ray of love from the sphere of the real, the "Thou" relation is shown to be the manifestation of an unconscious strife of wills. Thus Heim refers to the sense of joy and freedom, which accompanies the relation, in the following words: "We see in it release from the burden of opposition and of suffocating constraint, which are characteristic of the "Thou" relation in its original state" (p. 166). Elsewhere, he refers to the awareness of a "Thou" as being the feeling of "his silent presence as a dynamic opposition." Finally, in referring to the reversions to primitivism which civilized men may experience in times of stress, he says: "It is the primitive feeling that the dead "It"—world is but the secondary precipitate of the Reality whose primary form we live as the struggle of will against will."

It is important to notice this vital difference between the two accounts of the "Thou" relation, because Heim, who quotes copiously and approvingly from Buber, does not seem to be aware of the fact that the views of the Jewish mystic are irreconcilable with his own.

As to the relation of God to nature, the two philosophers are clearly in disagreement. Heim does not accept Buber's postulate, "The extended lines of relations meet in the eternal Thou. Every particular Thou is a glimpse through to the eternal Thou; by means of every particular Thou the primary word addresses the eternal Thou." (I and Thou, p. 75) Heim insists that the relation of God to the world is transcendent in a higher sense than the "I-Thou" relation is to the "I-It" world. To be sure, in describing the act of turning to God, Heim does employ the phraseology of Buber. (See God Transcendent pp. 218, 219, 220.) Yet, it may well be doubted whether he accords the same meaning to those phrases. For, to Buber, addressing oneself to man is not, toto genere, different from speaking to God. (M. Buber, "Die Frage an den Einzelnen," p. 31)

Among American thinkers, the philosophy of Prof. Hocking comes closest to the thought of Buber. It is the contention of Hocking that, implied in our common experience, there is an awareness of God. We recognize the presence of other persons only on the silent assumption of the presence of a Being, not ourselves, in the world. The basic insight of Hocking differs from the "Thou" relation, in that the former appears at its purest in a cognitive situation, whereas the latter is experienced only in an ethical or esthetic situation.

CHAPTER IV, SECTION (*d*)

Note 1.   A discussion of the religion of childhood is given in J. B. Pratt's "The Religious Consciousness" Chapter 5. It is the opinion of the author and of many investigators cited by him that there is no warrant for the view that children have any attitude at all toward the Determiner of Destiny, though, he admits, children do show a worshipful attitude toward their parents. The concensus of opinion among psychologists appears to contradict the thesis of Buber.

In a larger sense, the assertion of the "inborn Thou" puts Buber among the ranks of those investigators who postulate the existence of a "religious instinct" or a "mystic sense." The meaning of such a faculty varies, of course, with the different thinkers who have assumed it. Psychologists as a rule refuse to admit the existence of any such innate capacity or striving.

Note 2.   There are narrower conceptions of mysticism based upon dogmatic assertions of what "it really is" that would exclude the "Thou" relation. Such, in fact, appears to be the usage of Buber. Perhaps the clearest expression of this view is found in E. Lehmann's "Mysticism in Heathendom and Christendom," p. 8. "The true mystic refuses to think of himself as standing before his God as an 'I' to a 'Thou,' but rather as an 'I' to a higher 'I.' Or better, he wants to be so absorbed so made one with his God, that there exists no longer either 'I' or 'Thou.'" This view is unjustified on a strictly empirical basis, as it would exclude a large group of Christian mystics who took the imagery of the Song of Songs to be symbol of the perfect mystic union.

(As protagonists of a religious instinct, see Morris Jostrow, "The Study of Religion" and Evelyn Underhill, in "Mysticism," who speaks of a "mystic sense.")

Note 3. To classify the mystic way into stages is, of course, an arbitrary task, since no classification will fit all recorded adventures into the mystic quest for reality. Catholic mystical theory is based on a threefold classification. Delacroix has a fourfold division. For our purpose, a more detailed analysis from the standpoint of its development is obviously more useful. But whatever scheme is formally adopted, the "Thou" relation would still have to be classified as a milder form of mysticism.

Note 4. The contention that mysticism bears no practical fruits would probably be contested by all great mystics and by many students of the subject. The great mystics have displayed extraordinary vitality in dealing with the knotty problems of the day. Outside India and Greece, the end of the Mystic Way was assumed to lie in the field of human relations. Even in India, the test of the "purity" of Samadhi was good works, as James relates in "Varieties." Still there is this to be said on behalf of Buber's condemnation of ecstasies: that no proof exists for the claim that these experiences are the cause of the increased vitality of the mystics. The psychological elements which account sufficiently for the increased power of the mystics are the concentration of the personality about some altruistic ideal, that is especially relevant to the needs of the moment, and the sense of certitude concerning one's aims and methods. These elements occur in their pure and unalloyed state in the "Thou" relation. Again, the Mystic Way cannot be regarded as a way of life for all people. (See E. Underhill in "Mysticism," the chapter on "The Unitive Life" for a view which connects ecstasy with practical life. See H. Bergson in "Two Sources of Religion and Morality," for a view which finds the source of all creativeness in human society in the mystic experiences of ecstasy and which offers a metaphysical basis for this contention.)

Not all mystics described ecstasy as a union with the All. Some have contended that even in ecstasy the two beings remain essentially distinct. See especially the quotation from Ruysbroeck in E. Underhill's "Mysticism," p. 505—"The Union is brought about by love; but the creature sees and feels between God and herself an eternal and invincible distinction."

CHAPTER VI, SECTION (a)

The views of D. Neumark are of especial interest in this connection. In a series of articles in the Hebrew magazine "HaShiloah," Neumark expounded the thesis that there are two distinct ways of constructing a philosophy of life. One may begin with the subjective valuations of good and bad and proceed to search for the ultimate grounds of these value-judgments. Or, one may begin with the attempt to understand the objective order of the physical universe. While he recognizes that the two starting-points imply each other, he insists that it makes a vital difference in the final result as to whether one starts with the problem of the purpose and meaning of human life, *Hashkofath Hachayim,* or whether one begins with the study of the nature of existence, *Hashkofath Haolam.*

In the first case, he points out, two alternatives are open to the thinker. He may either assert that our moral conscience is but the faint echo of the Will of God. On this assumption, the meaning of human life is ultimately to be sought in an extra-human Source, Who is yet perforce understood in terms of the human personality. Or he may take up the atheistic hypothesis and declare that morality is altogether a human affair. Nevertheless, having put down, at the base of his thought, the distinction between good and evil, even the atheistic philosopher of this school remains a moralist. The theistic thinker, impressed with the all-embracing Will of God, will find it easy to proceed from morality to ritual, there being no reason why certain actions may not have been ordained by God, Who is primarily conceived as the Supreme Lawgiver.

If a thinker, however, bases his philosophy of life upon the contemplation of the objective universe, then he is never able to arrive at the conception of a personal God. He, too, may decide to adopt either the theistic or the atheistic hypothesis. But, the theism of the universe-philosopher is really no more than deism. His God is the "Cause of Causes," the Prime Mover, in general, the principle of order in the universe. Such a God can have no interest in the affairs of men. At most, it may be claimed, on this view, that human rational thought is a Divine and eternal faculty, since it is the instrument whereby man apprehends the immutable laws of God.

No genuine reconciliation between these two attitudes in philosophy is possible. In history, these two extreme viewpoints were represented in Greek philosophy and Jewish religious thought respectively. Numerous attempts were made, at different times, to effect a unified world-view out of the contrasting hypotheses of Judaism and Hellenism. The supreme attempt was made in the medieval era, when it was sought to proceed from universe-philosophy to religion—that is, to prove the existence of a worshipable Deity out of the axioms of natural philosophy. That attempt finally ended in failure. Kant dealt the death-blow to all the scholastic proofs for the existence of God. At the same time, Kant launched a new endeavor to effect the same synthesis which the Medievalists failed to attain. In his "Critique of Practical Reason," he attempted to reason in the Jewish manner, from morality to cosmology. But, Kant's synthesis, Neumark concludes, is little better than that of his predecessors. The chasm between the two viewpoints is now as wide as ever. "Two views there are: the cosmological view which leads rationally to a blind metaphysical Being and a view of life which represents a cosmic doctrine to us as true, through a direct and immediate intuition." [1]

Is the religious view of Judaism sufficient unto itself? Is the direct intuition of Judaism so clearly authoritative as to require no corroboration from natural philosophy? Neumark seems to believe that this is indeed the case. The Jew apprehends directly the truth that "ethical and cosmic Being are one." For this intuition he is impelled ever and anon, through the influence of foreign cultures, to seek rational justification, but, in strictness, this intuition is in itself the only and sufficient ground for his faith.

Accordingly, Neumark formulates the problem of modern Jewish philosophy in the following manner:

(a) To show the relation of Judaism to modern ideas.

(b) To defend the real nature of Judaism.

(c) To examine and to refute the arguments of the atheistic

---

[1] "HaShiloah," vol. 11, 1903, p. 431.

philosophers, who profess to "prove" the non-existence of the cosmic Idea (God).[2]

It will be seen that this program does not envisage the task of proving the correctness, reliability and authority of the alleged Jewish intuition. Neumark appears to maintain that the intuition of the unity of the spirit carries the seal and proof of its own authority. Development of Jewish philosophy is hence possible only along the path of polemics. Every new challenge is met and illumined from the standpoint of Judaism. In this way, the different implications of the Jewish intuition are brought into the open. But, the loyal Jew does not attempt to probe behind this intuition.

Thus, in his outline of the development of Jewish philosophy, Neumark describes the evolution of Jewish thought as being a series of fresh unfoldings of the one intuition of Israel, occasioned by the need of combating different foreign ideas. Jewish philosophy, he contended, was intrinsically one through the ages. It was only its expression that has varied in accordance with the need of overcoming the varying challenges of different cultures. Summing up his researches, he declares that "the history of the development of the religion of Israel is the memory of its holy wars against mythology."[3]

It is clear, therefore, that Neumark's philosophy of Judaism is based upon the assertion that the Jewish intuition of the unity of the spirit in all its intellectual and moral phases is so distinct and so valid, as to require no additional proof.

In our opinion, Neumark failed to touch the heart of the problem. Having arrived at the conclusion that Jewish religious thought was based upon a unique intuition, he should have proceeded to describe those psychological characteristics of this intuition, which entitle it to the claim of being the one avenue of metaphysical knowledge. The term intuition obviously covers a multitude of sins. When not defined and circumscribed in detail, it is little more than a euphemism for irrationality or naiveté.

Neumark does not appear to regard the intuition of the unity of the spirit as an experience at all. He speaks of it as a speculative

---

[2] "HaShiloah," vol. 13, 1904.
[3] "Toldoth HaPilosophia b'Yisroel," p. 3.

idea, especially in his Hebrew "Toldoth HaPilosophia b'Yisroel." [4] As an idea, it cannot be regarded as anything more than a hypothesis. The fact that this idea was held by a whole people for many generations does not constitute proof of its truth.

In brief, Neumark failed to deal with what he conceived to be the essence of Judaism as a present hypothesis, to be tested and proven true in the light of common human experience. In a series of articles in the "HaToren," [5] he criticized scathingly the philosophy of religion of Herrmann Cohen, contrasting it with the genuinely "Jewish" system of critical idealism. The essay was written more from the historical than from the philosophical viewpoint. It does not outline an original system of thought. Neumark's contributions to the study of Jewish philosophy are invaluable; he never became, however, an independent philosopher.

---

[4] P. 4.
[5] Years 1923, 1924.